Gary Gentile started his diving career in 1970. Since then he has made more than 1,000 decompression dives, over 100 of them on the *Andrea Doria*.

Gary has specialized in wreck diving and shipwreck research, concentrating his efforts on wrecks along the East Coast, from Newfoundland to Key West, and in the Great Lakes. He has compiled an extensive library of books, photographs, drawings, plans, and original source materials dealing with ships and shipwrecks.

Gary has written dozens of articles for such magazines as *Animal Kingdom*, *Sea Frontiers*, *Sterns*, and *The Freeman*. He has published thousands of photographs in books, periodicals, newspapers, brochures, advertisements, corporate reports, museum displays, film, and television. He lectures extensively on wilderness and underwater topics, and conducts seminars on advanced wreck diving techniques and high-tech diving equipment. He is the author of twenty-one books: ten novels, and eleven nonfiction works on diving and nautical and shipwreck history. The Popular Dive Guide Series will eventually cover every major shipwreck along the East Coast.

In 1989, after a five-year battle with the National Oceanic and Atmospheric Administration, Gary won a suit which forced the hostile government agency to issue him a permit to dive the USS *Monitor*, a protected National Marine Sanctuary. Media attention that was focused on Gary's triumphant victory resulted in nationwide coverage of his 1990 photographic expedition to the Civil War ironclad.

The epic battles of the *Monitor* are the subject of a separate volume.

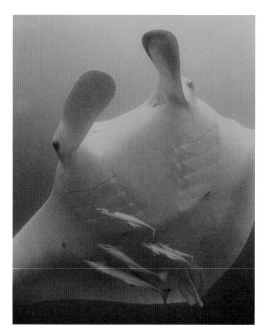

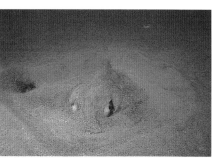

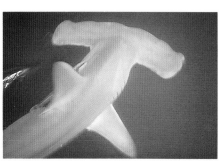

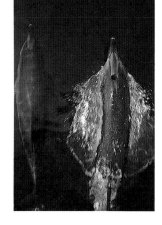

THE POPULAR DIVE GUIDE SERIES

Shipwrecks
of
North Carolina

from the Diamond Shoals North

by Gary Gentile

GARY GENTILE PRODUCTIONS
P.O. Box 57137
Philadelphia, PA 19111
1993

GARY GENTILE PRODUCTIONS
P.O. BOX 57137
Philadelphia, PA 19111

Additional copies of this book may be purchased from the same address by sending a check or money order in the amount of $20 U.S. for each copy (postage paid).

Picture Credits

The front cover photo of the *Carl Gerhard* is courtesy of the National Archives. The back cover photo is courtesy of the National Oceanic and Atmospheric Administration. Every attempt has been made to contact the photographers of pictures used in this book where the name was known, and to ascertain the name of the photographer where unknown; copies of many pictures have been in public circulation for so long that the name of the photographer has been lost, or the photographer's present whereabouts are impossible to trace. Any information in this regard forwarded to the author will be appreciated. Apologies are made to those whose work must under such circumstances go unrecognized. Uncredited photographs, including all marine life examples typical to the area, were taken by the author.

The author wishes to acknowledge Jon Hulburt and Barb Lander for reviewing and editing the manuscript, and Drew Maser and Pat Stewart for proofreading the galleys.

International Standard Book Number (ISBN) 0-9621453-7-8

First Edition

Printed in Hong Kong

CONTENTS

Cape Hatteras

INTRODUCTION

The Diamond Shoals have long been recognized by mariners as a treacherous area. For centuries, ships of wood and ships of steel have run afoul of the long, conelike projection of sand that acts as a deadfall to the unwary sea captain.

Often shrouded in fog, always beset by current, the Diamond Shoals seem to attract ships to destruction much as the mythical Sirens sang to ancient mariners and drew their frail craft onto the rocks.

The shoals are an underwater extension of the barrier islands that protect the Pamlico Sound. North of Cape Hatteras the coastline runs north-south, south of the cape it trends northeast-southwest; from the air it looks like a giant boomerang. The shoals bisect the angle of directional change, thrusting outward into the Atlantic where the cold Labrador current running south bucks the warm Gulf Stream current running north. This meeting of two opposing water masses is the cause of constant turbulance; the temperature differential frequently causes fog. For the purpose of designating this mixing zone as a location, the names Cape Hatteras and the Diamond Shoals are usually considered synonymous.

Readers should note that there is not as much water mixing as one would expect. Because cold water is denser than warm water, at the junction of the two ocean masses of differential temperature the cold water settles to the bottom as the warm water rides over top. This "layered" effect often results in sharp thermoclines (what begins as a wonderfully warm dive becomes a chilling experience), and unexpected and dissimilar currents that may change in speed and direction as one descends to the bottom. An anchor line may make a three-dimensional zigzag on its way to the sand.

The back cover satellite image was taken with heat sensitive film. Cold water shows up green while warm water shows up red. The photo clearly depicts the cold northern water meeting the warm southern water at the Diamond Shoals. Throughout the year, as the temperatures rise and fall, and as the Gulf Stream undulates closer to and farther away from shore, the hues vary in intensity. This fluctuation (the delineation of the edge of the Gulf Stream) can be seen in sequential photographs taken during different seasons.

There are actually two shoals under the beam of Cape Hatteras light: the Outer Diamond Shoal and the Inner Diamond Shoal. Sometimes ships, either because of their draft or the tide, have sneaked through the troughs of the outer shoal only to come to grief on the inner shoal. Usually, once ensnared, wind and waves worked a ship until the wooden beams splintered, or the steel plates popped their rivets. After a hull flooded it quickly broke up in the pounding surf.

The shoals themselves are not the only cause of shipping losses. During two world wars German U-boats lurked there because tankers and freighters following the near shore route were funneled past Cape Hatteras by the way it jutted out into the ocean. This heavy concentration of merchant shipping attracted the enemy the way carcasses attract flies. So many ships were sunk in the vicinity during the first six months of 1942 that the area became known at "torpedo alley."

In 1942, war correspondent Robert Casey published a firsthand account of the war in the South Pacific. He called the book *Torpedo Junction*. The same title was later used by Ben Dixon MacNeil in his book about the U-boat action off the Diamond Shoals. The corruption stuck and has been copied ever since, causing untold confusion since the appellation also applies to the passage between Iceland and Newfoundland, and to Port-of-Spain, Antigua, where U-boats were similarly active.

In just retribution, two of the marauding U-boats met their fates in the shallow waters north of the Diamond Shoals. Both the *U-85* and the *U-701* are covered in this volume. The depth where the *U-576* was sunk, southeast of the shoals, is commonly given as over 700 feet, although the possibility exists that it lies in shallower water. Their rusted remains serve as sunken monuments to human folly and foreign aggression. For a complete action chronology of the east coast U-boat war, read this author's book, *Track of the Gray Wolf*.

North of the Diamond Shoals to the Virginia border lie many more wrecks: the result of strandings, collisions, and casualties of war. The ultimate tragedy, however, is not the loss of property, but of life. The pages that follow are filled with drama as men, women, and children, thrust upon a savage sea, struggle for survival against uneven odds. This is not my story, but theirs.

Shipwrecks are not always isolated events. The tale of one may be interdependent upon that of another. These interdependencies are not always confined to wrecks lying within the borders of a single state. Therefore, in order to add perspective, I often refer the reader to companion volumes in the Popular Dive Guide Series.

Mixed in with true tales of shipwrecks and survivals along the North Carolina coast are myths that persist to this very day. Books describing and charts depicting these fallacies come about because their compilers relied on secondary source materials that were themselves poorly researched. Inevitably, this leads to a mass of misinformation that is carried on in the tradition of "I read it, therefore it must be true."

If it is read in official records the writer may be forgiven. After all, no historian actually knows the truth of a particular event, only what available documentation discloses. In circumstances where original data is contradictory, the historian must make interpretations which of necessity include inaccuracies. In many cases I have quoted directly from my sources; this not only preserves the flavor of the language and usages of the past, but offers the facts as they genuinely appeared.

I do want to dispel a few falsehoods, however: during World War Two neither the *Malay* nor the *Chester Sun* were sunk off the North Carolina coast. The *Malay* was viciously shelled and torpedoed by the *U-123*, and five of her men were killed; but the tanker outran the U-boat and made safe harbor. The *Chester Sun* was part of a small convoy that was attacked, but she herself was not fired upon. These incidents are related in *Track of the Gray Wolf*.

In this regard one must accept U-boat crews and commanders for what they were: heroes, perhaps, in Germany; but dreaded adversaries preying on innocent bystanders to the men of the merchant marine, and to the women and children passengers who died because of their actions. Undoubtedly, the lucky survivors and families of the dead did not idolize the men behind German torpedoes; assuredly, those killed did not. In an act of war, hero worship is a point of view. Many widows and fatherless children paid a severe price for the enemy's ambition of world domination.

In my research of the final resting places of those ships sunk during World War Two, I have relied heavily upon the wreck reports prepared by Eastern Sea Frontier. Surveys conducted during the summers of 1943 and 1944 attempted "to locate all wrecks lying within the 100-fathom curve in the Fifth Naval District, and to obtain as much information as possible about each wreck." These surveys were not always successful, were often inconclusive, and were sometimes inaccurate. Nor was the entire ocean surveyed: only selected areas in the proximity of a ship's last known or suspected position.

Survey vessels located wrecks from a distance using sonar gear and magnetic anomaly detectors, examined them with fathometers, wire drags, and underwater cameras (bulky affairs lowered by winch and fired blindly as the survey craft hovered above the target), and recorded their positions by loran, or, in most cases, by ranges and compass bearings off buoys, channel markers, and lighthouses. Equipment that was sophisticated at the time is equivalent to petroglyphs by today's standards, sometimes leading to great disparities in positional data.

As an example, by surveying the wrecks and exploring their remains, I have determined that the positions given on modern charts as the *Buarque* and *Equipoise* have been reversed, that the wreck commonly known as the *Ciltvaira* is probably the *Mirlo*, and that the *Ciltvaira* is as yet unfound. Uwe Lovas and Steve Lang have been instrumental in sorting out some of the discrepencies among wrecks lost in various localities on the Diamond Shoals.

To contradict local lore, the *Tenas* was sunk south of the shoals, on March 16, 1942; it was a wooden barge and of little interest. Pieces of the wreck washed ashore; the rest of it may have broken up and become scattered. On July 2, 1944 the Coast Guard cutter *Gentian* located what was believed to be a piece of it, in 45 feet of water, at 35-08.9N and 75-32.0 W. Today, nothing may exist at the spot marked on the charts. Yet divers and fishermen continue to look for the site as if it were of great importance.

The same holds true for most of the wooden windjammers that grounded on uncharted shoals, or stranded on lonely stretches of beach. Often, a vessel was left high and dry after the storm that drove it ashore moved on. State-appointed wreckers oversaw that salvaged cargo and rigging was returned to the owner, or was sold, and the proceeds banked in his name. Hulls were either dismembered and carted off (legally) by local inhabitants, or disjoined and disseminated by the forces of nature. Many large sections of keels and adjacent bottom planking were buried; today, storms and slowly shifting sand sometimes disinter these wreck fragments and refloat them. These so-called "buoyant wrecks" might come aground again several miles downcurrent. Be wary when tracking down the final resting places of wrecks found in books and charts, because they either may not exist any longer or they may have been moved.

One could conceivably write a whole series of books on the shipwrecks of North Carolina: tarheel winds luffed the sail of many a clipper whose voyage ended prematurely on the Outer Banks. With hundreds of wrecks to choose from I have written primarily about those whose names are more widely known among divers, fishermen, and local historians. In addition I have selected wrecks with enlightening or instructive stories behind them, that demonstrate uncommon valor or cowardice, or that expound upon the indefatigable efforts of the men of the Life-Saving Service or its successor organization, the Coast Guard. Also, I have included in this volume the tales of those vessels most likely to still exist—such as the many steel-hulled steamers that gasped their last on the Diamond Shoals.

If you plan to visit these wrecks you should know that between the shoals and the northern border of the State there is great diversity in the conditions of the water. There is no distinct line of demarcation, but a gradual blending as one moves from south to north: from the clear, warm, blue Gulf Stream water to the dark, cold, green Labrador water.

The deep-water wrecks just south of the shoals are quasi-tropical island environments that support amalgamated ecosystems: not as colorful as the luxurious coral reefs found farther south, nor as populated by many-hued tropical fish, although the water can be nearly as warm. The bottom often consists of a thick layer of silt that is easily stirred, reducing visibility quickly from twenty or thirty feet to near zero. The current is often "ripping" from the surface right to the bottom.

The Diamond Shoals itself is a mixing pot. Conditions can vary widely from day to day, even from hour to hour. A diver might go down the anchor line in flawless conditions, and minutes later be subjected to horrendous currents. As a rule of thumb, a summer surface temperature of 75° usually implies little or no current; 80° means that the Gulf Stream is in and is tearing across the bottom. Be prepared.

North of the Diamond Shoals the water is cooler and darker, and, although one can find visibility approaching seventy-five to one hundred

feet, it is not the norm: the average is forty to fifty feet. You will find more sea bass on the wrecks and fewer tropicals. The hulls more closely resemble halftones instead of gayly decorated impressionistic paintings such as one would see off Morehead City. The bottom consists largely of granulated sand that is moderately reflective and not so easily stirred.

From Oregon Inlet north the water is definitely not tropical. Corals and sea fans exist, but are not nearly as prolific as in the south. The water has a bite to it that can make a diver shiver after long immersion, even in a wetsuit. Generally, a thermocline separates the colder water on the bottom from the warmer water at the surface. An indication of the trend in marine life can be deduced from the fact that I once caught a five-pound Maine lobster (Homerus americanus, the kind with claws) on the *U-85*.

As you approach the Virginia border you will encounter the raw chill generally ascribed to more northern wrecks, with similarly attendant cold-water marine life. In July, the temperature on the *Buarque* was only 46°. Even the fish were sluggish.

Due to these less amenable conditions the wrecks from the Diamond Shoals north attract fewer members of the wreck diving community, most being content to amble about the wrecks in the more tropical waters from Hatteras Inlet south. Yet, despite adverse conditions, the wrecks off the northern part of the State offer the underwater explorer a full panoply of challenges and fascinating experiences, especially now that the pace of discovery is increasing.

I would like to thank those people who have helped me in the preparation of this volume, either by opening museum and archival files, pointing me toward sources of information, or granting interviews. They are, in alphabetical order: Gina Akers, Denny Breese, Danny Bressette, Laura Brown, Wynne Dough, Roger Huffman, Art Kirchner, Donny Lang, Steve Lang, Fil Nutter, Brian "Doogie" Pledger, Bill Quinn, Helen Shore, Charlotte Valentine, Angie Vandereedt, Mike Walker, Anne Wilcox, and Barry Zerby.

Deserving special thanks are Richard Lawrence, of the North Carolina Underwater Archaeology Unit, at Fort Fisher, Kure Beach; and Uwe Lovas, who has done more than his share to add to the fund of knowledge of the wrecks in the proximity of the Diamond Shoals. His magnetometer searches and subsequent diving surveys have located and helped put names on many previously unknown or unidentified wreck sites. With this information in hand others must carry on the tradition of inquiry and exploration. To both Richard and Uwe I owe a great debt of gratitude. Through shipwreck research we have become close friends.

This book does not purport to be the last word on any of the wrecks covered; in shipwreck research there can never *be* a last word. I have merely begun to unravel for the reader some of the mystery surrounding vessels lost during the age of sail and early steam, and exposed some of the possible identities of tankers and freighters lost during two world wars. With this information in hand others must carry on the inquiry and exploration. As Laura Brown says, "Don't wait for perfection. Go ahead and publish. Let others see the results of your work and add to it."

Join me in the following pages as we open together a new era of wreck research in what may prove to be the hottest dive spot on the American east coast—from the Diamond Shoals north.

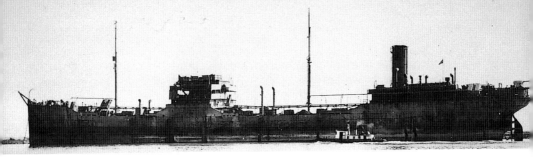

Courtesy of the National Archives.

AUSTRALIA

Built: 1928
Previous names: *Mary Ellen O'Neil*
Gross tonnage: 11,628
Type of vessel: Tanker
Builder: Sun Ship Building and Dry Dock Company, Chester, Pennsylvania
Owner: The Texas Company
Port of registry: Wilmington, Delaware
Cause of sinking: Torpedoed by *U-332* (Kapitanleutnant Liebe)

Sunk: March 16, 1942
Depth: 110 feet
Dimensions: 509' × 70' × 39'
Power: Twin diesel engines

Location:	26883.5	Bow	40250.2
	26883.3	Stern	40250.4

   Captain Martin Ader was uncommonly cautious with his ship and her valuable cargo of heavy fuel oil, particularly as he approached the dreaded Diamond Shoals—dreaded not as they had been during the days of sail, when foul weather, tricky currents, and poor navigational aids often contributed to a ship's demise, but because of the U-boat menace. March 1942 saw the height of enemy activity. The *Australia's* 110,000 barrels of oil were valued at $140,076, and was bound from Port Arthur, Texas to New Haven, Connecticut.

   In the dark morning hours on the fifteenth both the *Olean* and the *Ario* were torpedoed. The *Olean* was abandoned, but later reboarded and anchored until salvage tugs towed her to the shipyard for repair. The *Ario* (see *Shipwrecks of North Carolina: from Hatteras Inlet South*) was shelled and filled so full of holes that she finally slipped beneath the waves. When Captain Ader heard this the *Australia* was some forty-six miles from Frying Pan Shoals.

   "Since both of these distress messages were sent from the immediate area into which the *Australia* was proceeding, Captain Martin Ader ... decided to turn back in order to allow a certain amount of time to elapse before proceeding through the danger area.

   "Accordingly, the *Australia* returned south of Frying Pan Shoals and remained there until about 1200 on Sunday, March 15, 1942. She then proceeded north, but instead of taking a course straight for her position south of Cape Lookout, she proceeded to follow the coast through Onslow Bay, hugging the shore line as closely as safety would permit. Proceeding this way until she was just off Beaufort Inlet the ship found itself in a heavy fog and bad weather. Accordingly, the *Australia* turned back a second time and remained in the area of Lookout Bight for approximately two hours before continuing on her original course north around Cape Lookout.''

Routing instructions from the Port Director at Port Arthur directed that ''an area of thirty miles on each side of Cape Hatteras be passed in the daylight hours during which time the ten fathom curve was to be followed. Leaving Cape Lookout the *Australia* traveled close to Ocracoke Inlet and then proceeded eastward at a speed of 11 knots, zigzagging, to round Diamond Shoals.''

If Captain Ader's confidence was buoyed by the patchy haze that partially hid his vessel, or by the ships four miles ahead and the one four miles behind—both of which had already passed the tip of the Diamond Shoal—he entertained a false sense of security.

Under those conditions the *U-332* must have been close—lying in wait for a juicy target worthy of a torpedo, before giving away its position and being forced to run for cover.

The explosion that blew in the starboard side of the engine room killed four duty personnel: two engineers, a wiper, and a pump man. Crew men resting in their rooms above were knocked out of their bunks. ''The compartments filled so quickly with water that it rose to the ankles of the men between the time they reached their feet and the time they made their way out of the cabins. ... Within a few seconds the after portion of the main deck was awash.''

Radio Operator Zim Elkins tapped out a wireless message which the Coast Guard immediately answered. Then Captain Ader gave the order to abandon ship; he also placed his routing instructions and all code books ''in a bag equipped with a zipper and containing 30 pounds of lead,'' and dropped it over the side.

Only seven minutes after the attack the remaining thirty-six men got away safely in lifeboats. They rowed for thirty-five minutes before they were picked up by the *William J. Salman*, which had bravely reversed course despite the danger in which she placed herself.

Because the *Australia* sank with her bow and bridge showing above water, the Navy Salvage Service sent the tug *Relief* (SP-2170) to inspect the hull for possible salvage. Oddly, it reported that ''the vessel had burned and sunk and considered it a total loss.'' The *Australia's* crew made no mention of fire. When did the wreck burn?

A possible explanation may be local boaters, who stripped the wreck of everything worthwhile before it slipped into deeper water. A fire may have been started accidently during illegal salvage operations.

The *Australia* slowly settles before breaking in two. (The black and white photos are courtesy of the National Archives.)

The wreck was marked with a red nun buoy. According to the Coast Guard, "one mast was still visible above water in the summer of 1944 when demolition work was commenced." The wreck was cleared "in excess of 42 feet by the Navy Salvage Service." Divers take note: "Numerous bombs were dropped on the wreck by training planes." There may be some duds lying around.

The wreck of the *Australia* is in two upright pieces a couple hundred feet apart, separated by a low-lying field of debris not distinctive enough to follow from one end to the other. The anchors are prominent on the bow: the port anchor is tight in the hawse pipe, the starboard anchor is buried except for the shackle that connects it to the chain which climbs six feet into the hawse pipe. The weight of the windlass has caved in the forward deck. About thirty feet aft of the point of the bow the wreck breaks down completely into a broad field of debris that averages six feet in relief.

The stern section rises some twenty feet off the bottom, and is canted about thirty degrees to starboard. The fantail and upper decks are gone; one can swim into the after steerage compartment where the steering quadrant is prominent. The starboard propeller is buried, but two bronze blades of the port propeller protrude from the tangled wreckage. The engines have fallen on their starboard sides. Large flasks, some four feet across and fifteen to twenty feet long, lie haphazardly in the high debris between the engines and the stern. The main structure of the wreck appears to terminate a few feet forward of the engines; because a large scattered debris field stretches from there on, a boat anchoring into the wreck may find itself hooked into disarticulated hull plates spread across the sand.

Those seeking souvenirs should know that chinaware embossed with the Texaco logo is found just aft of the engine on the starboard side. You have to dig a bit to find intact plates and saucers, but the rewards make the effort worthwhile.

As with all wrecks on the Shoals, the current can be severe. One phenomenon I observed was a current hitting the upright hull plates with such force that it created "sand devils"; like desert dust devils, these swirls of sand spun with the fury of a midwest cyclone. The miniature twisters spun dark sand in circles that could have lifted Dorothy's house and deposited it somewhere over the rainbow.

On January 27, 1943, Oberleutnant zur See Eberhard Huttemann replaced Liebe as captain of the *U-332*. Under his command the *U-332* was lost with all hands on May 2 or 6, 1943, in the Bay of Biscay. Credited with the kill was RAAF Squadron 461.

BEDLOE

Commissioned: July 25, 1927
Previous names: *Antietam*
Displacement tonnage: 241
Type of vessel: Cutter
Builder: New York Ship Building Corp. (division of American Brown Boveri Electric Corp.), Camden, New Jersey
Owner: U.S. Coast Guard
Cause of sinking: The Great Atlantic Hurricane of September 1944
Location: 26940.8

Sunk: September 14, 1944
Depth: 80 feet
Dimensions: 1.25' × 24' × 7'
Power: Twin diesel engines

Official designation: WSC 128

40687.3

JACKSON

Commissioned: February 14, 1927
Previous names: None
Displacement tonnage: 241
Type of vessel: Cutter
Builder: New York Ship Building Corp. (division of American Brown Boveri Electric Corp.), Camden, New Jersey
Owner: U.S. Coast Guard
Cause of sinking: The Great Atlantic Hurricane of September 1944
Location: Unknown

Sunk: September 14, 1944
Depth: Unknown
Dimensions: 125' × 24' × 7'
Power: Twin diesel engines

Official designation: WSC 142

The *Antietam* (later *Bedloe*) and the *Jackson* belonged to a class of thirty-three cutters designed for the express purpose of interdicting rum runners. They were built in the heyday of the Volstead Act, better known today as the era of Prohibition, gangsters, speak-easies, and flappers: the Roaring Twenties. Smuggling was big business that was so profitable that it was possible to earn back the cost of a boat on one successful run of the gauntlet; many considered such a reward well worth the risk of getting caught and going to jail.

In order to protect themselves from the downside of capture, those trafficking in illegal liquor armed themselves with machine guns and high-powered rifles. Shootouts were common. Therefore, in addition to small arms, Coast Guard cutters carried a 3-inch cannon mounted on the deck forward of the wheelhouse.

Bedloe. (Courtesy of the U.S. Naval Institute.)

In 1933, when the Twenty-first Amendment to the Constitution repealed the Eighteenth Amendment, bootlegging became obsolete, and law-enforcement cutters were freed to pursue other duties: to aid vessels in distress and to save lives at sea. They continued in this occupation until the onset of World War Two. Most of the cutters were re-engined in the late 1930's.

When German U-boats began attacking merchant vessels off the U.S. east coast, in January 1942, all available Navy and Coast Guard craft put to sea as part of a massive anti-submarine warfare (ASW) campaign. *Antietam* and *Jackson* were no exceptions; both were assigned to the Eastern Sea Frontier. They were fitted with depth-charge racks on the stern: stingers that carried a deadly venom to marauding U-boats. During the next six months of intense U-boat activity, the cutters saw plenty of action.

In the dark morning hours of March 10, the *Antietam* was patrolling off Barnegat Light, New Jersey when the tanker *Gulftrade* was torpedoed by the *U-588*. Almost immediately the ship broke in two. The *Antietam* was only half a mile away when her crew was struck abash by oil-fed flames nearly a hundred feet high. She sounded the general alarm, warned off approaching ships by radio, and drove in to the rescue. No sooner had she stopped to pick up survivors in a lifeboat than a torpedo sped by, missing her bow by barely fifty feet. She ignored the obvious danger in order to save the *Gulftrade's* captain and eight of the crew. The *Antietam* then chased after the stern section of the tanker as it drifted off; a group of survivors huddled in the cold on the after deck. As the *Antietam* nudged under the tanker's fantail her port propeller was fouled by a line from the wreckage; she was unable to maneuver on one engine, and could not take off the remaining survivors. She remained in the vicinity until the Navy tender *Larch* appeared on the scene to effect the rescue. (See *Shipwrecks of New Jersey* for more details.)

Three weeks later came the *Jackson's* turn to assist the merchant marine in the deadly U-boat war. On April 1, off Virginia Beach, the *U-754* stalked the *Tiger* until the tanker slowed to take on a pilot, then launched a torpedo into the hull of the unprotected ship. The crew got away in lifeboats as the tanker slowly settled aft. The *Jackson* arrived shortly thereafter and took the abandoned ship in tow. For six hours the *Jackson* struggled with her charge to reach shoal water—to no avail. The stern sank deeper and deeper until it came to rest on the bottom; only the bow and midship remained afloat. The Navy tug *Relief* took up the hawser, but even with her more powerful engines she could not save the tanker. The *Tiger* eventually sank, and later had to be demolished as a menace to navigation. (See *Shipwrecks of Virginia* for more in that regard.)

The *Antietam* had another close encounter shortly after midnight on June 1, 1943. While leading a convoy of five ships out of the Chesapeake Bay, the lead ship in the convoy, the freighter *John Morgan*, collided with the inbound tanker *Montana*. The *John Morgan* was loaded with more than a thousand tons of dynamite and nearly 400,000 high-explosive shells; the *Montana* was heavily laden with aviation fuel. Sparks caused by steel scraping against steel ignited fires on both ships. A few moments later the bow of the *John Morgan* was vaporized when flames detonated the cargo in the forward holds. Once again the *Antietam* was only half a mile from the scene of disaster. "The force of the explosion blew the windows out of the pilot house and showered the U.S. Coast Guard Cutter *Antietam* with debris." (For the complete story see *Shipwrecks of Virginia*.)

By coincidence, the same day that the *Antietam* was helping to rescue survivors from the *Montana* and the *John Morgan*, her name was officially changed to *Bedloe*.

Launching of the *Jackson*. (Courtesy of the U.S. Coast Guard.)

Skip to September 12, 1944, about twenty minutes after the witching hour. The Liberty ship *George Ade* was steaming northward with the Gulf Stream between Frying Pan Shoals and Cape Hatteras, North Carolina. By this time the U-boat war off the U.S. east coast was practically nonexistant. The undersea killers had been whipped out of the Eastern Sea Frontier in July 1942; since then only infrequent incursions got past ever-alert anti-submarine warfare units, and in more cases than not the invading U-boat had been sunk.

Nevertheless, the *U-518* found the *George Ade* about a hundred miles offshore, and launched a torpedo that hit the Liberty ship aft. The force of the explosion damaged the rudder, destroyed the steering engine, drove the propeller shaft forward, and knocked the main power plant out of line; there was some minor flooding. A second torpedo passed under the counter but did not explode.

The German code was an open book to Allied Intelligence. The Submarine Tracking Office was well aware of the U-boat's presence off the eastern seaboard and was trying hard to pinpoint its position. The baby flattops *Core*, *Croatan*, and *Guadalcanal* were already on the scene. Dispatched immediately upon receipt of the distress call were eight destroyer-escorts, the HMNS *Van Kinsbergen*, and three patrol vessels organized as a killer group. Ordered to the *George Ade's* relief were the minesweeper *Project* and the tugs *Relief* and *Escape*, the *Natchez* and the *Temptress* from New York, and the *Bedloe*, *Jackson*, and rescue tug *ATR-6* from Morehead City. With nearly two dozen vessels and hundreds of aircraft converging above its conning tower, being chased first by gunfire then by depth charges, the U-boat wisely slunk off for less protected waters.

Meanwhile, the *George Ade* wallowed out of control on the broad Atlantic swells; she could turn her engine, which knocked badly, but could not maneuver. Nevertheless, the valiant crew refused to abandon ship. That afternoon the *ATR-6* took the wounded merchantman in tow and headed for Cape Henry, with the *Bedloe* and *Jackson* acting as escorts. It was slow going: four knots at best. All night long and all the next day the tug, tow, and escorts crawled northward.

At the same time another situation was developing, this one caused by Mother Nature: a hurricane. What came to be called the Great Atlantic Hurricane of September 1944 (there was another one in October) was already beating up the Florida coast. The storm could just as well have been called the Great Ship Destroyer of 1944, for in the course of twenty-four hours it caused the destruction of six ships and the loss of more than three hundred lives at sea.

First to go down was the USS *Warrington* (DD-383). The destroyer had the great misfortune to be heading south along the Florida coast as the hurricane was moving north. The ship was pounded so severely that she took massive amounts of water through her vents, which resulted in the loss of electrical power first, then her main engines. The crew abandoned ship in the teeth of the storm, shortly after noon on the thirteenth. Only seventy-three were rescued, and then only after a prolonged search; two hundred forty-eight men were lost.

The storm swept the Atlantic coast with devastating effect. On the fourteenth came the rest of the casualties. The Naval auxiliary *YAG-14* went aground near Salvo, North Carolina. The tanker *Thomas Tracy* was driven ashore at Rehobeth Beach, Delaware. Heroic action on the part of local Coast Guardsmen saved both crews by use of the breeches buoy. (See *Shipwrecks of Delaware and Maryland* for the story of the *Thomas Tracy*.) The *Vineyard Sound* lightship was dragged from her moor and disappeared without a trace; she took with her twelve men.

The situation was no better ashore. Ninety-mile-per-hour winds drove mountainous seas against beach resorts; wiped out piers and boardwalks; razed houses, restaurants, and public buildings; toppled trees; washed hundreds of small boats far inland; disrupted telephone service from North Carolina to Rhode Island; knocked down power lines and plunged tens of thousands of homes into darkness; and sank automobiles as highways were drowned under six feet of water. New York City and Long Island were demolished to the tune of $34 million worth of damage; it took three weeks just to clear the roads of fallen trees.

While this large-scale catastrophe was taking place on the mainland, our little convoy was transiting the worst of all possible places: the Diamond Shoals. The normally sleepy Hatteras Island was hit hard by the storm: the road was washed out between Hatteras and Avon, ninety percent of the houses were knocked off their foundations, and nearly all drinking water was contaminated by the sea. Dead cattle, sheep, and horses littered the land. Albemarle Sound was "obstructed to navigation by innumerable logs and telephone poles." People were stranded everywhere by washed out bridges and beach roads. "Receding tides left Ocracoke and Portsmouth Island split into many small islands."

Dawn on September 14 found the convoy north of the Cape, off

YAG-14 ashore near Salvo. (Courtesy of the National Archives.)

Wimble Shoals. "A submarine was estimated to be in the immediate vicinity, and it was considered that the possibility of an attack on the comparatively helpless tow made an anti-submarine escort mandatory. The group was cautioned to expect winds of high intensity and to keep plenty of sea room. Weather reports received the evening of the thirteenth predicted the actual storm center would pass well clear of the group, about 100 miles east of Cape Hatteras. By the morning of the fourteenth it became evident that the storm had deviated from the predicted path and would pass very close, but this information came too late to allow the escorts time to run for shelter. Moreover, the exact condition of the *Ade* was not known; there was a possibility that she might founder in the storm; and the escorts, if on station, would be available for rescuing the crew. Accordingly they were not directed to seek shelter."

At five-thirty a.m. the towing bridle parted. The *Escape* re-established a tow line and took over the job. By eight o'clock the *Escape* noted in her log that the wind was in excess of 125 miles per hour. Lieutenant (jg) F.K. Merrick, Executive Officer of the *Jackson*, cited "visibility zero, raining extremely hard, and . . . from about 0900 on the waves were running from fifty to one hundred feet." None of the ships were in actual sight of each other, but radar contact placed the *Jackson* one mile on the *George Ade's* port beam (inshore) and the *Bedloe* one mile on the starboard beam. The ships by this time were approximately twelve miles off Bodie Island.

At about ten o'clock the tow line parted again. Because the storm was at the height of its severity there was no way the *George Ade* could be re-attached: she could not even be seen. The Liberty ship dropped both anchors. "One hook carried away but the second with 60 fathoms of chain held while engines were run slow ahead. Wind velocity over 100 knots and seas 50' high were reported. During the storm #2 and #3 lifeboats and 4 liferafts were washed overboard."

The situation on the *Jackson* was worse. Lieutenant Merrick's debriefing was summarized with typical bland military descriptive technique: "that the *Jackson* capsized at about 1030; that the starboard hatch was open and the port hatch closed; that the *Jackson* turned over on her port side; that at that time the *Jackson* was headed due East, sea was Northeast, wind was Northeast; that he and the Commanding Officer, the Helmsman, the radioman, Ens. Hainge, the radarman, the radioman on watch, and the soundman, all managed to get out of the starboard hatch; that one life raft was cast loose and floated free and one of the enlisted men went after it and brought it back to where the men were standing on the side of the ship; that they got into the life raft and paddled away; that the *Jackson* stayed on her side for a short time and then turned keel up and floated from twenty to thirty minutes when sight was lost of her; that at the time of the capsizing the *Jackson* was estimated to have been about three-fourths of a mile from the tug and tow; that there were four life rafts afloat, all crowded; that the tug was sighted about thirty minutes later within about half a mile from the survivors; that the Commanding Officer shot off flares from his raft, red, white and green; that also later, flares were fired from his raft; that the tug seemed to be headed toward the survivors; that at the time the weather was terrific, it was raining hard and waves were from fifty to one hundred feet; that for about twenty minutes the survivors were in a lull in the storm shortly after getting in the life rafts at which time the tug could be seen clearly; that the weather then became bad again and remained so until about 1500–1600 that afternoon at which time the storm cleared away; that the life raft turned over some eight or ten times; that upon one occasion he came up some fifty yards from the life raft and had a terrific time in getting back.''

If the men from the *Jackson* were anticipating a quick rescue from their brethren aboard the *Bedloe*, they were in for a long wait. The *Bedloe* had difficulties of her own. She managed to survive the morning blow that sank the *Jackson,* but had no idea that her sister ship had dived into Davy Jones's locker. The eye of the hurricane brought a few moments respite just before noon. Then the winds became variable and gusty. ''The *Bedloe* was cruising back and forth trying to keep with its mission, but finally the weather became so bad that the main objective was to keep the ship afloat.''

The summary of the statement made by Lieutenant (jg) August Hess, Commanding Officer of the *Bedloe,* was as laconic and shorn of graphic detail as that of Lieutenant Merrick. At about three p.m. the cutter ''became unmanageable and got out of control with her beam to the wind; that the sea and the wind did not agree; that he held the ship until finally one big wave struck; that the ship got in the trough and at about 1306 capsized on its port side; that he escaped through the hatch on the starboard side; that all of his men got out and were standing on the side of the ship; that it was noticed that two of the men did not have life jackets whereupon Peters went back into the ship and obtained life jackets for the two men who had none; that three rafts were cut loose, four or five men getting into the first raft and several getting into the second one; that he slipped off into the water and came up swimming some fifty or seventy-five yards from the life raft, to which he swam; that after the ship capsized it remained afloat for about two and a half minutes and then went straight down; that the wind at the time was one hundred knots or more, with waves of from sixty to sixty-five feet; that he was able to get two of the life rafts together but not the third raft, upon which there were six men; that several men were seen bobbing around in life jackets and these were picked up; that he got about thirty men on these two rafts ... that there were so many hanging on to the two rafts that there was barely room enough for the men to hold on to by using only one hand; that the rafts kept turning over; that the men kept slipping off one by one ... that effort was made to recover any man whose hold slipped from the raft but that utter exhaustion finally prevented efficient rescue work.''

The men of both cutters were in desperate straits, not the least of which was being cast adrift on constantly overturning life rafts in the worst storm to hit the east coast in the memory of man.

The weather moderated toward nightfall. On the morning of the fifteenth it was recorded in the *Escape's* log, "Making preparations and maneuvering to pass tow line to SS *George Ade*." The tow line was secured by 0900, parted at 1130, and resecured at 1500. The *ATR-6* acted "as drag on tow" for steering purposes, by hanging back off the Liberty ship's stern on a 2-inch wire cable. On September 16, at 0407, tugs and tow passed the Currituck Beach Light. At 1100 they entered the Chesapeake Bay. The tow line parted once again, but by 1930 they were safely moored at the Norfolk Navy Base.

This was two full days after the *Jackson* and the *Bedloe* had gone down. What of the survivors cast into tempestuous seas?

Since no official word had been received about their demise, or even about the possibility that the cutters might have foundered in the storm, no one was sent to look for them. Neither cutter had transmitted a distress call, and radio silence otherwise was routine. Furthermore, land-based Coast Guardsmen were overcome with the work of rescuing civilians stranded along the Outer Banks: people who were without food, water, or shelter. The massive clean-up was hampered by the lack of transportation, for only jeeps, amphibious vehicles, and trucks fitted with oversized tires could navigate the soft, sandy dunes in the absense of paved roads. Besides, the storm was still raging at sunset on the fourteenth. The wind lessened somewhat by dawn of the fifteenth, but at that time the rescuers themselves were still digging out of the mess left by the hurricane. Movement was at a virtual standstill, and with power lines and telephone poles down all along Hatteras Island, the only communication was by radio.

What this meant, for the moment at least, was that the men from the *Jackson* and *Bedloe* were left to their own devices. One official report that was classified "secret" stated that, "Although some anxiety was felt for the *Bedloe* and *Jackson*, it was thought that they had been blown farther to sea and would rejoin later." Blown to sea they were, but without their ships.

How horribly the men suffered can hardly be imagined. Only the hardiest survived the ordeal of overturning rafts; one by one the weak and the injured lost their grips, dropped or were flung off, and drowned. The presence of sharks and the darkness of night increased the anxiety of those who managed to live through the storm's aftermath. They spent the night without relaxing for a moment, for to lapse into sleep meant to be washed off their precarious perch. Waves constantly inundated them, and more than one sailor breathed involuntary gulps of sea water—then vomited it back up. It was a night of agony.

By morning of the fifteenth the number of survivors was halved. The ocean began to calm down, but there were new tortures to endure. Now came the unbearable heat from the sun, unquenchable thirst, and the unrelenting pain caused by the stings of Portuguese men-of-war. The men were blistered severely by sunburn and stinging tentacles. Their entire world was one of unceasing pain. The emergency rations with which the rafts were equipped did not go far.

The day passed, and so did another night.

By this time there was concern for the safety of the Coast Guard cutters. "With all attempts at radio contact unsuccessful, an air search by twenty-six planes and four blimps was begun in the afternoon of the fifteenth and continued until dark. Although flying conditions had been improving since the storm, visibility was still poor and hardly permitted an effective search. Forces available for searching were limited because many of the planes and blimps evacuated before the hurricane had not yet returned to their bases. The blimp, *K-20*, did sight an empty lifeboat and scattered wreckage at 35-18N 75-11W at 1604, but no trace of survivors." The drift was southward, nearly to the Diamond Shoals.

Morning on the sixteenth brought flat seas, more heat, less men. Many had died during the night from exposure and exhaustion. The rafts had drifted apart, each a lonely island surrounded by an endless horizon. Hope for rescue was evanescent: those still alive were weak and full of despair. Under those conditions, none had long to live.

At seven a.m. came the drone of a plane. All eyes turned skyward.

A massive air-sea rescue operation was in full swing, consisting of "a total of one hundred and sixteen planes and six blimps." Fortunately, the aircraft in use were OS–2–U seaplanes. The first to spot survivors was flown by Roy Webber. He radioed his position to base, landed on the sea, and taxied up to a raft on which three men lay more dead than alive. "He and Radioman Third Class Philip Pincus shed their clothes and dove into the water to drag the men onto the plane." The aircraft could not take off with the weight of three additional men, so it stood by while a rescue boat charged out from the Oregon Inlet Coast Guard Station.

A second plane landed and lashed itself to a raft bearing twelve survivors. A third plane found another raft, this one with five men. From overhead, a Navy blimp dropped emergency supplies. These twenty men were all who were left from the *Jackson's* crew of thirty-nine. The *Jackson's* captain, Lieutenant (jg) N.D. Call, was not among the survivors.

Motor lifeboat *CG-30340* (a 36-foot rescue launch) reached the scene at noon. The *Jackson* survivors were so weak that they had to be helped aboard. They were given first aid, food, water, and stimulants.

One trenchant story was related by William McCreedy, a Coast Guardsman who assisted in the rescue. He saw "a man doubled up in a small raft, his eyes resembling 'a couple of blue dots in a beefsteak. He flashed a beautiful smile that couldn't be missed. I felt I had looked at something a man sees once in a lifetime—sort of thought I had come to the edge of heaven. Then, as though his last will to fight had been lost when he saw us, he slumped into the water. The radioman grabbed him and held him in the raft. I went overboard to help and the three of us dragged the raft down. The unconscious man's foot was twisted in the lines, but I cut him free and we put him in the boat.' Just before reaching shore, the severely injured man reached up, stroked McCreedy's face and mumbled, 'We made it,' then died."

The four most seriously injured were transferred to a PBM and flown to the base hospital at the Norfolk Naval Air Station.

The search for survivors continued with the addition of six Navy vessels: the tugs *Sciota* and *ATR-8*, the minesweepers *Fulmer*, *Inflict*, and *Thrush*, and the destroyer escort *Jordan*. A "secret" document gives a succinct account of the results.

"At 1823 an SB2C signalled the ship to follow it, and when telephone communication was established reported there were two groups of survivors in the water about eighteen miles away. On nearing a raft with ten men on it, the plane dropped a float light to mark the position and the *Inflict's* motor whaleboat was gotten away and set out to pick up the men. The ship continued on for four miles, following the plane, which dropped a second float light marking the position of a small raft carrying two men. The ship

picked up the men and returned to its motor whaleboat, which was picked up with the first group of survivors. The rescue was completed at 2030. All of these men were from the *Bedloe*. The plane first contacted the ship about sunset and the rescue was completed after dark."

That document also stated that "all survivors suffered from exhaustion due to exposure and from necrotic ulcers of the legs due to immersion, but responded speedily to treatment. In addition, one man had a dislocated shoulder, another two broken ribs, and a third suffered considerable injury and destruction of tissue on the right leg which will require treatment for an estimated six months."

The massive search mission continued on the seventeenth, but no more survivors were found. Four bodies from the *Bedloe* were recovered. "Of the five officers and thirty-one enlisted men aboard the *Bedloe* on sailing, the Commanding, Executive and Engineering Officers and nine men were saved. Of the thirty-nine officers and men aboard the *Jackson*, the Executive Officer, one Junior Officer and seventeen men survived." A Coast Guard historical account gives different figures: twenty-six lost from

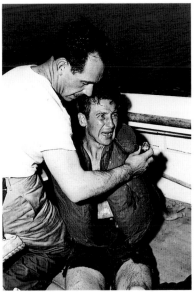

Anguish and exhaustion are evident on the faces of men plucked out of the sea after two horrible days adrift. The original photos are uncaptioned, but the survivors appear to be from the *Jackson*. (Both pages are courtesy of the National Archives.)

the *Bedloe*, twenty-one from the *Jackson*. Whatever the tally, these deaths were all the more tragic since every man had managed to escape from both cutters, only to die a slow and lingering death in the sea.

When the events of the double catastrophe were reconstructed later, it was the opinion of the men serving on the *Escape* that the wrecks lay in less than fifteen fathoms, and that therefore an effort should be made to locate and salvage the vessels. However, after due deliberation, the recommendation that was handed down was against any such attempt because the cutters could probably be replaced for what it would cost to locate, salvage, and rebuild them. The *Bedloe* and the *Jackson* were therefore written off the books.

Fil Nutter says he found one of the cutters by accident in 1988, but was then unable to relocate it. Brian "Doogie" Pledger found it in 1991. The wreck is now dived regularly.

It is broken in two, with the forward section consisting of about one quarter of the wreck separated by about thirty feet from the after section, which comprises the remaining three quarters. The bow section is angled about 45° to starboard with respect to the stern. The bow lies over on its starboard side, the stern sits upright.

The port anchor is visible on the bow, as is a considerable amount of ammunition: 3-inch gun shells, 30 caliber bullets in clips, and 20 millimeter machine gun shells. At the forward end of the break on the stern section are batteries and miscellaneous junk, with the deck gun lying some ten feet off the starboard edge of the wreck. The relief at this point is about one foot. The highest part is the engine: about fifteen feet. Otherwise, the level of the sand is even with the top of the hull, making the wreck appear like a sunken bathtub the bottom of which is actually deeper than the depth of the surrounding sand—which explains why the wreck is so difficult to find.

What appears to be a fuel tank about eight feet square sits in the middle of the stern section: baffle plates are visible through the rust holes. Both diesel engines are exposed, with the propeller shafts extending behind them. At the extreme stern are the depth-charge racks, still loaded with depth charges.

No positive identification has been made. A careful reading of the circumstances of the two sinkings reveals that the *Jackson* was last observed in an inverted condition, and that her bottom was visible for half an hour before being lost to sight. It would seem likely that the wreck would have settled upside down.

The *Bedloe*, on the other hand, rolled over on her port side, then stayed in that position for two or three minutes before going down. Although "capsized" was used to describe the way the cutter was lost, the word appears to have been misused, as she seems to have rolled over on her beam ends. She could have righted before hitting the bottom.

Further exploration—of the wreck as well as of historical documents—may provide the final clue. The location of the other cutter is still unknown.

BREWSTER

Built: 1903
Previous names: None
Gross tonnage: 1,517
Type of vessel: Freighter
Builder: Akt. Burmeister & Wain, Copenhagen, Denmark
Owner: H.H. Schmidt
Port of registry: Hamburg, Germany
Cause of sinking: Ran aground
Location: Southeast point of the Inner Diamond Shoal

Sunk: November 28, 1909
Depth: 14 feet
Dimensions: 249′ × 34′ × 15′
Power: Coal-fired steam

The *Brewster* was on a routine voyage from Port Antonio, Jamaica to New York when she was blown off course by a fierce northeast gale. She stranded on the Inner Diamond Shoal late at night on November 28, 1909. Captain F. Hinz, master, saw that his position was precarious. He ordered an officer and four men to launch a lifeboat and go for help while he and the rest of the crew took care of the ship.

By the time the wreck was discovered by a surfman at dawn, the weather was worsening and waves were breaking over the vessel fore and aft. The Life-Saving Service was galvanized into action. Boats from the Cape Hatteras, Hatteras Inlet, Creeds Hill, and Big Kinnakeet stations set out for the *Brewster* despite mountainous seas. The Creeds Hill boat was disabled, so the men transferred to the Cape Hatteras boat. However, even with additional men at the oars the life-saving crew could not make sufficient headway. Neither could the Hatteras Inlet power boat fight the wind and the sea. The men had the will, but their boats were simply too small for the task at hand.

Fortunately, H.L. Gaskill, fishing from his large power boat, saw their struggles and came to their aid. The Creeds Hill men transferred again, this time to the Hatteras Inlet power boat. Then Gaskill took the Cape Hatteras boat in tow toward the wrecked steamship. Because of the huge swells and breaking waves he was unable lay up alongside the *Brewster*. With skillful maneuvering he approached in the steamer's lee as near as he dared.

The *Brewster's* crew lowered a buoy into the raging torrent, and paid out the attached rope as the current dragged the buoy to the life-savers in the fishing boat. The Life-Saving Service report is all too brief and somewhat unclear on ensuing events: "By means of this line the seamen were hauled into the lifeboat one at a time. After 10 or 12 had reached the lifeboat they were transferred to the power lifeboat. which remained near by, and then another boat load was taken off and transferred in the same manner. When the entire ship's company had been taken off, the power lifeboat, with 16 of the rescued party, started for Hatteras Cove with the Cape Hatteras lifeboat in tow, which had the remaining 12 seamen on board. Counting the 5 men who were later taken from the lightship, the Cape Hatteras crew cared for 21 at their station." All thirty-three crewmen were thus accounted for.

Elsewhere it was reported that the life-saving crews "succeeded in landing at noon today Capt. Hinz and 28 members of the crew, who remained aboard the *Brewster*, only four members of the crew having left the steamer during last night and boarded *Diamond Shoals* lightship." It was also reported that "as soon as the steamer struck, six men from her crew managed to reach Cape Hatteras lightship and asked for assistance. The lightship, equipped with wireless notified Norfolk and the Merritt-Chapman Wrecking Company detached the tug *Foley* to assist the stranded vessel."

The disparity in numbers notwithstanding, all the *Brewster's* men were saved and well cared for; they received dry clothing and hot food and drink.

That same day the revenue cutter *Onondaga* and the Merritt and Chapman Wrecking Company's tugs, *I.J. Merritt* and *William Coley*, left Norfolk to lend assistance to the stranded steamer. When abandoned, the *Brewster* was still in good condition with her watertight integrity maintained. Initial hopes that she could be lightered and refloated soon waned when salvage tugs found it impossible because of increasing seas to get close to the wreck. The *Onondaga* lay to nearby until she lost her anchor and fifteen fathoms of chain.

The storm continued to rage. It was well that Captain Hinz and his crew had been taken off, for, "swept by mountainous seas, with only her deck and splintered spars showing at intervals, the wreck of the German steamer *Brewster* ... was fast breaking up." For miles "the coast was strewn with bananas and cocoanuts," her cargo. Finally, after two days of pounding, the *Brewster's* hull cracked. She filled with water until she "settled down so that only her masts and smokestacks were showing above water." The sunken ship represented a $75,000 loss, and $36,000 worth of bananas and cocoaunts were ruined.

On December 1 it was reported that "the steamer *Hermod*, passing *Diamond Shoals* lightship this evening took off from the lightship an officer and four men of the stranded steamer *Brewster* and will land them at Baltimore."

Encomiums were quick in coming. Captain F. Hinz and three of his officers wrote of the life-savers: "We must say that their conduct on this occasion is worthy of the greatest praise, and the manner in which the rescue was carried out worthy of American seamen. We also thank them for the kindness and hospitality extended to us while at the life-saving stations, and assure you that we will never forget same."

Perhaps they did not realize that Gaskill was a private citizen not in the employ of the Life-Saving Service, or they might have extended their commendation to include him as well.

The wreck of the *Brewster* is now part of the ever-shifting sands of the Diamond Shoals at a position then given as "seven miles offshore."

Sand tiger shark.

BUARQUE

Built: 1919
Previous names: *Scanpenn, Bird City*
Gross tonnage: 5,152
Type of vessel: Freighter
Builder: American International Ship Building Corp., Hog Island, PA
Owner: Lloyd Brasileiro
Port of registry: Rio de Janeiro, Brazil
Cause of sinking: Torpedoed by *U-432* (Kapitanleutnant Schultze)
Location: 26843.5

Sunk: February 15, 1942
Depth: 250 feet
Dimensions: 390′ × 54′ × 32′
Power: Oil-fired steam turbine

40999.3

The *Buarque* was a tramp freighter that gathered cargoes from various South American ports for transportation to purchasers in the United States. Starting in January 1942 she picked her way north from Rio de Janeiro, and gradually filled her holds with castor seed, timbo root, bauxite, coffee, cotton, and sheepskins from the Brazilian coastal cities of Bahia, Maceio, Pernambuco, Cabadelo, Natal, and Ceara. On her decks she carried rubber, aluminum ore, beryllium, drums of oil, and tanks of oxy-acetylene. In Belem she took on passengers. After a day and a half in La Guaira, Venezuela where she onloaded sabadilla seed, and a brief pause in Curacao, she threaded a path through the Caribbean Islands and struck out for her final destination of New York. Her cargo was valued at over half a million dollars.

Aboard the *Buarque* were eighty-five people: Captain Joao Joaquim de Moura, seventy-three officers and crew, and eleven passengers. Because Brazil was not militarily engaged in the world-wide war, she ran fully lighted at night and had huge Brazilian flags painted on her hull; the Brazilian ensign flying from the taffrail was illuminated by a brilliant floodlight. The ship was unarmed. Indeed, according to international treaty she had nothing to fear from marauding German warships. Even though Brazil had severed diplomatic relations with the Axis powers, neutrality laws protected the country's shipping.

That was why, when the lookout sighted a submarine off Wimble

Courtesy of the U.S. Coast Guard.

Shoals, Captain de Moura slowed his engine. The U-boat matched speed and closed to within two hundred feet of the lumbering freighter. In the darkness the enemy appeared as a ghostly silhouette. After several minutes of observation, the U-boat proceeded north on the surface and disappeared. If the captain and crew breathed a collective sigh of relief that they had passed the neutrality test, two American passengers were not so mollified.

Walter Shivers and John Dunn were Pan American Airline employees who were well-informed about the recent spate of torpedoings off the U.S. east coast. In the previous month more than two dozen ships had been attacked, and most had been sunk. For two days Shivers and Dunn had pleaded with Captain de Moura to black out his ship; the captain had firmly but courteously declined from engaging in what could be construed as hostile action.

Shivers and Dunn took it upon themselves to inspect the ship's safety equipment. They found the lifeboats in poor repair and improperly secured. "Not one member of the crew was instructed in any of the duties of lifeboat launching, care or handling."

The evening wore on uneventfully until just after the witching hour. Most of the people were asleep, Shivers and Dunn fitfully, when a tremendous explosion ripped out the *Buarque's* port side between holds No. 1 and 2. "The entire ship shook like a terrier would shake a rat," said Shivers. All the ship's lights were knocked out by the concussion.

Confusion reigned.

A Navy report summarized events. "The ship's passengers were uninstructed and ignored, even pushed aside by the crew in their hurry to get into the lifeboats. In the inky blackness, hand flashlights were the only illumination."

Episodes telescoped. "The ship faltered, stopped, took a list to starboard, and started down by the bow." In those last desperate moments Dunn "ran with his life belt on to the deck. There he found Mrs. Adrian Ferriera, an American woman passenger, with her 5-year old son, Freddie, in a lifeboat but without belts. He rushed back to her cabin for belts and additional blankets, returning immediately, and awaited orders to embark. No instruction came, and time drew short. Both Shivers and Dunn climbed down the Jacob's ladder to the No. 4 lifeboat which had been lowered very unevenly and was now in a precarious nose-down position. Mrs. Ferriera and her son were already in this half-launched boat; the rest of the crew and passengers had left the *Buarque* in three other lifeboats.

"In the confusion and disorganization of the abandonment, Shivers and Dunn were forced to take the initiative. Heavy ground swells were causing their boat to crash continuously into the mother ship. The officer in charge, Shivers observed, apparently had never been in a lifeboat before. The Americans spoke no Portugese, but motioned and yelled to lower the boat away, and proceeded to take general charge. The Brazilian sailors used no hooks or oars, and the boat was in danger of being crushed or swamped. Many gestures finally got them away from the ship's side. Dunn and Shivers then unlashed the oars and began rowing, shouting to the crew in the other three boats to do likewise.''

Dunn: ''There were eighteen of us in the boat. We had pulled about 100 yards away from the ship when a second torpedo struck amidships. . . . There was a terrific screaming sound as the water rushed into the ship's open spaces. I think she was ripped in half by the explosion.''

Shivers: ''A young tidal wave which followed the explosion almost swamped our lifeboat. The screaming of that sinking ship was almost human. It was the most eerie sound I've ever heard. It made my blood run cold.''

The *Buarque's* bow dipped beneath the surface, her stern rose high into the air, and like a steel knife sliding through soft butter the ship sank into the depths. Despite Shiver's and Dunn's admonitions about the crew's lack of proficiency, everyone managed to evacuate the freighter during the ten minutes between the first torpedo strike and the final submergence.

Dunn: ''We were leery of showing lights because we didn't know whether the submarine would machine-gun us. Later, however, we showed a flashlight and we saw flashlight beams from two other lifeboats. We remained in communication for a while. Then the boats became separated. After daybreak Sunday we saw the boat containing the two Venezuelan women.'' These two lifeboats stayed close, although ''not close enough to get some of the cognac they had aboard.'' In Dunn's lifeboat, ''Freddie became seasick; he was cold, wet and cramped, but he didn't complain and he smiled when any one spoke to him.'' The radio operator made paper boats to amuse the lad.

At 7 a.m. the two lifeboats were spotted by a land-based plane flying a partrol in response to an SOS received shortly after midnight. The plane radioed its position to base. Other planes circled the boats throughout the day, but salvation did not arrive until 5 p.m. when the Coast Guard cutter *Calypso* hove into view and took aboard the survivors. Said Dunn, ''We got a good break on the sea and the weather.''

However, the other two lifeboats did not get as good a break. They drifted all day of the fifteenth, that night, the next day, and that night. The seas were calm, but the thermometer hung only slightly above the freezing point. A steady rain poured down on them for forty hours; soaked and shivering, the men huddled together as best they could for protection from the elements.

It was not until 10:30 in the morning of the seventeenth that the Socony-Vacuum tanker *Eagle* came upon one of the lifeboats. By that time Manuel Rodriguez Gomez was already dead from exposure. The others were suffering from shock and frostbite.

That afternoon, after more than sixty hours adrift, the U.S. destroyer *Jacob Jones* (DD-130) found Captain de Moura's lifeboat. The survivors ''were able to scramble up the cargo net and walk with some assistance. All were well clothed except for two who had no shoes. In this group there was no evidence of shock, hysteria or delirium.''

Lieutenant Commander Hugh Black and some of his officers signed the back of a picture postcard of the *Jacob Jones*, and gave it to Captain de Moura as a souvenir. Eleven days later the *Jacob Jones* was torpedoed and sunk by the *U-578*, resulting in the deaths of every officer and most of the crew: one-hundred thirty-four fatalities; there were only eleven survivors. (See *Shipwrecks of Delaware and Maryland* for details.) Upon hearing the tragic news, Captain de Moura lamented, ''I feel more sorry at the loss of the destroyer than for my own ship, because no lives were lost on my ship.'' (He must have forgotten Gomez.)

Besides the political furor in Brazil caused by the loss of the *Buarque* (for details see *Track of the Gray Wolf*, by this author), the insurance companies lost quite a bit of money due to arrogant German transgression. Reinsurers were further incensed when Lloyd Brasileiro put in a claim for lost shipping fees resulting from nondelivery.

The back of the *Buarque's* bill of lading stated that ''the freight, whether payable by the shipper or by the consignee at the port of destination is fully earned and belongs completely to the carrier at the time of receipt of the merchandise into the custody of the vessel and if paid in advance is not returnable and if to be paid by the consignee remains payable even if ship and/or cargo are lost.'' This was a win/win situation for the government-sponsored company that operated the *Buarque*. It meant that Lloyd Brasileiro expected to get paid even if it failed to deliver the goods.

The opinion rendered by Bigham, Englar, Jones & Houston (the legal firm retained by the American Cargo War Risk Reinsurance Exchange) differed from the wishes of Lloyd Brasileiro. The lawyers ruled that the ''pay anyway'' clause was invalidated by two declarations: on the face of the bill of lading was typed ''Freight payable at destination;'' stamped below it was ''Freight to be paid at port of destination two hours after the arrival of the vessel.''

Bigham, Englar, Jones & Houston: ''The ordinary rule in the absence

Passengers and crew of the *Buarque* are landed after their ordeal at sea. (Courtesy of the National Archives.)

of any clear provision to the contrary is that collect freight is not earned or payable unless and until the cargo is delivered at destination. The foregoing clause, *printed on the back of the bill of lading*, in the absence of any other inconsistent clause, is sufficiently clear to overcome the ordinary rule that freight is not due until delivery. However, the *stamped* provision *on the face of the bill of lading* to the effect that the freight is to be paid two hours after the arrival of the vessel, in addition to the *typed* provision *on the face of the bill of lading* that the freight is payable at destination, is, in our opinion, inconsistent with the lost or not lost clause printed on the back of the bill of lading. Therefore, in view of the well recognized rule of construction that a stamped or typewritten clause overrides an inconsistent printed clause, we think the carrier is not entitled to any collect freight because the vessel never arrived at the port of destination.''

This was not the end of the matter. If Brazil could not collect from the insurance carriers, it could exact a toll from the Germans responsible for the monetary loss. The sinking of the Brazilian freighter *Olinda* only three days later sharply exacerbated the situation. (See *Shipwrecks of Virginia* for details of that casualty.) Brazil seized German property and froze German assets, and made a formal protest to the Axis powers. Germany issued a formal apology for its indiscretions, but continued to attack ships flying the Brazilian flag. On March 7, the *U-155* sank the *Arabutan*; on March 8, the *U-94* sank the *Cayru*.

The *Cayru* is covered in *Shipwrecks of New Jersey*. There were some curious coincidences between the *Cayru* and the *Buarque*: they were identical sister ships built at the same yard in the same year; the *Cayru's* first name was *Scanmail*, the *Buarque's* first name was *Scanpenn*; the *Cayru's* second name was *Chickasaw*, the *Buarque's* second name was *Bird City*; after a long career both were bought by Lloyd Brasileiro, which owned them at the time of their demise; and they were sunk within three weeks of each other, only a couple hundred miles apart.

Hostilities escalated between the two countries and reached a fever pitch among the Brazilian citizenry. Eventually Brazil was forced to declare war on Germany and her allies.

What of the *Buarque*? In 1943, *Sub Chaser 664* (SC-664) found a wreck hoped to be a sunken U-boat. However, investigation alleged that it was more likely the wreck of the *Equipoise* (q.v.). The USCG *Gentian* surveyed the area the following year, relocated the wreck, and lowered an underwater camera to examine the site. That report states, ''A further check into the source of the information which placed the sinking of the *Equipoise* in this area reveals that it is a composite of widely divergent positions given by various of her nine survivors, none of whom were officers. A study of the underwater photographs and other information available relative to the wreck does not shed any light on its identity. Its designation on the wreck list has therefore been changed from ''Probably *Equipoise*'' to ''Probably *Buarque*.''

The coordinates given were 36-16.1 N/74-51.1 W. Modern nautical charts show a wreck symbol very close to that position. The depth given by the *Gentian* was 225 feet, with the wreck standing as high as 165 feet. Today that wreck is well known by fishermen, who fish it regularly and call it the *Equipoise*. But it was not until July 3, 1992, that divers first descended to the rusted hull. Those who made that discovery dive were, in alphabetical order, Mike Boring (Captain of the *Sea Hunter*), Ken Clayton, Peter Feuerle, Steve Gatto, Jon Hulburt, Tom Packer, and the author. A pair of gauges recovered by the author seem to bear out the *Gentian's* deduction of "Probably *Buarque*." The gauges were manufactured by the Moeller Instrument Company of Brooklyn, New York, and were stamped "Made in U.S.A."

Because the *Buarque* was built at Hog Island, Pennsylvania, while the *Equipoise* was built in Glasgow, Scotland, the gauges presented a strong indication that we had in fact dived the *Buarque*. However, the final piece of evidence was provided by Hal and Penny Good. I had never dived the wreck being called the *Buarque*, in 140 feet of water, but I knew that they had. I called them for a description. Not only did they tell me that the wreck they dived had a triple expansion reciprocating steam engine (which the *Equipoise* had; the *Buarque* had a steam turbine) but they had recovered the helm stand, the head of which was stamped "The Pepper Steering Geer," "R. Roger & Co.," and "Stockton-on-Tees." In my mind, that made the identification of both wrecks definite.

Fifty years of immersion in sea water has taken a hard toll on the *Buarque*. On our necessarily brief exploration of the wreck we found the hull basically upright at a depth of 250 feet, rising no more than twenty feet off the bottom. There appears to be a slight tilt to port, born out by an inboard lean of the upper starboard hull plates, an outboard lean of the upper port hull plates, and a debris field to port from the midship superstructure. Otherwise, the decks have collapsed down into the hull, giving the effect of a giant steel bathtub filled with broken support beams, disjointed decking, and machinery. The wreck deserves a great deal more attention.

On the same patrol the *U-432* also sank the *Olinda* (see *Shipwrecks of Virginia*), *Azalea City*, *Norlavore* (q.v.), and *Marore* (q.v.). It returned to the American coast in June 1942, but sank only two samll fishing boats. It was sunk in the North Atlantic on March 11, 1943, with twenty-six crewmen killed and twenty captured.

Courtesy of the National Archives.

BYRON D. BENSON

Built: 1922
Previous names: None
Gross tonnage: 7,953
Type of vessel: Tanker
Builder: Oscar Daniels Company, Tampa, Florida
Owner: Tide Water Associated Oil Company
Port of registry: Wilmington, Delaware
Cause of sinking: Torpedoed by *U-552* (Oberleutnant zur See Topp)
Location: 26923.6

Sunk: April 7, 1942
Depth: 105 feet
Dimensions: 465' × 60' × 36'
Power: Oil-fired steam

40864.9

1942 was not a good year for the *Byron D. Benson*. On January 10 she rammed and sank the freighter *Continent* off the New York bight. Captain John MacMillan, master, was exonerated of all blame when the Bureau of Marine Inspection and Navigation found that "the collision was due to the failure of the *Continent* to keep out of the way of the *Byron D. Benson* which was the privileged vessel under the circumstances." (For complete details, see *Shipwrecks of New Jersey*, by this author.)

On April 4, Captain MacMillan was equally as innocent, although this time the casualty was the fault of the *Byron D. Benson* in not keeping out of the way of a German torpedo.

The tanker finished onloading 100,000 barrels of crude oil on March 27, at Port Arthur, Texas. She steamed across the Gulf of Mexico, rounded the southern tip of Florida, and headed north along the coast bound for Bayonne, New Jersey. She traveled independently, and ran a zigzag course which under many circumstances confused U-boat commanders and their target bearing transmitters. Nights found the ship with her navigation lights off and her ports tightly sealed, lest any stray glimmers of light give away her position to the enemy.

On April 4, off the coast of North Carolina, where U-boat activity was pronounced, Captain MacMillan found an escort craft blinking at him. She was the USS *Hamilton* (DD-141). A graphic account of ensuing events was related in an official Navy report that was written in a style unusual in formal military historical briefs.

"At first, the officers aboard the tanker were unable to figure out the message which the sub-chaser blinked at them. The captain hurried back to the chart room and returned with the code book which he kept carefully filed away in the wheel house. One mate said the code looked like 'AA', someone else was sure it was 'L', and another piped in that he was just as certain that the code letter was 'O'. The captain looked at the code book and, unable to find an answer to his pressing problem, slammed the book down disgustedly with a slight outburst of ocean-going profanity.

"Apparently noticing the confusion aboard the tanker, the sub-chaser ran up some letters, and then noting that the tanker still did not understand the hoist, the escort came close aboard, and, by the use of a megaphone, the Commanding Officer called out, 'You and the other tanker will receive escort throughout the night. Do you follow me? Follow behind me!' With that, the sub-chaser and another patrol craft with it disappeared astern."

The other patrol boat was the HMS *Norwich City*, an armed British trawler. They dropped behind long enough to issue similar instructions to another tanker, the *Gulf of Mexico*. The latter ship had had a U-boat encounter only the month before, and only a hundred miles south of her present position. At that time she had been machine-gunned. Now, the *Gulf of Mexico* drew up parallel with the *Byron D. Benson* while one patrol boat led the way and the other followed behind. The miniature convoy groped through the dark at eight knots.

With a lookout on the bow and two on the bridge, a large tanker by her side, two escorts, and a plane circling overhead, the *Byron D. Benson* semmed well protected. Nevertheless, Erich Topp boldly maneuvered his U-boat into position for an attack; at 9:45 that night he launched a deadly fish into her starboard side amidships, between No. 7 and No. 8 tanks. "The explosion was devastating and everything seemed to catch afire on the starboard side of the ship as soon as the torpedo hit. Burning oil spouted out of the gaping hold," which extended from below the water line all the way up to the main deck center-line.

"Members of the crew ran out from their compartments to find the forward part of the ship already on fire which was moving aft through the passageway and the scuppers on both sides."

Flames fanned the deck, and acrid fumes curled into the air making it difficult to breathe. The men were smoked out of their quarters and duty stations. The tanker was out of control. She "continued to proceed underway and bore off to the starboard spewing burning oil aft of the vessel." Captain MacMillan wasted no time ordering abandon ship. He had to shout in order to be heard above the clamor of the conflagration.

Both lifeboats on the starboard side were burned to a crisp. The crew worked furiously against advancing flames to launch the port boats. Twenty-six men crowded into lifeboat No. 4 as it was released from its falls. As the twenty-seventh tried to get in, the first engineer, in charge of the boat, told oiler John Austrauske that they were already overloaded, and sent him on to the forward boat. The men bent to the oars and pulled away from the blazing tanker.

Austrauske was too late. By the time he reached the other station the lifeboat was gone. Aboard were the captain and all the deck officers. Austrauske's despair turned to horror as the undermanned boat struggled to get away. The ship's forward momentum was still unchecked so that it moved inexorably past the lifeboat; the pool of burning oil spread out behind the *Byron D. Benson* like a living, breathing beast of destruction. The raging oil slick overtook the lifeboat and engulfed it flames. All nine men were consumed by fire.

Austrauske spent nearly an hour on the burning tanker, coughing in the noxious fumes. His last hope was to get away on an emergency life raft. With a fire axe the oiler chopped apart the ropes holding the raft in place, threw it over the side, and jumped over after it. Immediately he found himself in the same situation as the lifeboat. Alone, he was unable to keep the raft away from the encroaching flames. The blazing oil caught up with the raft and set it afire.

Austrauske leaped off his temporary refuge. He swam away with the strong, sure strokes borne of the fear of death. Still the oil kept coming, faster than he could swim. With fire crackling around him, with the heat searing his lungs, with the air filled with smoke, he almost succumbed. When flames licked his face he ducked underwater and swam until he found a water-filled hole in the slick—like a seal popping its nose through a hole in arctic ice. Again and again he dived, and eventually he outdistanced the flames. Then, nearly exhausted, he "just lay to."

As he gasped for air, he "claims to have heard a drone that seemed to him to sound like an airplane engine, but which might have been that of a submarine. . . . After that he thought he saw some bright illuminating lights. . . . that it might be an airplane dropping flares. They were bright bluish white lights and traveled down slowly into the water. He didn't know where they came from."

While this might seem like a near-death fantasy, an incident occurring only three miles away lends authenticity to his powers of observation. The fishing trawler *Isaac Fass* had just set her nets when the *Byron D. Benson* was torpedoed. The crew was aghast to see "bright flames licking through billowing, thick smoke," and "red flames rise from close to the water on each side of the fire." The ship was being shelled.

"Eight or ten shots were heard. Both the captain and the engineer declared that each shot jarred the *Isaac Fass* and that the vibration was so great that a wedge between the exhaust stack and a hole through the roof of the pilot house jarred loose and fell to the deck.''

They hastened to haul in their nets, and did it in the dark instead of switching on the deck lights as they usually did. ''While the nets were being hauled in, the men noticed two bright red running lights coming toward them from the direction of the burning vessel. These lights appeared to be very steady and therefore could not have been on a lifeboat or a fishing trawler. The smoke was blowing from the burning tanker toward the trawler, so that the red lights were often obscured.''

As soon as the nets were aboard, they skedaddled.

By this time the *Gulf of Mexico* was far to the north, hopefully out of range of any follow-up torpedoes. The *Hamilton* and the *Norwich City* scoured the dark, smoke-filled sea for survivors; neither of the escort vessels saw any signs of submarines, or fired any shots. Less than two hours after

Courtesy of the National Archives.

leaving their vessel, the men in lifeboat No. 4 were rescued by the *Hamilton*. Austrauske was picked up by the *Norwich City*. The survivors were taken to the Norfolk Naval Operating base; two men were hospitalized for burns.

Among the survivors were two who were not seamen at all. Monor Mabry was a 19-year-old plebe at the U.S. Military Academy; he had joined the crew in order to regain his health after a serious eye infection had debilitated him. Merlin Johnson was a free-lance writer who signed on to get story material. What one did not get the other certainly did.

Dawn found the million-dollar tanker still afloat and spewing her valuable cargo into the ocean. Thick, black smoke boiled thousands of feet into the air. The *Byron D. Benson* did not sink that day, nor the next. Not until April 7 did she give up the ghost and settle into a watery grave. By that time she was a burned out, useless hulk.

Erich Topp had quite a successful patrol, sinking in all six vessels within the confines of the Eastern Sea Frontier; total tonnage amounted to 39,475. Further depredations of the *U-552* include the *Lancing* (q.v.), and three ships covered in *Shipwrecks of North Carolina: from Hatteras Inlet South: Atlas, British Splendour*, and *Tamaulipas*. Topp is infamous for torpedoing the U.S. destroyer *Reuben James* (DD-245) six weeks *before* Germany and the United States were at war. One hundred fifteen American sailors were killed because of Topp's premature aggression.

Topp relinquished control of the *U-552* to his successor on September 8, 1942. The U-boat survived the war only to be ignominiously scuttled by its crew upon Germany's capitulation.

On March 10, 1945 the wreck of the *Byron D. Benson* was wire-dragged as a hazard to navigation; it was cleared to a depth of fifty-eight feet. On April 24 two prowling destroyers made a sonar contact with the sunken hull, and buoyed it. Thus its identity has come down through history.

The wreck is huge and contiguous along its keel, although a wide break in the hull resulting from torpedo damage seems to make it appear as if the wreck is split in two. The distance across this break is about fifty feet.

The stern section contains the boiler room and engine room. The fantail and the port side along the machinery spaces is somewhat broken down and caved inward, while the starboard side rises some thirty feet off the bottom. The engine room and boiler rooms can be entered easily from above because the superstructure has been swept away. Gauges abound on the bulkheads, and conger eels thrive in every available nook and cranny.

Forward of the break the wreck is less interesting. With the wheelhouse gone there is very little left except the tanks, some of which have collapsed while others maintain their structural integrity and rise to a depth of 90 feet. The bow section has the shape of a ship and some of its deck gear, but very little else. The very tip of the bow is broken off so that the hawse pipes and anchors rest against the sand. The wreck is not visited as much as it should be.

Carl Gerhard to the left, the remains of the *Kyzickes* to the right. (Courtesy of the U.S. Coast Guard.)

CARL GERHARD

Built: 1923
Previous names: None
Gross tonnage: 1,505
Type of vessel: Freighter
Builder: Larvik Slip & Verksted, Larvik, Sweden
Owner: Trelleborgs Angf. Nya Aktiebolag (F. Malmros, Managers)
Port of registry: Trelleborg, Sweden
Cause of sinking: Ran aground
Location: One mile north of Kill Devil Hills Coast Guard station

Sunk: September 24, 1929
Depth: 15 feet
Dimensions: 244′ × 39′ × 17′
Power: Coal-fired steam

Difficult as it may be to believe, in these days of sophisticated electronic aids to navigation, Captain A. Ohlsson blamed the stranding of his vessel on being lost at sea for five consecutive days: he could not sight the sun by day nor fix the stars by night; his sextant and logarithm tables were useless. Add to this a northeast gale and malfunctioning steering gear, and you've got a recipe for disaster.

He did not see the watchful Coast Guardsman firing rockets to warn him away from the shoal. The first that Captain Ohlsson realized that the *Carl Gerhard* was headed for shore was when the ship grated over the outer bar off Kill Devil Hills. Then it was too late. The great combers washed the ship straight toward the beach.

There came a loud, rending crash and the screech of steel on steel. By some crude cosmic coincidence the *Carl Gerhard* struck the battered hulk of the *Kyzickes* (q.v.), which had gone aground two years earlier. As the *Carl Gerhard's* port side scraped across the *Kyzickes'* jagged hull plates her side was stove in. Then the Swedish steamer came to a sudden, grinding halt as she bottomed out a hundred yards from the beach. The time was 7:30 a.m.

Huge waves pounded the *Carl Gerhard* relentlessly; the hull began to break apart. Soon there converged upon the scene the crews of four Coast Guard stations: Bodie Island, Kill Devil Hills, Nags Head, and Paul Gamble Hill. "Capt. Herman Smith, of Bodie Island station, was in command. . . . The coast guardsmen, unable to launch their life boats in the seething surf, resorted to the use of the Lyle life line, and the breeches buoy which is a part of the life saving outfit.

"When the line, shot with remarkable accuracy from the shore, fell across the deck of the helpless craft it was seized by eager hands and made fast to the foremast of the *Gerhard*. Then, the breeches buoy or basket was hauled out to the ship. Mrs. Ethel Adehard, wife of First Mate Adehard, was first to come ashore in the basket. The life line sagged considerably and several of those who took the wild ride in the basket were dragged through the sea for several feet."

No sooner had the last person been brought ashore than the ship broke completely apart. The people "reached shore in fairly good condition and were given food and dry clothing at the Kill Devil Hills Coast Guard station." Twenty men and one woman owed their lives to the valiant members of the U.S. Coast Guard.

At the time of her loss the *Carl Gerhard* was carrying 1,504 tons of crushed gypsum rock on a voyage from Mabou, Nova Scotia to Tampa, Florida. Although the cargo was valued at only $6,000, the vessel was worth a quarter of a million. It was afterward suspected that the freighter had suffered bottom damage when she grounded temporarily in the mud "just before she started on the voyage that ended so disastrously." That concussion may have strained the steering gear.

The wreck of the *Carl Gerhard* has been pummeled throughout the years by a crashing surf. It serves today as a haven for fish and marine life, and as a snare for surf fishermen with an exceptionally long cast. Divers can access the site from the beach. The wreck is known locally as one of the Triangle Wrecks.

CARROLL A. DEERING

Built: 1919
Previous names: None
Gross tonnage: 2,114
Type of vessel: Wooden-hulled five-masted schooner
Builder: G.G. Deering Company, Bath, Maine
Owner: G.G. Deering Company, Bath, Maine
Port of registry: Bath, Maine
Cause of sinking: Ran ashore
Location: Diamond Shoals

Sunk: January 31, 1921
Depth: Unknown
Dimensions: 255' × 44' × 25'
Power: Sail

The stranding of the *Carroll A. Deering* is one of the strangest and most perplexing cases on record: a seafaring mystery that was never solved. There is much speculation on the cause of her demise, but the documented facts are few and unsatisfactory.

The schooner cleared Rio de Janeiro under the command of Captain Willis Wormell who "is reported to have been experienced as a navigator and thoroughly reliable." With him was a crew of ten. Without cargo the windjammer rode high and light. On January 9, 1921 she put into Barbados "for orders, but, receiving no different orders, proceeded on its voyage to Norfolk." As she worked her way north she was undoubtedly spotted by many ships but as a typical sight of the day none took special notice of her until the twenty-third, when she reached the coast of North Carolina.

A letter later circulated among American Consular Officers at seaports along the windjammer's route offered particulars. "On January 29, 1921, the American schooner *Carroll A. Deering*, sailing at the rate of about five miles per hour, passed Cape Lookout Light Ship, North Carolina. ... at the time ... a man on board, other than the Captain, hailed the Light Ship and reported that the vessel had lost both anchors and asked to be reported to his owners. Otherwise the vessel appeared to be in very good condition."

On January 30, Captain Henry Johnson, master of the SS *Lake Elon*, "sighted a five-masted schooner about two points on our starboard bow, the wind was S.W. moderate and she had all sails set and steering about NNE making about seven miles. We passed her about 5:45 p.m. about one-half mile off on our port side we were then about twenty-five miles S.W. true from the Diamond Shoal Light Vessel, from the description of the *Deering*, we think that this schooner was her but we could not read her name, there was nothing irregular to be seen on board this vessel but she was steering a peculiar course. She appeared to be steering for Cape Hatteras."

These two sightings a day apart are about eighty miles distant.

Surfman C.P. Brady was on lookout duty the next morning when he sighted a five-masted schooner "with all sails set" riding a sandbar on the Diamond Shoals. He put out a call for help. As was customary in the case of a vessel in distress, lifesavers from the adjacent Coast Guard stations pooled their resources. The two surfboats that pounded through the waves toward the stranded schooner carried members of Big Kinnakeet, Cape Hatteras, Creeds Hill, and Hatteras Inlet stations.

They found the ship "driven high up on the shoal ... in a boiling bed of breakers." Unable to reach the schooner due to the crashing surf surrounding her, they scanned the wreck for signs of life to be saved. They found none. Nor did they observe any lifeboats in their davits. A dangling ladder implied that the crew had escaped.

Foul weather continued for the next two days. On February 2 the Coast Guard cutter *Seminole* braved the breaking seas by backing to within three-quarters of a mile from the wreck. According to her log "the surf was running high over the shoals and occasionally breaking over the schooner's poop. It was impossible to read her name, But it appeared to be a long one, and the home port looked to be Bath, Me., however this could not be positively made out. ... Practically all her sails are set except the flying jib. She lies pointed about N x W and on the S. side of the Outer Shoal in about 35° 08' 30" N., 75° 28' W. She was not pounding so far as could be seen, and she is staunch as yet. No wreckage alongside of her was seen. She is listed to starboard 4° or 5°."

By February 4 the seas moderated enough for the Coast Guard cutter *Manning* to anchor nearby. She lowered a boat and took soundings. Surfboats from stations 182 and 183 arrived on the scene. Together the Coast Guardsmen explored the wreck. They found the *Carroll A. Deering* "in fair condition although fast going to pieces." Her papers were still aboard but she appeared to have been looted: "All provisions, clothing, and supplies of the vessel has been removed."

The *Manning* looked for debris as she worked her way toward the Chesapeake Bay. "The *Carroll A. Deering* carried a motor lifeboat and a dory, but neither of them has been picked up and no wreckage from them has been found."

Nor was any wreckage, or any survivors, *ever* found.

Five executive branches of the United States federal government initiated investigations into the matter: the Departments of Commerce, Justice, Treasury, State, and Navy. Contradicting the Light Ship report, Shipping Board Commissioner Edward Plummer learned that "both anchors were on the vessel when she was found ashore, the kedge anchor lashed under the bowsprit. Furthermore, the man who hailed the lightship was not the captain, for he had red hair, and, according to the records of the owners, there was no red-haired man in the crew."

It can logically be concluded that the crew did not abandon ship *after* she stranded, for they certainly would have taken in the sails in order to stabilize the ship and help prevent her grinding on the bottom. This deduction infers that the men left the ship before she ran aground.

One suspicious event disclosed by official inquiry came from the *Cape Lookout* lightship. "A short time after the schooner passed the Light Ship, a steamer, the name of which can not be ascertained, which was passing, was asked to stop and take a message for forwarding, and in spite of numerous attempts on the part of the master of the Light Ship to attract the vessel's attention, no response to his efforts was received."

A minor point, perhaps, unless taken in conjunction with a bottle found on the beach near Cape Hatteras on April 11, that contained the following message: "*Deering* captured by oil burning boat something like chaser taking off everything handcuffing crew crew hiding all over ship no chance to make escape finder please notify headquarters of *Deering*."

Enter Lulu Wormell, the captain's daughter. Not satisfied with the lack of positive results of the official investigation she eagerly pounced on this peculiar piece of evidence. She took the note to the homes of each crew member's relatives, to track down the hand that wrote it. The hastily penciled strokes appeared to have been made by the schooner's engineer, Herbert Bates. A handwriting expert who compared the note with letters written by Bates agreed that the script was similar.

However, further analysis contested the resemblance, and subsequent examination revealed that the handwriting looked suspiciously like that of Christopher Columbus Grey, the fisherman who found the bottle. Grey finally admitted he had faked the message; then he ran off and hid in the swamp. He was not prosecuted because no law existed under which he could be punished.

Meanwhile, government agents theorized that a much more sinister plot was afoot: piracy. Not just ordinary pirates, but Bolsheviks.

Taking into account that no less than eleven ships—and possibly as many as twenty—were lost without a trace off the Carolinas in the first six months of 1921, coincidence was ruled out. A bottled message supposedly from the SS *Hewitt* claimed that she too had fallen victim to nefarious hijackers. (The *Hewitt* was carrying sulphur from Sabine, Texas to Boston, and last wirelessed her position some two hundred miles southeast of Cape Hatteras.) The *Carroll A. Deering* provided the only tangible evidence that a human agency, and not the dreadful forces of nature, was responsible for the numerous catastrophes.

This was not just an early case of communist paranoia; there was substantiating evidence. In April 1920 Russian mutineers took over the Cuxhaven fishing vessel *Senator Schroeder* and drove it to Murmansk, where it was declared confiscated in the name of the Soviet government. The captain and two officers were returned to Germany. The following month the remaining crew members stole the ship back and returned to Cuxhaven with the newly appointed Russian officers, who were then tried and sentenced to prison.

Despite that singular incident, it is stretching a point to blame all unexplained ship disappearances on Iron Curtain holders.

Weather Bureau meteorologist F.G. Tingley surmised that winter storms were more likely the cause than Russians. "We are not worried about Bolshevik submarines or pirates."

So what happened to all those sailors unaccounted for? Were they kidnapped? Did they drown? Were they forced to walk the plank? Did they run afoul of rum runners? Or were they scooped up by the mysterious powers of the Bermuda Triangle? One unconfirmed report claimed that the only living creature found aboard the *Carroll A. Deering* was a parrot—but it refused to talk.

Perhaps even more ridiculous was the wild speculation that the pirate vessel in question was the long-lost Navy collier *Cyclops*. *(In 1918 the Cyclops* left Brazil with a load of manganese ore bound for Norfolk; also on board were 308 passengers and crew. The 19,360 ton bulk cargo carrier put in at Barbados—and was never seen again.) This hypothesis gained support due to the mistaken belief that forty-seven life-term prisoners being transferred to American custody broke out of confinement and took over the ship. In fact, only five prisoners were aboard. Believers also surmised that a 542-foot-long ship could surreptitiously pull into little-used inlets along the eastern seaboard and hide from the authorities. Left unexplained is how the *Cyclops* refueled during the three years of her absence.

During the spring of 1921 the derelict schooner was designated a menace to navigation, and was dynamited by the Coast Guard. The bow fetched up on the beach; the wreckage was still visible in 1950. Today, all vestiges of the ghost ship lie beneath the sand; and, were it to resurface above the crystal granules, it would be classified as a "buoyant wreck" whose wooden remains might be refloated by the encroaching tides and taken once again to sea—to sail along the shore until it fetched up elsewhere, or until the hulk could be harnessed with hawsers and towed beyond the reach of danger.

The case of the *Carroll A. Deering* remains an unsolved riddle, the fate of her crew a mystery. Perhaps somewhere among the sandy shoals, where bleached bones berth, lie answers to the questions that have been passed down to this generation—and will probably be passed on to the next.

The bow of the *Carroll A. Deering*, photographed in 1950. (Courtesy of the Outer Banks History Center.)

CHENANGO

Built: 1918   Sunk: April 20, 1942
Previous names: *War Hamlet, Newaster, Kurikka*   Depth: 140 feet
Gross tonnage: 3,014   Dimensions: 342' × 46' × 22'
Type of vessel: Freighter   Power: Coal-fired steam
Builder: Irvine's Ship Building and Dry Dock Co., West Hartlepool, Eng.
Owner: United States Maritime Commission
Port of registry: Panama
Cause of sinking: Torpedoed by *U-84* (Kapitanleutnant Uphoff)
Location: 26872.3   41104.8

But for fortuitous circumstances the *Chenango* would have been one of those ships lost without a trace. She was carrying a cargo of manganese ore from Rio de Janeiro (via the Virgin Islands) to Baltimore when she was struck by a torpedo fired by the *U-84*, Oberleutnant zur See Horst Uphoff. The warhead detonated at the port side water line with such violence that topside personnel and loose equipment were hurled overboard. In a torrent, water poured through the huge hole in the hull. The ship was dragged down within two minutes.

No distress signals were sent, all but one of the lifeboats went down with the ship (and that one capsized), and the emergency life rafts had been improperly stowed on the deck: they were smashed up by the rigging (they should have been stowed above it). Luckily, one raft floated free, and to this two survivors clung. James Bradley and Joseph Dieltiens were all who remained out of a crew of thirty-three.

Alone in the untamed sea, they clambered aboard an open raft that had been condemned; it was fitted with a single cask of water and one fishing line. Bradley was Irish, Dieltiens was Belgian; neither understood the language of the other. They communicated in the silent tongue of men fighting for survival.

Dieltiens incurred internal injuries during the blast; he was hemorrhaging internally. Bradley was strong. When help did not arrive immediately, they decided to ration their water and fish for food. Day after day they eked out a precarious existance. Cold water washed over their raft,

Opposite: Above, two exhausted survivors wave at the rescue plane. Middle, the plane taxies close to the raft. Bottom, the survivors are offloaded on stretchers. (All courtesy of the National Archives.)

drenching them constantly; they lay exposed to the chilly air with hardly any clothing for protection.

Time and again they were disappointed as patrol planes droned by—only to fly off when their pilots failed to see the lone raft bobbing gently in the Atlantic swells. The fishing was poor, their water insufficient. Gradually, both men weakened.

It was not until the twelfth day adrift that an Army plane spotted the raft. Although the *Chenango* sank just south of the Virginia border, the raft was found southeast of Oregon Inlet, North Carolina. The plane dipped low enough for the pilot to see both men waving frantically. The distress call sent back to base prompted an immediate response. Captain Richard Burke proceeded "to the area in a PH-2 seaplane, he made a successful landing in confused cross seas and, after many difficulties, succeeded in removing the semi-conscious and delirious survivors."

Both men were taken directly to the Marine Hospital at the Norfolk Navy Base. Bradley rallied, and was soon on his feet. Despite medical treatment, Dieltiens weakened: he was too far gone from internal bleeding compounded by exposure and lack of food and water; two days later he died.

The *Chenango's* position was not known until after the war, when the Allied Command correlated German U-boat records with merchant ship losses. In 1956, the wreck was wire-dragged to a least depth of one hundred feet.

Few divers have visited the *Chenango* due to its location: far offshore, and midway between Rudee Inlet and Oregon Inlet. It is a long boat ride from either direction. Yet it is a wreck that deserves closer scrutiny.

The hull is broken in two in the shape of an "L", with the break occurring at the forward end of the boiler room. The two extensions of the "L" are separated by about twenty feet. Both parts are upside down: the forward part perfectly so, the after part at an angle that is not easy to measure. The bow rises less than five feet above the sand, but the stern sticks up about fifteen feet. The boiler rooms are easily entered; one can go completely through the wreck and come out the other side. The engine room is somewhat cluttered due to collapse of the machinery.

The propeller shaft is visible on the starboard side for the last fifty feet of its length. It goes through the gland in the stern, but there is no propeller on the end of it; the clean terminus makes it appear that the propeller was salvaged. The rudder stands intact in the stern post with its pintles resting perfectly in their gudgeons; because the rudder lies over at about a forty-five degree angle, it appears that the hull is similarly twisted to the side.

Divers should note that this is a cold water dive, akin to wrecks found in Virginia, the extension of whose border is not far north. The *Chenango* is shrouded in anemones, not warm water coral and sea fans. Fisherman, both rod-and-reelers and spear-wielders, should note that the wreck is inhabited by the largest tautog—and the most plentiful—I have ever seen.

CILTVAIRA

Built: 1905   Sunk: January 21, 1942
Previous names: *Twyford, Vironia, Twyford, President Bunge, Endsleigh*
Gross tonnage: 3,779   Dimensions: 346' × 50' × 23'
Type of vessel: Freighter   Power: Coal-fired steam
Builder: J.L. Thompson & Sons, Ltd., Sunderland, England
Owner: Latvian Shipping Company   Depth: Unknown
Port of registry: Riga, Latvia
Cause of sinking: Torpedoed by *U-123* (Kapitanleutnant Hardegen)
Location: Unknown

    The east coast U-boat war was only five days old when Reinhard Hardegen created a night of terror that saw two ships sunk and one damaged—and many lives lost. It began when he torpedoed the *City of Atlanta* (q.v.). Within thirty minutes he spotted the tanker *Malay* running in ballast; during the ensuing gun battle five seamen were killed and others injured, but the *Malay* outran the U-boat and lived to tell the tale. Not so lucky was the *Ciltvaira*.

    Proceeding from Norfolk to Savannah with a load of paper, the aged freighter plodded along at eight knots—hardly fast enough to get out of her own wake, much less outdistance a charging U-boat. It was five o'clock in the morning and "clear, calm, and dark" when the unseen torpedo struck the *Ciltvaira* on "the port side of the engine room, pierced the boilers, and flooded the boiler room and No. 2 hold." There was a hole four feet in diameter at the water line.

Killed instantly were two firemen: Carl Gustaefssen and Rolf Semelin. Radio Operator Rudolph Musts found himself locked in his room. "The door was jammed. Everything was black out and everywhere was hot steam. I managed, somehow, to force open the door and that way I get to a lifeboat."

Seaman Nick Creteu said, "All of a sudden something happened. The whole night was filled with fire. Some kind of noise happened. I don't know how to say it. I was knocked straight up off my feet, about two feet in the air. But it didn't knock me out."

Captain Skarlis Kerbergs ordered abandon ship. In high aplomb considering the circumstances, the men launched lifeboats and stood off their wounded vessel. Among the survivors were the ship's mascots: a cat named Briska and a dog named Pluskis.

At seven o'clock came the northbound passenger liner *Coamo*. The *Ciltvaira* survivors signaled for help with flashlights. "The *Coamo's* master was evidently aware of the new dangers off the coast; he continued on at full speed." Captain Nels Helgesen was wise to be cautious. Before the year was out his ship was sunk with all hands—one hundred thirty-four souls— by the *U-604*.

Although she was sorely wounded, the *Ciltvaira* did not sink. She floated idly "ten miles south of Wimble Shoals buoy, at a point nine miles from shore." Captain Kerbergs and a crew of hardy volunteers reboarded their ship. They could not shore up the damage hole but two hours later, when the Brazilian freighter *Bury* hove into view, they worked a towing hawser around the bitts and thumbed a ride. Said Leon Lusis, "The ship was then practically sinking under us."

The newly appointed tug and tow made very little headway. The *Bury* asked to be relieved. She continued on to New York with the portion of the *Ciltvaira's* crew she had taken aboard. Captain Kerbergs gathered the men's passports and the ship's papers. According to Seaman Leon Da Salva, "We hoisted a signal flag—SOS—and went back to the boat again. We looked back and saw now the ship was broken in the middle with a big hole. She was filling fast with water. About 9 o'clock, four hours after we were hit, we were picked up" by the tanker *Socony Vacuum*, which took them to Charleston, South Carolina.

When the USS *Osprey* (AM-56) arrived she stood by the sinking freighter until the ocean-going tug USS *Sciota* (AT-30) could resume the tow. From this point the records regarding the fate of the *Ciltvaira* become confused, and the ship's final moments were only cryptically noted.

One official document states that "the vessel remained afloat and drifting for two days, from all reports, and was last seen, almost sunk, at 2100 on January 21. The location was 35-46N; 74-37W."

Another document is even more perplexing in that it appears to be a compilation of various memoranda put down without concern for order:

With her back broken, the *Ciltvaira* sinks ever lower in the water. (All courtesy of the National Archives.)

"Standing by *Ciltvaira*. Vessel apparently broken amidship but floating. Entire crew has abandoned vessel.

"*Ciltvaira* retorpedoed 35 miles NNE of Cape Hatteras. Attacked sub in vicinity. From Fleet Air.

"Ship taken in tow but lost in heavy sea. Ship settling and believe unsafe take in tow again. From *Sciota*.

"Request ships vicinity destroy vessel by gunfire. From *Sciota*.

"Believe *Ciltvaira* torpedoed only once when found ship sagging and awash amidship. Settling slowly. From *Sciota*.

"Fleet Air, at 1615/20, giving position 3552–7516, reported *Ciltvaira* about 3 miles E and 3 miles S of above position and drifting rapidly to SE. A DD, PC and *Sciota* were standing by.

"Passed over *Ciltvaira* still afloat although her back is sadly broken in 3546–7437. From CG plane V175."

Where did the *Ciltvaira* finally come to rest? Most definitely not at the loran coordinates most commonly circulated (26847.8/40450.8) because that wreck has a deck gun mounted on its stern. Aerial photographs taken while the *Ciltvaira* was under tow clearly show that she carried no such gun. (See *Mirlo* for further discussion in that regard.)

An examination of the *Sciota's* deck log for January 20 reveals that the towing operation was extremely hazardous. Three men were injured while being transferred to the *Ciltvaira*; one suffered a fractured tibia and fibula, one a sprained ankle, one a strained leg muscle. The *Sciota* took the freighter in tow at 12:25 p.m., but the tow wire parted an hour later. She left the *Ciltvaira* at 3:45 p.m. "in danger of breaking in two," and headed back to Norfolk at 9.7 knots on a course of 308°; she passed Bodie Island Light at 6:20.

Extrapolation of the *Ciltvaira's* drift pattern is complicated by this wealth of contradictory evidence.

The 1944 wreck survey proved negative. "Derelict was last sighted drifting seaward beyond 100-fathom curve." But then, the survey made the same statement concerning the *Byron D. Benson* (q.v.). It is possible that the wreck only tentatively identified by the *Gentain* as the *San Delfino* (q.v.) could prove to be the *Ciltvaira*. An open mind, a diligent search, and direct observation of that wreck or newly-acquired hang numbers will someday lead to its discovery.

Reinhard Hardegen survived the war and is alive today. On June 5, 1942, command of the *U-123* was given to Oberleutnant zur See Horst von Schroeter. According to the log of the *U-123*, it was decommissioned in Lorient on August 19, 1944.

As she originally appeared. (Courtesy of the Steamship Historical Society of America.)

CITY OF ATLANTA

Built: 1904

Previous names: None

Gross tonnage: 5,269

Type of vessel: Passenger-freighter

Builder: Delaware River I.S.B. & Engineering Works, Chester, PA

Owner: Ocean Steam Ship Company of Savannah, New York, NY

Port of registry: Savannah, Georgia

Cause of sinking: Torpedoed by *U-123* (Kapitanleutnant Hardegen)

Location: 26894.8

Sunk: January 19, 1942

Depth: 90 feet

Dimensions: 378' × 49' × 35'

Power: Coal-fired steam

40399.7

The *City of Atlanta* had a long and perhaps too notorious career, spending nearly as much time in the news as she did on the ocean. For many years she served the coastal trade, and was revered for her efficiency if not for speed and luxury. In addition to passenger staterooms occupying her two upper decks, with both a shaded and sunlit promenade, her cargo holds were large and commodious and usually full of general merchandise.

After much of her passenger accomodations was removed. (Courtesy of the Steamship Historical Society of America.)

It was not until October 29, 1920 that the *City of Atlanta* first encountered catastrophe: one that changed the course of her life. On that night she was without passengers, carrying only pig iron from Savannah, Georgia to Providence, Rhode Island. As she entered Narragansett Bay she collided with the outbound concrete ship *Cape Fear*. Steel evidently proved stronger than concrete, for the *Cape Fear* sank in about three minutes. The *City of Atlanta* survived with a badly crumpled bow. There were no casualties.

During the time the *City of Atlanta* was drydocked for repairs her owners re-evaluated her usefulness in the shipping business. With the passenger trade on the wane they had her upperworks cut back, and space allocated to providing services for passengers was converted into cargo compartments. Accomodations were more than halved.

On February 10, 1925, the *City of Atlanta* was involved in another collision. This time she ran down the barge *Juniper* in a dense fog off York Spit, Baltimore. The barge sank in thirty feet of water; the *City of Atlanta* received a broken guard rail and a dented side.

May 14, 1930 found the *City of Atlanta* once again victorious against a lesser antagonist. This time she rammed the schooner *Azua* some forty-seven miles southeast of Barnegat, New Jersey. The schooner went to the bottom with her captain and one crewman.

If the *City of Atlanta* was a headache to insurance companies during peacetime, she became a major casualty once German U-boats replaced accident with intent. The freighter left New York for Savannah on January 17, 1942 with a varied cargo consisting of moist coconut, dried coconut, soap, brassware, sardines, dates, date-nut bread, orange-nut bread, gingerbread mix, Devil's-food mix, poultry feed, macaroni, metal cots, spring assemblies, sole leather, shoe tops, fish, rubber products, drug products, scoured wool, and three cases of Kings Ransom Scotch Whiskey—all insured for $453,896. The hull was worth another $400,000.

Captain L.C. Urquhart commanded a crew of forty-six; there were no passengers aboard. Only three days before leaving port the German U-boat arm made known its presence by sinking the tanker *Norness* off Long Island, New York. America was in an uproar. The Navy issued instructions for the *City of Atlanta* to hug the shore and dim her navigation lights.

She was doing just that when an explosion "shook the ship from stem to stern." The time was 2:15 a.m. According to Chief Mate George Tavelle, the watch officer, the torpedo "struck on the port side, a little abaft of the engine room bulkhead in number 3 hold. There was a great flare of flame on the explosion, and there was debris in the air, and a very heavy concussion. The concussion blew in the pilot house windows, shattering them."

The blast also knocked out the lights and blew up the radio shack. An emergency relay system kicked in and automatically switched on lights that brightly illuminated the bridge. Tavalle immediately turned them off, "fearful that we might be machine-gunned." He shoved the telegraph handles to the "engine off" position. He rang the alarm bell, but it shorted out after a couple of seconds.

The *City of Atlanta* listed so abruptly that it was message enough for the crew to assemble at their lifeboat stations. Oiler Robert Fennell "was asleep when the torpedo hit. When I got some clothes on and was almost up to the deck I remembered that I didn't have my wife's picture. So I went back to my bunk and got it."

Tavelle had to kick his way out of the bridge because the doors had been jammed by the force of the explosion. He began launching his assigned lifeboat barely a minute after the torpedo hit.

"The men were already gathering on the deck when I came out on the starboard side, and with considerable difficulty, because of the rapid listing of the ship to port, we managed to get number 1 and 3 boats swung out, but by the time the davits were swung out the ship had listed to port so sharply that the boats rested on the starboard side and we could not release the gripes. ... I do not know what was going on on the port side. ... Between four and five minutes after the impact, the submarine came around our stern and up on our starboard quarter and stood off perhaps 75 feet from where we were at the boats, but close under the stern. She played a small searchlight over us."

The U-boat crew watched with grisly fascination as the freighter's men fought for their lives, as if the rolling ship were a carnival sideshow.

In trying to release the jammed falls, "one of them slipped and broke my hold, and I fell into the water on the starboard side in the space between the two lifeboats. I managed to get out from between the boats and swam away from the ship. ... Within ten minutes—not more—after the explosion the ship turned over. She first lay on her port side for a moment or two and then turned keel up."

Fennell's lifeboat station was on the port side. The boats were stuck in their davits. The men were still trying to free the falls when the ship's gunwale dipped beneath the waves. The belt of Fennell's sheepskin coat caught on something and dragged him underwater. "It looked bad for a while." He held his breath as he struggled against the unseen snag. He broke free and reached the surface with his last gasp. Fortunately, the sinking ship generated no suction. Fennell grabbed a floating skylight that kept his head above the surface if not his entire body. This saved him until he found a bench that offered more support.

Tavelle added that the searchlight "was still on us when the ship was turning over and I got into the water." He grabbed a piece of wreckage that turned out to be the frame of the port dining salon door. "Though there were a number of men around the submarine in close proximity calling for help I saw nothing to indicate that any effort was put out to save any of the crew."

Reinhold Hardegen had more important things on his mind than saving lives. He tore off at high speed after another juicy target, the tanker *Malay*, which he engaged with his deck gun. The *Malay* outran the U-boat, but not until five of her men were killed by shellfire. Hardegen then torpedoed the Latvian freighter *Ciltvaira* (q.v.).

Tavelle closed his affidavit laconically. "I never saw Captain Urquhart after I got into the water. I remember seeing him and the first officer on the starboard side while we were trying to get the boats over. While I was in the water I helped Chief Engineer Kenney get some wreckage, and he and some fifteen others of the crew were clinging to wreckage nearby. All these men were drowned."

From his improvised raft Tavelle saw flashes in the distance and heard the reports of gunfire.

Six hours after the *City of Atlanta* took her final plunge the freighter *Seatrain Texas* hove into view. She put over a boat and picked up survivors. Only four men were still alive, and of these Assistant Engineer John York soon died from exposure to the cold water. Earl Dowdy, a wiper, was the other survivor. Ultimately, ten bodies were recovered from the debris field. Captain Urquhart and forty-three good seamen joined the ranks of the dead.

When doctors examined George Tavelle they found numerous glass cuts from the shattered bridge windows, as well as a deep cut on his leg he got during his fall from the sinking hull, but they could not explain his badly discolored neck. "I got that from turning around in the water so often trying to see a ship."

The wreck of the *City of Atlanta* was depth-charged on May 11, 1942, when its sunken hull was spotted from the air by a Navy pilot and thought to be a submerged U-boat. On June 21, 1944 the wreck was wire-dragged to a least depth at mean low water of forty-three feet.

Despite George Tavelle's observation that the ship rolled over keel up before she sank, the wreck is upright. There is no doubt that the wreck is that of the *City of Atlanta*, for Lynn DelCorio recovered several of the brass letters from the collapsed fantail. The engine and boilers are visible, and reach a height of some twenty feet, but forward of that there is little more than spread out debris. Portholes found face up imply that the hull plates have collapsed outward.

However, if one keeps swimming across the sand away from the stern and along the longitudinal axis, the bow will eventually come into view. The wreck is actually contiguous, held together by the keel which is buried by the sand. The bow lies on its starboard side and is completely intact. It is largely unexplored. Bales of wire found on the bottom are part of the cargo. The wreck deserves more attention than it gets.

Reinhard Hardegen survived the war and is alive today. On June 5, 1942, command of the *U-123* was given to Oberleutnant zur See Horst von Schroeter. According to the log of the *U-123*, it was decommissioned in Lorient on August 19, 1944.

CONSOLS

Built: 1898
Previous names: None
Gross tonnage: 3,493
Type of vessel: Freighter
Builder: Bartram & Sons, Sunderland, England
Owner: Consols Steam Ship Company (W. Thomas, Sons & Company)
Port of registry: Liverpool, England
Cause of sinking: Fire
Location: 27042.8

Sunk: February 4, 1912
Depth: 90 feet
Dimensions: $350' \times 46' \times 16'$
Power: Coal-fired steam

41011.2

At Galveston, Texas the holds of the *Consols* were filled with asphalt, cottonseed meal, and 9,500 bales of cotton, intended for Hamburg, Germany. The ship made a routine crossing of the Gulf of Mexico, rounded the Florida coast, and headed north to Norfolk where she intended to take on coal for the Atlantic crossing.

While off the coast of South Carolina someone smelled smoke.

Courtesy of the Steamship Historical Society of America.

Investigation soon disclosed flames in the forward hold, among the cotton. Fire hoses were brought to bear against the smoldering bales. All afternoon and night the crew fought the slowly expanding conflagration.

The next day, Captain Jones, master of the *Consols*, alerted the steamship *Texas* of his ship's plight. The *Texas* then wirelessed for help. The call was picked up by the Revenue Cutter *Onondaga*, which was escorting the damaged *Pomona* into Newport News. (The *Pomona* had collided with and sunk the *Allegheny*.) The *Onondaga* reversed course and headed for the distressed *Consols*, which was maintaining its northerly course. Also dispatched to the scene was the Merritt-Chapman wrecking and fire-fighting tug, *Rescue*.

Meanwhile, the British steamer *Castle Eden* rushed to the *Consols'* aid. Sparks spread from hold to hold until nearly the entire ship was ablaze. By this time both the ship and the fire were out of control. A towing hawser was passed from the *Consols* to the *Castle Eden*, which attempted to haul the flaming ship toward shallower water. Eventually, every hold was a fiery cauldron, and the crew was forced to abandon ship. All thirty-four officers and men made a safe transfer to the *Castle Eden*.

Said Captain Jones, "I shall never forget the fight against that fire. I shall never forget the brave men who stood by me and endured the heat and strain of the desperate struggle. For hours the deck was so hot beneath our feet that shoes were no protection and nothing could be touched that was not first drenched."

That afternoon the *Onondaga* took over the tow, but to no avail. The *Consols* was ablaze from stem to stern; she burned practically to the water line; then, twenty hours after the fire began, she slipped hissing under the waves.

The *Consols* was last reported to be thirty-three miles south of Cape Henry, and eighteen miles off Currituck beach. Mike Boring has dived a wreck called the 1800 Line Wreck that he thinks may be the *Consols*. It is twelve miles offshore and just south of the Virginia-North Carolina border.

The wreck lies upside down and is buried so deep that what is normally below the water line of a ship is now what appears above the sand. The stern is intact, rising some twenty feet from the bottom; the propeller shaft runs horizontally just above the sand. At the engine room the hull breaks down so that the engine and both boilers are exposed. The sides of the engine have fallen away, revealing the cranks. One boiler lies in the normal position, the other sits on its end.

Forward of the boilers the wreck breaks down almost level with the sand. After twenty to thirty feet of low-lying debris what appears to be the flattened hull plates of the bow come into view. There is no recognizable point. The entire wreck is very narrow, as if the hull plates have fallen inward. A minor debris field exists on either side.

Verification of identity awaits the recovery of some part of the wreck that has the ship's name or builder's information.

DIAMOND SHOALS

Built: 1897
Previous names: None
Gross tonnage: 590
Type of vessel: Lightship
Builder: Bath Iron Works, Bath, Maine
Owner: U.S. Lighthouse Service, Department of Commerce
Official designation: LV 71 (Light Vessel No. 71)
Cause of sinking: Shelled by *U-140* (Korvettenkapitan Kophamel)
Location: 35-05 North

Sunk: August 6, 1918
Depth: Unknown
Dimensions: 112′ × 28′ × 13′
Power: Coal-fired steam

75-20 West

The Diamond Shoals has long been known as a perilous place. Besides being the junction of opposing currents (the Labrador from the north, the Gulf Stream from the south), the area is along the track of West Indies hurricanes. This combination of reefs, shallow water, confused seas, tricky currents, and awful weather, has conspired to strand countless vessels during the early centuries of exploration and the later years of commerce.

According to Commissioner of Lighthouses George Putnam, as early as 1824 an attempt was made to maintain a lightship off the dreaded Diamond Shoals, but it was driven ashore and wrecked after three years on station. "In 1852 a bell boat was moored nine miles and a buoy three and one half miles from the lighthouse, but within four months both had disappeared." Then, "A whistling buoy was placed off the shoals in 1883. In 1884 a gas buoy was moored off Cape Hatteras, but a later report states that it 'remained in position but a few months and has since been drifting about the Atlantic'; and remarks, 'it is evident that such a buoy cannot be maintained at this point.'"

As traffic and the number of ship losses increased, "Congress in 1889 authorized the construction of a lighthouse by contract on the Outer Diamond Shoal at a cost not to exceed $500,000. The contractors built at Norfolk a caisson fifty-four feet in diameter and forty-five feet high. The caisson was towed to the site by three powerful tugs and grounded in water twenty-two to twenty-five feet deep on July 1, 1891." Within days the current scoured the sand from the caisson's base, tilting it awkwardly. "The storm of July 8 carried away the machinery and the upper part of the caisson, and the contractors abandoned the work."

In 1894 the Lighthouse Board tried to erect a lighthouse on the shoals. "As a preliminary measure a skeleton iron frame supported by wrought-iron piles with large disks at their lower ends was built, floated to the site on pontoons, and successfully placed in position." This structure was merely a work station from which test bores a hundred feet deep were dug into the substratum. However, permanent construction was halted when Congress decided that the real solution lay in a floating station. Thus began the era of Diamond Shoal lightships.

LV 69 became operational on September 30, 1897. She was moored in thirty fathoms of water thirteen miles off Cape Hatteras, a point beyond the outer shoal. Thus a ship could pass offshore of the lightship without fear of grounding. Unfortunately, LV 69 was dragged off station and washed ashore in a terrible hurricane only two years later. She was left high and dry, but otherwise not badly damaged. A trench was excavated between the ship and the sea, and LV 69 was subsequently salvaged and towed to drydock for repairs. She lived to take up other stations.

Meanwhile, sister ship LV 71 dropped her mushroom anchor off the shoals and, except for repair sessions and temporary alternate duty situations, served as the *Diamond Shoals* lightship for the next two decades. (She spent short intervals on Tail of Horsehead (Virginia), Winter Quarter Shoal (Virginia), Overfalls Shoal (Delaware), Cape Lookout Shoals (North Carolina), Nantucket Shoals (Massachussetts), and Cape Charles (Virginia). When off station, LV 72 guarded the Diamond Shoals.

LV 71 cost the government $70,700. Her composite hull consisted of a steel frame and topsides with a wood bottom. Her single cylinder steam engine was fired by a Scotch boiler eleven feet in diameter and twelve feet long. The four-bladed, eight-foot-diameter propeller could move the ship through the water at better than eight knots.

Heavy duty framing, extra bulkheads, and compartmentalization ensured watertight integrity. Hull lines were designed to control both rolling and pitching: steadiness and ease of motion were more important than speed.

Her two masts were each topped with a lantern gallery that contained a cluster of three 100 candlepower lens lanterns. In fog she could signal her position by either a 12-inch steam whistle or a hand operated 1,000-pound bell.

Modifications throughout the years included the installation of wireless telegraph and radio, the addition of meterological equipment, and the replacement of the cluster lights with single 375-millimeter electric incandescent lights.

While day-to-day activity on board the lightship was relatively boring, with the crew spending a lot of time playing cards, sea duty was sometimes punctuated by incidents of great excitement and moments of sheer terror. In 1900, the *Diamond Shoals* was dragged off station no less than nine times. (She returned unassisted on each occasion.) On January 9, 1912, she was rammed by the schooner *John Bossert*; considerable damage was inflicted upon the lightship's starboard hull plates and engine room machinery, but she survived the blow. On April 24, 1915, she provided shelter, food, and clothing for the master, his wife, and the crewmen from the wrecked five-masted schooner *M.D. Cressy*, until they were transferred to a passing vessel.

Courtesy of the North Carolina Division of Archives and History, Raleigh.

Unquestionably, the most intensely thrilling encounter for the crew of LV 71 came during the Great War. Coastal shipping increased dramatically as tramp freighters and heavily-laden tankers hugged the shore in order to avoid prowling German U-boats. Despite the flood of enemy incursions, the lonely sentinel remained on station.

The *Diamond Shoals* was a defenseless ship: ungunned, moored semi-permanently, and with her boilers unfired. Her lights burned brightly at night, her bell clanged melodiously in wave-tossed seas, her crew kept a diligent watch for ships straying too close to the shoals. It was during the normal course of duty that the *U-140* was spotted after opening fire on the *Merak* (q.v.).

The shot "attracted the attention of the First Mate of the *Diamond Shoals* lightship and the submarine was then discovered, between 3 and 4 miles East North-East of the Lightship and about 4 miles from the steamship."

While the *U-140* continued its pursuit of the *Merak*, the lightship sent a warning broadcast: "KMSL S.O.S. Unknown vessel being shelled off *Diamond Shoal* Light Vessel No. 71. Latitude 35-05, longitude 75-10." (The position was that of the U-boat, not the lightship or the *Merak*.) Although the message was repeated three times, no acknowledgment was received.

However, Korvettenkapitan Kophamel, captain of the *U-140*, was aware of the transmission, for he recorded in his log: "She sends radio signals during shelling of the other steamer. In order for my operations to remain undisturbed, she must be captured quickly."

In steering an evasive course the *Merak* ran aground and was therefore helpless. Kophamel redirected his attention to the lightship.

The lightship crew later issued this statement: "At 3:25 PM submarine commenced shelling Lightship, firing six shots, none of which had effect. The period during which the six shots were fired was about five minutes. The crew of the Lightship, twelve in number, left the Lightship in one life boat just before the sixth shot was fired. The life-boat was about 25 yards from the Lightship when the sixth shot was fired." This last shell "exploded a few feet from the side of the Lightship and filled the upper deck with water from end to end. When the shells hit the water they threw the water up 75 or 100 ft. The sub was apparently using shrapnel."

Seeing the lightship crew abandoning ship, Kophamel went back to the *Merak* and finished her off. The *U-140's* log continued succinctly: "Proceeded back to the lightship, which had already been abandoned by the crew. Sank her."

The lightship crew's report was more detailed: "The submarine then returned to the vicinity of the Lightship and fired seven shots at the Lightship, commencing at a distance of about 2 miles from the Lightship and extending over a period of about ten minutes. The boat containing the crew of the Lighship was then five miles away from the Lightship. The submarine then stopped firing for about 45 minutes and then commenced again, firing about 25 shots up until 9:00 o'clock.''

What the lightship crew could not see through the haze was that the *U-140* had already sunk the *Diamond Shoals* and had gone on to bigger game: it chased the *Bencleuch* and the *Mariners Harbor*. It lobbed shells at the *Bencleuch* but did no damage, and did not get within range of the *Mariners Harbor*. Both got away. Fortunately, Kophamel did not have time to board the lightship, for the crew departed in such haste that they left behind the Radio Code Book and the Merchants Ship Cipher—documents that could have been valuable to the German naval command.

After rowing some ten or twelve miles, the lightship crew "landed one mile to the North of Cape Hatteras and proceeded to Coast Guard Station #183.''

A different view of events was later published by Rene Bastin, the second officer of the tanker *O.B. Jennings*; Bastin was on board the *U-140* as a prisoner. He claims to have been brought on deck during the action, and to have observed the "Diamond Shoal Light Vessel at a distance of 150 yards. At the same time I saw three steamers on fire and the submarine was shelling the Light Vessel with her two 6-inch guns at 150 yards. I noticed the smoke of these shells was yellow and I think the shells fired on the *O.B. Jennings* were smokeless. I concluded, therefore, that the submarine was firing gas shells at the *Diamond Shoal*. I think she did that in order that none of the Light Vessel crew might escape. The Light Vessel blew up in a few minutes and I saw her lee boat pulling away at a few hundred yards distance. The submarine was shelling the boat with a four-inch gun but missed it and the submarine could not go any further in as it was shallow water. That is how the Shoal Light boat escaped.''

Bastin's account does not correspond to circumstances otherwise related and known to have occurred, thus throwing much doubt on either his powers of observation or honesty in reporting. For more on this enigmatic character, see *O.B. Jennings* in *Shipwrecks of Virginia*.

For the duration of the war a lighted gas buoy was established in place of Lightship No. 71. When hostilities ceased, a relief lightship (No. 72) was moored on station until 1920, when a new lightship named *Diamond Shoals* resumed the duties of her namesake. This later ship was wisely pulled off station during World War Two, in order to prevent a recurrence of events; she was stationed at the entrance to Hampton Roads, checking inbound and outbound traffic, when she was rammed and sunk by a barge towed by the tug *P.F. Martin*. All twenty-eight Coastguardsmen were rescued by nearby naval vessels. Lightships have been superceded by technology; today, a beacon tower guards the dangerous Diamond Shoals.

Due to LV 71's SOS, the position of her sinking was listed on original Navy documents as that of where the *U-140* first opened fire. However, the depth of water at that location is 360 feet. All records state consistently that the lightship was moored thirteen miles off Cape Hatteras in thirty fathoms, or 180 feet. A 1954 Navy hydrographic survey placed the wreck ten seconds to the west, in the proper depth. A wreck symbol on the chart purports to represent the site of the *Diamond Shoals* lightship; it deserves to be investigated more closely.

The *U-140* returned to Germany after a successful cruise. When the war ended, the U-boat was turned over to British authorities, and subsequently given to the United States and commissioned into the U.S. Navy. Along with five other U-boats, the *U-140* made the Atlantic crossing under an American crew. It then toured the east coast as part of the Victory Loan campaign. People were allowed to take tours of the U-boats, and were encouraged to buy bonds in order to alleviate the country's war debt.

On July 22, 1921, the *U-140* was sunk by shell fire from the U.S. destroyer *Dickerson* (DD-157). For the complete account of that event, see the Special Report on Billy Mitchell in *Shipwrecks of Virginia*, by this author.

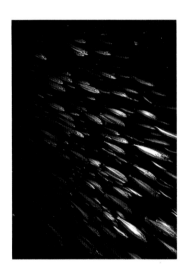

EMPIRE GEM

Built: 1941
Previous names: None
Gross tonnage: 8,139
Type of vessel: Tanker

Sunk: January 23, 1942
Depth: 140 feet
Dimensions: 463' × 61' × 33'
Power: Twin diesel engines

Builder: Harland & Wolff, Ltd., Glasgow, Scotland
Owner: Ministry of War Transport (British Tanker Company, Ltd., Mgrs.)
Port of registry: Glasgow, Scotland
Cause of sinking: Torpedoed by *U-66* (Korvettenkapitan Zapp)

Location:	26903.5	Bow	40173.0
	26903.5	Stern	40172.6

The *Empire Gem* was only three months old when she ran into the fireworks off the Diamond Shoals on the night of January 23, 1942. Her tanks were filled with 10,600 tons of gasoline picked up at Port Arthur, Texas. Captain Francis Broad held his ship's course for Halifax, Nova Scotia where he expected to join an eastbound convoy for England.

During the day the careful captain followed a zigzag pattern in accordance with instructions from British Naval Control at Galveston. An alert gun crew maintained stations at the 4-inch gun aft, the 12-pound anti-aircraft gun, and six machine guns; their fingers were itchy because only four days previous the *Ciltvaira* and the *City of Atlanta* had been torpedoed and sunk a few miles north, and the *Malay* had been shelled unmercifully.

The *Empire Gem's* masthead and side lights were dimmed: a compromise between total blackout to hide from the enemy, and full lights needed to avoid a collision. (During the night action against the *Ciltvaira*, *City of Atlanta*, and *Malay*, the freighter *Brazos* sank after colliding with the HMS *Archer* when both ships were blacked out.) Ahead, the navigation lights of the freighter *Venore* were faintly visible. The bright moon shone down on a moderate sea.

Lurking under the calm surface was Richard Zapp in the *U-66* who within the past week sank the *Allan Jackson, Lady Hawkins,* and *Norvana* (q.v.). He was looking to flesh out his bag before returning triumphantly to Germany.

The *Empire Gem* passed the *Venore*. As the tanker approached the Diamond Shoals Light Buoy, Captain Broad ordered the helm altered to the progressive leg on the zigzag course, then retreated to the chartroom to plot the next leg. Two minutes later, at 7:45 p.m., a tremendous explosion ripped out one of the after tanks on the starboard side, instantly engulfing that portion of the ship in flames.

Captain Broad raced into the wheelhouse to find "the ship's wheel hard to port. The officer of the watch, who was the chief officer, and the helmsman apparently had sighted a submarine or a torpedo track, and sought to avoid it. As the torpedo struck, their posts were deserted."

Radio Operator Ernest McGraw and his assistant, Thomas Orrell, reached the bridge at the same time and tapped off one quick SOS before the radio went dead. Three miles astern, the *Venore* picked up the call for help and passed it on.

Captain Broad gave no specific order to abandon ship, but with a full load of flammable gasoline spreading flames over the waves, the crew took it upon themselves to get away before the ship blew sky-high. Orrell reported to the captain that the chief officer and helmsman had launched the port midship lifeboat along with fourteen others, but that it capsized upon striking the water because the ship's engines were still running and the tanker had too much way on. Captain Broad called the engine room but got no response on either the telegraph or telephone.

The captain and the two radio men "attempted to launch a boat but the davit carried away. . . . The trio then attempted to release a raft on the starboard foremast rigging, but the painter carried away and the heat became so intense on the bridge that the men were forced to move to the forecastle. Here they set up a portable transmitter they had been able to salvage from the radio shack, and two messages were sent which were picked up by shore stations in the Fifth Naval District.

"All this time the *Empire Gem's* engines were running, taking the vessel on a westerly course. Three hours after the submarine attack, the engines stopped. The three officers anchored the still-burning vessel in 28 fathoms of water, about 15 miles south of Cape Hatteras. As dawn of the next day crept over the horizon, the torn and gutted after half broke away and sank."

Meanwhile, the *Venore* had also been zapped by German torpedoes (q.v.) and broadcast a call for assistance. A motor lifeboat from the Ocracoke Coast Guard Station was dispatched in response, but because the *Empire Gem* was closer and so highly visible—she was still burning furiously—life-saving personnel approached the floating bow section and spotted Captain Broad, McGraw, and Orrell waving for help.

The intrepid Coast Guardsmen drove in to the rescue. "Flaming gasoline surrounded all but the forepart of the battered hulk, and high seas contributed to making the operation impossible. Seeing that this was the case, the trio jumped into the sea to swim to the rescue boat. Captain Broad and Orrell made it, but the angry seas swept Ernest McGraw back into the burning fuel. He was not seen again."

Of a crew of fifty-seven only these two survived.

Upon interrogation, Captain Broad admitted that confusion was so great after the explosion that "although two decoding tables had been thrown over the side in weighted bags, other documents such as routing instructions, zigzag tables, confidential books, and Navy merchant codes were still aboard in a weighted box in the wheelhouse. In response to this, an officer from the District Intelligence Office was dispatched to the scene of the wreck on January 28th. He found the entire wheelhouse, chart-room, and bridge quarters under water, with the port wing of the bridge exposed, but entirely awash. Thus it was impossible to obtain the papers."

At this point the bow was still afloat and right-side up. The Coast Guard cutter *Orchid* placed a quick flashing red "C" buoy near the wreck. "About a week later it was observed capsized with the anchor chains wrapped around the bow but still holding fast. Exactly how long she remained derelict is unknown, but one report mentions sighting her still above water on 7 April 1942."

Hatteras was soon designated a danger area, surrounded by a defensive minefield, and the wreck site was placed off limits. Although the buoy was swept away, "an extremely heavy slick still marked the scene in the summer of 1944." A survey conducted at that time found the wreck broken in two halves less than one hundred yards apart, lying in 132 feet of water with a least depth of 90 feet. Wire-drag clearance was considered unnecessary because the wreck presented no hazard to navigation.

The *Empire Gem* is more commonly known as the Smell Wreck because of the distinctive odor noticeable upon approach to the site. The wreck is found in two major parts. If you can smell the wreck, you are more likely over the bow section, which comprises approximately two thirds of the length of the hull. It lies upside down. The highest point of relief is the tip of the bow, which stands some twenty feet off the bottom; from there

Leaking oil continues to burn from the partially sunken tanker. (Both courtesy of the Naval Historical Center.) The men without hats are the only two survivors. (Courtesy of the Outer Banks History Center.)

the wreck slants aft until it disappears into the sand. Because the hull is so smooth the wreck is hard to hook, usually requiring divers to descend a buoy line to the bottom. A crack runs from port to starboard but is not wide enough to squeeze through; the interior is virtually sealed. A debris field lies off the port side.

Apparently, when the *Empire Gem* rolled over, the wheelhouse was knocked off. It was located by Roger Huffman when his grapnel slipped off the bow hull and caught in the bridge wreckage. It lies upside down. Quite a bit of the navigational equipment was removed by divers soon after its discovery.

The stern third of the wreck is the most exciting to explore. It lies upright with a slight tilt to starboard. The hull and upper decks have collapsed, exposing the giant diesel engines. I was befuddled on my first reconnaissance of the wreck because I expected to see two propellers and side-by-side diesels; usually, each engine drives its own shaft. Instead, I saw one large bronze propeller situated along the centerline in front of the in-place rudder, and only one diesel with gigantic rocker arms. Only upon close inspection did I determine that what looked like one long engine was in fact two in-line diesels mounted fore and aft of a connector block.

The stern section terminates about thirty feet in front of the forward engine, where it drops off dramatically twenty-five feet to the sand and a few bits of scattered wreckage. Beneath the distinctive cruiser stern a washout goes as deep as 150 feet. Off the starboard side of the fantail lies the gun platform and, lying next to it, the 4-inch gun; just in front of that lies a smaller barrel that might be the anti-aircraft gun. Because the upper decking is gone, the after steerage compartment is exposed and the rudder linkage visible.

Just forward of the poop deck is a huge boiler that seems out of place in a diesel driven vessel; it is ten to fifteen feet in diameter. It was used to generate steam not for propulsion but for pumps and other machinery. An extensive debris field lies off the starboard side of the engine area. There are portholes lying about but most of them are broken, undoubtedly because of the intense heat produced by burning gasoline just prior to the sinking of the ship.

Interestingly, due to the time difference between the sinking of the two parts, the fantail of the stern section faces the broken end of the bow section.

The *U-66* returned to the Eastern Sea Frontier in the summer of 1943, under the command of Kapitanleutnant Markworth, and sank the *Esso Gettysburg* and *Bloody Marsh*. On May 6, 1944, under the command of Kapitanleutnant Seehausen, the *U-66* was sunk off the Cape Verde Islands.

The *Empire Thrush* as the *Lorain*. (Courtesy of the Steamship Historical Society of America.)

EMPIRE THRUSH

Built: 1919
Previous names: *Lorain*
Gross tonnage: 6,160
Type of vessel: Freighter
Sunk: April 14, 1942
Depth: 65 feet
Dimensions: 395′ × 53′ × 31′
Power: Oil-fired steam turbine
Builder: Federal Ship Building Company, Kearny, New Jersey
Owner: Ministry of War Transport (Canadian Pacific Steamships, Mgrs.)
Port of registry: London, England
Cause of sinking: Torpedoed by *U-203* (Kapitanleutnant Mutzelberg)
Location: 35-11.8N   75-15.3W

The *Empire Thrush* was built for the U.S. Maritime Commission when it sorely needed ships. After World War One there was a glut of ship hulls: too many for the number of cargoes needing transport. As the *Lorain* she served her country during most of the twenties, but was finally laid up in Baltimore in 1929 as part of the reserve fleet. She was taken out of mothballs after twelve years of cold storage, and turned over to England in accordance with the Lend-Lease Act. May 1941 saw the beginning of new life for the *Empire Thrush*, serving another country, but still serving the cause of worldwide peace.

On April 14, 1942, the *Empire Thrush* zigzagged her way north along the Carolina coast, rushing to meet a transatlantic convoy in Halifax, Nova Scotia. Deep in her holds were 2,500 tons of rock phosphate, 2,500 tons of citrus pulp, 60 tons of citrus concentrate, and 745 tons of TNT and gunpowder. Captain George Fisk's routing instructions came from the port of origin: Tampa, Florida.

Since the *Empire Thrush* carried a deck gun she was called a British armed merchantman. She also carried two twin Marlins and two single Marlins. As an extra precaution in U-boat infested waters she had six lookouts on duty: one in the crow's nest, one on each bridgewing, one on the poop deck, and two on the after gun platform.

The morning dawned "clear and sunny, with a mild northeasterly wind. The ship rode easily on a slight swell, and visibility was good."

At 9:20 a.m. one sharp-eyed lookout spotted a torpedo broach the surface on the starboard side. He shouted a warning, but there was no time to take evasive action. The detonation blew in the hull at No. 5 hold. The rock phosphate muffled the blow, but the hatch cover was blasted off, the deck was buckled, and a jagged hole was torn in the freighter's side.

Captain Fisk knew that with all that trinitrotoluene in the adjacent holds he was sitting on a potential powder keg. He wasted no time giving the order to abandon ship. "All secret codes and confidential papers belonging to Captain Fisk were put in a tin box with holes punched in it and were thrown over the ship's side." Within ten minutes all fifty-five men were away in four lifeboats.

No SOS was transmitted because the radio was damaged in the explosion, but "four Coast Guard patrol boats apparently in formation were travelling about six miles off the port beam of the subject vessel. Realizing the situation, they immediately dispersed and proceeded to the general direction and location of the attacker where they dropped numerous depth charges."

One Coast Guard vessel approached the string of lifeboats to inquire if there had been any injuries. Since there were none, she returned to join the counteroffensive. The British tars hovered around their ship, watching helplessly as she sank lower into the water. Finally, two hours after the attack, the *Empire Thrush* settled to the bottom on an even keel with her funnel and masts above the surface.

Ten minutes later all the survivors were taken aboard the tanker *Evelyn*, which took them to Norfolk.

According to the Navy, "The superstructure and rigging were broken up slowly by the action of the sea until sometime in the summer of 1942 the last remaining mast disappeared below the surface." The wreck was relocated by the USCG *Gentian* in 1944 on June 29 and again on July 7. "Soundings indicated that the wreck was a menace to navigation, the least depth recorded being about 29 feet."

What followed must have been a spectacular pyrotechnic display as "demolition was accomplished quickly by the Navy Salvage Service which set off the *Empire Thrush's* cargo of explosives. When the *Gentian* revisited the scene on 24 July, all that could be found was a 30-foot hole where the wreck used to lie (and where the demolished wreck still lay, according to the Sonar gear and SMSD). The wire drag cleared the area at a mean low water setting of 42 feet; deeper drags were not attempted."

Uwe Lovas thought that finding the *Empire Thrush* was crucial to locating the *U-701* because survivors of the U-boat stated that they saw masts protruding from the water: masts that Lovas interpreted must be those of the *Empire Thrush*. (See *U-701*.) He found the freighter by magnetometer, and confirmed the Navy report of its condition. There is nothing left to see but the core of the wreck; it is hardly a dive site.

Rolf Mutzelberg, captain of the *U-203*, also sank the *San Delfino* (q.v.). Mutzelberg was killed accidentally on September 11, 1942. While the U-boat was stopped in the open Atlantic he and the crew took turns scrubbing themselves clean in the water. Mutzelberg dived off the conning tower, struck his head on the ballast tank, and broke his neck. Under the command of Kapitanleutnant Herman Kottmann the *U-203* was "lost in action against a convoy in the North Atlantic, Apr. 25, 1943, with 11 killed and 38 captured." Credit for the kill went to the HMS *Biter's* Squadron 811 A/C and the HMS *Pathfinder*.

Below: the name board clearly identifies the sunken freighter. (Courtesy of the U.S. Coast Guard.) Left: Captain George Fisk holding five-week-old pup Elizabeth, at Norfolk. (Courtesy of the National Archives.)

EQUIPOISE

Built: 1906   Sunk: March 26, 1942
Previous names: *Pietro Campanella, Chanda*   Depth: 140 feet
Gross tonnage: 6,210   Dimensions: 429' × 54' × 34'
Type of vessel: Freighter   Power: Coal-fired steam
Builder: Barclay, Curle & Company, Ltd., Glasgow, Scotland
Owner: U.S. Maritime Commission (International Freighting Corp. Inc.)
Port of registry: Panama
Cause of sinking: Torpedoed by *U-160* (Oberleutnant zur See Lassen)
Location: 26863.7   40932.9

In the early stages of the east coast U-boat war, prior to the implementation of the convoy system, independently traveling merchant vessels were required to follow routing instructions issued by the Navy. When the *Equipoise* left Rio de Janeiro with 8,000 tons of manganese ore, the Naval Routing Office at Rio issued a specific track the ship was to maintain.

The aging freighter lumbered along at eight knots, her destination Baltimore, Maryland. At night she ran blacked out. In addition to Captain John Anderson, master, the *Equipoise* carried a crew of fifty-two. Some of the men had been selected to operate the ship's defensive weapons: one 4-inch deck gun, two machine guns on the poop, and two machine guns on the bridge.

All this preparation and training came to naught when an unseen U-boat fired a torpedo into the ship's starboard side well below the water line, between No. 1 and No. 2 holds. A summary report stated, "It is believed that an entire bottom portion of the ship was blown out." The dense cargo of ore offered no reserve buoyancy.

The *Equipoise* sank in only two minutes.

The confusion of those two minutes was intensified by language problems among the polyglot crew of Finns, Danes, Swedes, Norwegians, Poles, Latvians, Estonians, Lithuanians, Hungarians, Portugese, Brazilians, and Americans. As fireman Kjeld Kristiansen stated, "Too many nationalities; they couldn't understand each other."

Most of the men were trapped below deck and drowned in the quickly rising water. "Remarkably, two lifeboats and two rafts were launched, though one of the lifeboats overturned as it reached the water." When the sea settled down after the ship was engulfed, only fifteen men were left alive, and some of them were injured.

No one knew they were out there, or that their ship had been sunk, because radio silence had prevented them from issuing progress reports, and because there had been no time to transmit an SOS. They were alone in the great wide sea.

That night one man succumbed to his injuries. The next morning Captain Anderson passed away, and his body was washed overboard "when the boat was nearly swamped in a high sea." The remaining survivors suffered horribly from the numbing cold. Anxiously they scanned the horizon for ships, and listened intently for the drone of a patrol plane. They saw nothing, heard nothing. The day passed.

The men endured a second night without food or water. Those in the lifeboat were cramped and uncomfortable; those on the rafts were constantly inundated by waves washing over the sides. Somehow, dawn found the thirteen men still alive—but barely.

It was not until late in the afternoon of their second day adrift that the U.S. destroyer *Greer* (DD-145) happened upon the lifeboat containing eight survivors. "An hour or so later the *Greer* found the two rafts carrying in all five men and the body of the carpenter." They were all brought to the Naval Operating Base at Norfolk, Virginia. Nine of the men were hospitalized.

Initially, the location of the *Equipoise* was confused with that of the

Toadfish.

Buarque. The evidence now in hand makes it likely that the wreck previously believed to be the *Buarque* is actually the *Equipoise*. (See *Buarque* for details of the 1944 *Gentian* survey, and for subsequent discoveries that led to its identification.) From this wreck, in 140 feet of water, Hal and Penny Good recovered a helm stand stamped "The Pepper Steering Gear," "R. Roger & Co.," and "Stockton-on-Tees," which, coupled with the gauges I recovered from the *Buarque*, lend strong support to the conjecture that the original identifications of the two wrecks were interchanged. Furthermore, the Goods sighted the triple expansion reciprocating steam engine by which the *Equipoise* was powered. (The *Buarque* was driven by a steam turbine.)

Hal and Penny describe the wreck as "visually spectacular." The hull is upright with the bow broken off and twisted so that it points up to a depth of 100 feet. Otherwise, the wreck is contiguous. Abaft the bow section lies a hundred feet of debris caused by the hull plates collapsing outward. The center section sits high with the lower deck levels easily accessible. The superstructure has large square windows but, surprisingly, no artifacts. The engine, two boilers, and condenser are exposed. The highest point on the stern is a cabin. The wreck has many recognizable features such as bollards, windlasses, and assorted deck gear. It is not dived as much as it should be.

The *Equipoise* was only the first of five ships sunk by the *U-160* during a fortnight of depredations. The others were the *City of New York, Rio Blanco, Malchace* (see *Shipwrecks of North Carolina: from Hatteras Inlet South*), and *Ulysses*. After three other successful patrols Lassen was retired from the *U-160*. It was taken over by Oberleutnant zur See Pommer-Esche in June 1943, and was sunk the following month in the Central Atlantic. There were no survivors.

Conger eel.

GLANAYRON

Built: 1889
Previous names: *Santon*
Gross tonnage: 2,577
Type of vessel: Freighter
Builder: C.S. Swan & Hunter, Newcastle, England
Owner: Glanayron Steam Ship Company (L.J. Mathias, Mgr.)
Port of registry: Aberystwyth, Wales (today's spelling)
Cause of sinking: Ran aground
Location: Outer Diamond Shoals

Sunk: May 22, 1896
Depth: Unknown
Dimensions: 303' × 39' × 20'
Power: Coal-fired steam

The stranding of the *Glanayron* could well be considered a textbook case, both in how a ship comes to grief upon a foreign shore, and how the men of the United States Life-Saving Service answer their call to duty. The facts were duly entered in the log of the Cape Hatteras station, unfortunately without embellishment or longed for detail:

"Stranded at 7.45 P.M. in heavy weather on the outer Diamond Shoals, about 9 miles SSE of this station, her master attributing the casualty to the fact that the light on the cape seemed to show indistinctly. A rocket sent up from the vessel was answered by the patrolman with his Coston light, and when the keeper was notified, a few moments later, he in turn displayed a signal, which, being responded to, confirmed his fears that a wreck had occurred. Cooperation was requested by telephone from the Big Kinnakeet and Creeds Hill Life-Saving stations, the station team being sent to the latter point to haul their boat to the north shore of the cape, the southwest wind making it too rough to launch from the southern beach.

"On the arrival of these crews, at 10.55 and 11.30 P.M. respectively, a consultation was held by the three keepers and it was decided, as the night was very dark and the breakers heavy, to wait until early morning before going off to the vessel. A little before daylight two of the surfboats were manned and set out for the scene, arriving alongside the ship at 5 A.M., the third crew being left on shore as a reserve in case of accident."

"The steamer's two lifeboats were lowered, laden with her crew's personal effects, and taken in tow, the men themselves, 23 all told, being distributed among the several boats, and the return trip safely accomplished by 11.45 A.M. On May 24 the Cape Hatteras surfmen again boarded the vessel and towed her small boat ashore, also bringing several articles for her master. The shipwrecked crew were maintained at the station until the 26th instant, when they left for Norfolk, Va. The vessel proved a total loss."

Against such manifest understatement Captain Evan Lloyd, master of the *Glanayron*, and six of the crew, had this to say to the General

Superintendent of the Life-Saving Service, the Honorable Sumner I. Kimball: "We, the undersigned, are under deep obligations to yourself and to Keeper P.H. Etheridge and his crew, as also to the keepers and crews of Big Kinnakeet and Creeds Hill life-saving stations for magnificent services rendered us when our steamship *Glanayron*, of Aberystwith, stranded on Diamond Shoals, off Cape Hatteras, on Friday, the 22d of May, at 7.55 P.M. On sending up rockets they were immediately answered by the patrol from the beach, a red Coston signal being burned, and ten minutes later a red rocket was sent up from the life-saving station. At daybreak the noble keepers and their crews came off to our assistance, which was a very difficult task, owing to the state of the sea and the breakers which prevailed at the time. However, they were successful in their work, rescuing all hands on board with their personal effects, and we wish to express to yourself and the keepers and crews of the above life-saving stations our appreciation of these services and our sincere thanks."

Thus ended the voyage of the *Glanayron*, bound from Fernandina, Florida to Rotterdam with 1,631 tons of phosphate. The vessel was valued at $130,000, the cargo at $36,000. Both steel ribs and rock lie on or beneath the shoals awaiting discovery.

Nets hung up on shipwrecks continue to catch fish.

HARPATHIAN

Built: 1913
Previous names: None
Gross tonnage: 4,588
Type of vessel: Freighter
Builder: Sunderland Ship Building Company, Sunderland, England
Owner: J. & C. Harrison, Ltd.
Port of registry: London, England
Cause of sinking: Torpedoed by *U-151* (Korvettenkapitan von Nostitz)
Location: 36–27.0 North

Sunk: June 5, 1918
Depth: 126 feet
Dimensions: 380′ × 53′ × 26′
Power: Coal-fired steam

74–58.0 West

The *U-151* was the first German U-boat to raid American coastal shipping after U.S. entry into World War One. In a whirlwind, month-long campaign Korvettenkapitan von Nostitz und Jaenckendorf sank twenty ships; to accomplish this feat he used torpedoes, mines, guns, and bombs placed on vessels by boarding parties. On one particular day he sank three schooners and three steamships. (See the Special Report in *Shipwrecks of New Jersey*, by this author.)

The *Harpathian* was on route from Plymouth, England to Newport News, Virginia, Captain Owens in command. Of the forty-one crew members, twenty-nine were Chinese: the black gang that had the dirty and onerous task of shoveling coal under the boilers. Captain Owens summarized events:

"The *Harpathian* was sunk without warning by a torpedo from an enemy submarine at 9:30 a.m. June 5, Cape Henry bearing N. 70 W. (true) ninety miles. The ship was torpedoed in latitude 36° 30′ N., 75° W.; sank in about seven minutes. All hands were saved. One member of the crew, a Chinaman, was struck between the eyes by a piece of the torpedo that sunk the ship. The captain did not see the submarine till after the ship was hit, and only a few of the crew saw the torpedo before it struck.

"The crew got safely away in the boats. The submarine commander called the boats alongside and asked if all were saved and if any were sick; he also asked if they had food and water. The Chinaman was given treatment aboard the submarine and was then returned aboard the lifeboat. The submarine commander gave each boat a bucket of water and asked the captain of the vessel if he had sent a wireless and on being told that there had been no time, gave the boats the course to the nearest land."

(Later that day, the *U-151* sank the Norwegian freighter *Vinland*.)

The crew of the *Harpathian* did not make it to shore; instead, they spent all day and night at sea. After more than twenty-five hours adrift, all hands were picked up by another British steamer, the *Potomac*. They reached Norfolk the night of the sixth.

The two positions sited by Captain Owens do not coincide. The lat/lon position is fifty-five miles southeast of Cape Henry, in 120 feet of water; the distance and compass bearing place the ship farther offshore, where the water is a thousand feet deep.

In 1944, during a wreck survey in the Fifth Naval District, the Coast Guard cutter *Gentian* found a "wreck standing about 20′ high in 126′ of water. Believed to be the *Harpathian.* . . . The wreck is a fair sound target, and a strong magnetic target. . . . Underwater photography showed the wreck to be extremely heavily fouled. The strength of the wreck's magnetic indications together with the fact that the fathometer did not show it to stand very high off the bottom are taken to be indicative of heavy sanding."

Although divers were not used to make a positive identification, "since the wreck shows signs of being of an age comparable to that of the *Harpathian*, it is being listed as probably that vessel."

As far as I know, divers have not yet checked out the location of what should prove to be a very promising dive site.

HESPERIDES

Built: 1884
Previous names: None
Gross tonnage: 2,404
Type of vessel: Freighter
Builder: R. & J. Evans and Company, Liverpool, England
Owner: S.S. Hesperides Company, Ltd.
Port of registry: Liverpool, England
Cause of sinking: Stranded
Location: 26910.1

Sunk: October 9, 1897
Depth: 35 feet
Dimensions: 286' × 38' × 24'
Power: Coal-fired steam

40236.5

The *Hesperides* was bound from Cuba to Baltimore with pig iron when she lost her way in a thick fog and came to grief on the Outer Diamond Shoals, on the morning of October 9, 1897. According to the official report, "As the weather continued thick all day she was not discovered by the life-savers until early next morning." Surfman D.W. Barnett raced back to the Cape Hatteras Life Saving Station to give the alarm. Meanwhile, the *Hesperides* sat high and dry in no immediate danger while the captain and crew waited patiently for rescue.

"Keeper notified the crews of Creeds Hill and Big Kinnakeet stations, arranging for the former to go direct to the wreck and for the latter to assist the Hatteras crew." The horses were hitched to the boat carriage and driven to the beach. "The surfboat was launched, and at 9:20 a.m. the surfmen boarded the steamer, followed by the Creeds Hill crew. As the steamer was hard aground, with 6 feet of water in her engine room, the keepers advised the master to abandon her, but he would not consent until two hours later, when the surfmen lowered three of the ship's boats, and after putting in them the crew of twenty-four persons, with their personal effects, started ashore and landed them on the beach abreast of station. The Big Kinnakeet crew aided in effecting the landing and unloading the baggage. Dry clothing was furnished to those in need. Eleven were sheltered and succored at the station until the 12th, the others being cared for at Creeds Hill Station until the 11th, and all were finally sent to Durants Station for passage to Elizabeth City. The vessel proved a total loss.''

Just another day in the Life-Saving Service. But for Captain Owen Williams it was a day of reckoning. When he lost his ship it was literally *his* ship, for he want not only her master but her owner. He bought her in 1895 for 6,000 pounds (when a British pound was worth about $5 U.S.) He made a good deal on her, for at the time of her loss she was valued at $70,000.

The *Hesperides* ''had two decks and was of the three island type— poop, bridge, and forecastle. Compound engines were fitted with two double-ended boilers and her speed was 11 knots. She was launched by Miss Kate Castle on March 13, 1884 and towed to Sandon Dock for engines to be installed by G. Forrester's Vauxhall Foundry, Liverpool for the River Plate Trade.'' Originally, she was owned by R.P. Houston & Company, of Liverpool, and was ''the first refrigerated vessel built for the Houstons for the South American meat trade.''

Apparently, Captain Williams did not compensate adequately for the current. The drift carried him north faster than he anticipated, causing him to reach the Diamond Shoals sooner than he expected and before he ordered the turn to starboard that would have carried his ship eastward and around the shoals. Lost with the ship was a $30,000 cargo that was never recovered.

One might think that the *Hesperides*, resting where it is on the ever-shifting shoals, might be covered with sand the way many of the other Diamond Shoals wrecks are covered. But for some reason it is completely exposed. It can be seen from the surface as a dark, elongated shape contrasting against the clear blue water. Caution must be exercised in approaching the wreck during times when the sea is running and the waves (and troughs) are high (and deep): the top of the engine comes to within seven feet of the surface, and the steering quadrant to within nine feet. Strong current can easily wrest control of a small boat and slam it down hard on the unforgiving iron. The bow points 240°.

The *Hesperides* is a near picture-perfect example of the way a wreck should look. The hull is upright and contiguous, and sits in a scour bowl that makes the wreck appear like a ship model sitting in a bathtub. With visibility averaging seventy-five to a hundred feet, the washout effect is obvious; the sand is built up into a tall dune on the starboard side, and is most pronounced around the bow and stern where it slants upward like the slope of an anthill. The port side of the wreck is in the lee of the prevailing

Above: left, the anchor stock sticks out over the port side of the bow; right, the anchor resting on the deck. Below left: the top of the engine is just below the surface. Below right: the propeller, rudder, and steering quadrant.

86

current, so the sand rises so subtly in that direction that the bowl effect is unnoticeable. Add to this the tremendous schools of baitfish (thick enough to plunge the bottom into darkness as they pass overhead), large sea bass, huge amberjacks, and miniature many-hued tropicals, and you have a site that divers and fisherfolk should not miss.

The after third of the wreck is the largest intact portion. The hull curves up out of the sand, becomes vertical, and stands as high as the lower deck. The superstructure has been scythed away. The steering quadrant dominates the view, seemingly standing up on its own. The delicate arch of the counter stern is somewhat truncated. Most of the rudder is visible, and it is complete except for rust holes in the facing. The two upper blades of the four-bladed iron propeller project above a washout that dips to a depth of forty-two feet.

About thirty feet forward of the stern the upper deck plates have completely rusted through, although the transverse beams outline where the deck used to be. This is the after cargo hold, made evident by the black rocks that comprise the cargo of iron ore. The winch has fallen onto the top of the shaft alley, which has a rust hole at its after end wide enough for a diver with doubles to enter. I was able to swim completely through the shaft alley, a distance of some fifty feet, to where the shaft reaches the open space aft of the engine.

As this point the hull plates have all collapsed outward and for the most part lie under the sand, as if the wreck had been peeled open like a giant banana. The shaft goes into the base of the two cylinder engine, itself a great iron tower whose sides have fallen away, exposing the inner workings. Bits of hull plate protrude out of the sand to port, but the largest debris field exists to starboard. The after mast, complete with spider ring

A boiler.

and belaying pins, lies parallel to the hull on the starboard side, and its top rests upon a fat iron cylinder.

The port boiler has rolled outboard off its bedplates, while the starboard boiler has been twisted around ninety degrees. Brass pipe lies everywhere amid the machinery spaces. Just forward of the boilers is a broad field of iron ore that has spread far beyond the perimeter where it was once confined by the hull. The only structural integrity here is the centerline bulkhead. The forward mast lies with its end close to this bulkhead, and extends forward at a forty-five degree angle to port.

About thirty feet of the bow is intact. A cavern effect is created by the decking; the inside is carpeted with soft sand, while basketball sized clumps of coral decorate the overhead. The weight of the windlass has caused the deck on which it resides to bend backward. Forward of that the forecastle deck has long since rusted away, made obvious by the port side anchor resting against the hull with its shank hanging out into space, and by the hawse pipes, which rise like fat conduits over the existing deck. Anchor chain from the starboard hawse pipe cuts in front of the stem and disappears into the sand on the port side. By looking out over the upper edge to starboard the deep scour is overtly apparent.

In addition to a steady current that commonly runs over the wreck from the north, one can encounter strong surges that buffet the diver about like the weight on the end of a pendulum. I got caught by a stream of water siphoning through upright iron plates and was at first sucked up against the opening and pinned there, then spit out like a watermelon seed in a carnival contest.

A dive on the *Hesperides* is a lot of work, but well worth the effort. Bottom time is limited only by one's control of hunger.

The shaft alley beneath the lower deck.

HURON

Built: 1875
Previous names: None
Gross tonnage: 541
Type of vessel: Third-rate gunboat
Builder: John Roach, Chester, Pennsylvania
Owner: U.S. Navy
Cause of sinking: Ran aground
Location: 200 yards off Bladen Street, Nags Head

Sunk: November 24, 1877
Depth: 25 feet
Dimensions: 175′ × 32′ × 15′
Power: Coal-fired steam

The *Huron* was the second Navy vessel to be named after the center lake of the Great Lakes. She was an iron-hulled sloop-of-war (that is, all her guns were on one deck) with limited armament: one 11-inch Dahlgren smoothbore rifle, two 9-inch Dahlgren smoothbores, one 60-pounder Parrott rifle, one 2-pounder rifled Howitzer, and one Gattling gun. According to the inventory in the ship's log, she also carried small arms for her complement of marines: sixty-three Remington rifles with bayonets, thirty-seven Remington pistols, twelve Colt revolvers, fifty cutlasses, sixteen boarding pikes, and eighteen battle-axes.

Although listed as an *Alert*-class screw-steamer, she was shorter by twenty-five feet and carried the Howitzer and the Gattling gun that the *Alert* did not. The *Huron's* simple two-cylinder steam engine was powered by five fire-tube boilers, each eight feet long and eight feet in diameter. At full revolutions the single propeller, twelve feet across, could drive the ship at ten knots. In addition, she carried three masts and was schooner rigged.

She was officially commissioned at the Philadelphia Navy Yard on November 15, 1875. During her first eight months of duty she served under the command of Commander Charles Carpenter. An uneventful cruise took her to Mexico where local insurrection was examined without involvement. Commander George Ryan assumed command in September 1876. Because Ryan had a background in astronomic observation, he and the *Huron* received orders to cruise the Caribbean in order to conduct scientific studies with new navigational equipment. The *Huron* ducked into many island ports, taking precise readings of latitude and longitude.

From August to October 1877 the *Huron* was refitted at the New York Navy Yard. She then sailed to Hampton Roads, Virginia to prepare for another scientific cruise off the coast of Cuba.

November 23 found the converted gunboat at sea, headed south. Immediately she ran afoul of heavy weather that reduced the ship's speed to five knots. Sails were set against a forty-knot wind. The fog grew so thick after passing Currituck Beach that the Bodie Island light was invisible. Only the sounding lead kept Commander Ryan apprised of his position: the recorded depth was plotted against the predicted depths on the nautical chart. The helmsman maintained a steady course, steering south-southeast, approximately paralleling the coast line.

As midnight of the 24th approached, Ryan retired to his stateroom; officer of the deck watch was Master Walter French. Shortly after 1:00 a.m., without warning of any kind, the *Huron* came to a grinding halt so suddenly that sleeping crewmen were catapulted from their hammocks. Commander Ryan rushed to the bridge to ascertain the ship's situation. At first it appeared that the *Huron* had grounded on an uncharted shoal some eight or nine miles offshore; but soon the sound of breakers was heard and land was spotted through the dark, swirling mist. The ship had come ashore on Bodie Island, at Nags Head.

This was no simple stranding. Due to the tremendous sea running, the *Huron* was hurled instantly into calamity. Huge waves crashed against the five-eights-inch-thick hull and washed completely over the exposed deck. First the foremast then the maintopmast broke away; the deck and superstructure became a tangled mass of rigging and broken spars. The steam whistle bleated stridently, calling for help for the beleaguered seamen at the mercy of the sea; but the feeble blasts were absorbed by the cacophony of the raging wind and churning water.

The tide was at dead low, so there appeared every chance of freeing the stranded gunboat by backing her engines. Firemen and the engine room crew remained at their posts and kept up steam for more than an hour. But the rising tide picked up the *Huron* and bumped it farther up the beach with each succeeding wave.

At that time Evan O'Neill left his home to shoot wild fowl. Through the fog he noticed a vessel's running lights where no ship had any right to

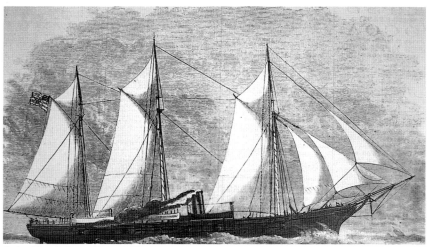

Under full sail. (From *Harper's Weekly.*)

be. He raced after the unknown ship "as she drifted and pounded along the outer edge of the bar." The *Huron* finally grounded abreast of Tillet's fish camp.

O'Neill heard the screams of the men aboard, and saw "three rockets go up, followed by Coston signals, which illuminated the vessel from end to end, so that even the light rigging as well as the men could be plainly seen." For thirty minutes he watched men fighting for their lives; then he went home and had breakfast.

No one came to the *Huron's* rescue. Only help from within could save the hapless sailors on the gunboat.

Commander Ryan tried everything to stabilize his ship and save his men. He ordered the mainsails reefed and a staysail set; he ordered the heavy guns thrown overboard; he ordered lifeboats launched. The crew hustled topside and worked with a will. However, the sails could not be handled in the howling wind. The guns were trussed with block and tackle but could not be lifted because the ship was rolling with the seas; and a gun loose from its mount might have pounded out the ship's side. Ensign Lucien Young stated that "all the port boats and the cutter had been carried away; the ship was lying on her port bilged broadside, inclined about 40°, and seas breaking clear over her." The cabin walls were stove in by force of the water.

What was worse, men were dying.

One reporter wrote vividly, "Amid falling spars, the howling of the tempest, the dying shrieks of the maimed and crushed, the furious waves swept the men into the seething surf, from which few emerged alive."

Torrents of water broke through rivet holes and ruptured hull plates. The ship's interior flooded. Men driven from the temporary protection of the inner hull fought to maintain a grip on loose gear, all the while being inundated by the raging sea. "The poor creatures huddled on the forecastle were washed overboard or killed by being dashed against the rail. Most of those who were forced to jump overboard were drowned in the surf. . . . the poor fellows under the forecastle had to stand the fury of the beating surf until their sufferings were ended by the forecastle being washed away, which took many of them overboard so bruised and mangled that they were powerless to help themselves."

Young rendered a stirring account of life and death during the *Huron's* last hours. "I had hold on the gattling gun, when a very heavy sea came over and washed myself and about five others down the leeward; all but myself went under the sail and they were drowned; I was caught in the bag of the sail and hurt both legs against the gaff; regained the gear of the nine-inch gun and worked myself forward; thought I saw Mr. French go in the main rigging; saw a number of men standing in the starboard gangway and on the first launch, and a number of men underneath the top-gallant forecastle; I succeeded in getting on the top-gallant forecastle with the assistance of the men there; a number of the men had on life-preservers and one rubber balsa was rigged on the forecastle; the top-gallant forecastle was full of men and officers; two or three men lashed themselves to the bowsprit.

"Everyone was perfectly cool and showed no signs of fear; the majority of us got close together on the upper side of the forecastle, suffering much from cold and exposure; the seas would break over us and nearly suffocate us; Mr. Conway, the watch officer, had on a blanket, and shared it with Mr. Danner, Mr. Loomis, and myself.

"We sounded over the side and found about six feet of water; a little while after we sounded again, and got seven and a half feet; saw lights about one point on the starboard bow, and we gave three cheers, and repeated them several times; we then saw that the flood tide was making in fast, and the sea was breaking over us more heavily.

"We saw the first launch, the only boat left, stove in, knocking Capt. Ryan and the navigator overboard; saw two men killed in the forecastle.

Weathering the gale. (From *Frank Leslie's Illustrated Newspaper.*)

"Mr. Conway suggested that we make some effort to get a line on shore. I said I would attempt it, and called for one to put the balsa over, when a three-inch line was made fast to the balsa and the same lowered overboard, but it fouled with the jibboom, foreguard and other spars, and I got down on the torpedo spar and worked about 10 minutes to clear the balsa, and called for some one to help me. Mr. Danner came down part of the way, and said he was too weak, and could not get on. I then told him that it was our only chance, and he had better try. He said he could not, and that he would in a little while. Williams, a seaman, then came down and said he would go. In about 10 minutes we succeeded in getting the balsa clear of the spars. I could get no main line, and the First Lieutenant, Mr. Simons, Mr White, and many others in the forecastle sung out to me, 'the line is out; cut it and get on shore if possible for assistance.'

"I had a small pen-knife, but could not open it, because my hands were benumbed. Williams opened it and I succeeded in cutting the rope. I was then struck several times by the spars, once in the small of the back and once in the hips. We thought the beach ran parallel to the ship. It was foggy and we could not see the shore. When the line was cut the balsa went toward the stern of the ship and we thought we were going to sea, one thing that deceived the majority of the ship's company.

"We paddled the balsa with pieces of paneling. Near the stern of the ship a heavy surf struck us and capsized the balsa end for end. My leg being jammed, it held me underneath the water for awhile. Both Williams and myself regained the balsa, when I told Williams to get on the end and we would then steer the balsa in fear of another capsize. We were thrown over

From *Frank Leslie's Illustrated Newspaper.*

again and the catastrophe threw Williams about 10 feet; my arm being jammed, I was thrown on my back. When we came up again it was rather still water. I swam and pushed the balsa toward Williams. He got on top and stood up, and looked around, and said that he saw the masts of fishing vessels ahead, which proved to be telegraph poles on shore. I told him I would steer for them. We capsized twice more, and before we knew it we were on the beach.

"I told him to haul the balsa up, as we might want to use it to send off to the ship. We landed about three-quarters of a mile up the beach from the wreck. Found two men inside the surf, but they were too weak to get up; went down and pulled them up; I then ran to the first house I saw, but found no one in it; started down the beach as fast as I could; legs hurting me very badly; found 10 or 15 people from shore standing opposite the wreck, looking at it. I told them to go further up the beach and do all they could to save the men, as they appeared to be landing up there, with the very strong current running up the coast. We pulled out several men.

"I asked them where the life-saving station was. They said one was seven miles up the beach and the other five miles down the beach. Saw a man on horseback; sent him to the upper station for aid and to telegraph to Washington for assistance to the wreck. This was about 7 o'clock in the morning. Then saw Mr. Conway who had landed.

"Asked these men on shore why the life-car was not there. They told me the life crew were at Roanoke Island. I asked them why they did not bring the car up; they said it was locked up in the station and they were

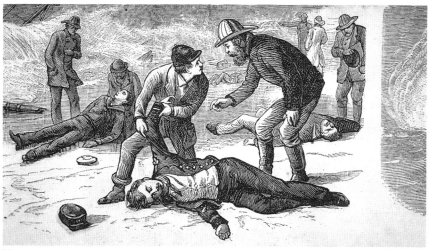

Members of the relief party check for signs of life. (From *Frank Leslie's Illustrated Newspaper.*)

afraid to break open the door. I told them that if they would come with me I would break open the door and get it out. Five of them volunteered to go; I asked them if they saw my signals and they said they did—even the first signal. I then walked and ran down the beach with these men, but saw a team coming down the beach, which proved to be that of Sheriff Buckley, of Dare City. I broke open the door, got the mortar and lines, broke open the locker, and found powder and balls, which Sheriff Buckley brought up with his team, but when I got back to the scene of the wreck, all the masts of the *Huron* were gone, and no one was on board.''

Of the 138-man crew, only thirty-four survived the ordeal.

Sheriff Buckley took the four surviving officers to his house. The enlisted men were succored at the life-saving station and given provisions, beds, blankets, and clothing. Also saved was a dog belonging to one of the *Huron's* officers; it swam through the seething surf with the sure strokes of a dog paddle.

Then came the grisly task of searching for the dead that washed up on

Survivors are treated at the Life-Saving Station. (From *Frank Leslie's Illustrated Newspaper.*)

the beach. All day the sheriff led patrols with his team of horses, and one by one the drowned sailors were stacked like cordwood in his wagon. Only eight bodies were recovered, but "twenty-five bodies are plainly seen from the shore, lashed to the main and mizzen rigging on the starboard side of the vessel, which is still held by the dead eyes to the chain plates."

On the 26th, the gunboat *Swatara* and the wrecking tug *B. & J. Baker* arrived at the wreck site. Both vessels anchored offshore, unable to approach the wrecked steamer because of monstrous seas. A surf-boat from the *B. & J. Baker* inched its way past the *Huron's* battered remains, but soon got out of control.

Again tragedy struck. "The surf-boat in attempting to make a landing passed the first line of breakers in safety, but at the second she broached to, and was capsized, her whole crew being thrown into the water. It is thought that two men were killed outright, others were drowned, and those who escaped did so by clinging to the boat until they were rescued by life lines thrown from the shore." One of the men drowned was Captain John Guthrie, Superintendent of the Life-Saving Service of North Carolina, there to oversee recovery operations.

The surf-boat overturning in the breakers. (From *Frank Leslie's Illustrated Newspaper.*)

The death toll rose from 104 to 110. (Note: the figures vary slightly according to the source, one of which gives a death toll of 98, plus the six lost on the lifeboat, totaling 104.)

That day, the steamship *Bonita* took the men and the recovered bodies to Norfolk. (Due to the still-raging storm, the steamer ran through the Albemarle and Chesapeake Canal.) There, the living were cared for aboard the sloop-of-war *Ossipee* and the frigate *Franklin.*

A Court of Inquiry convened in order to determine the cause of the disaster. Several findings of fault were attributed to the *Huron's* late Commander Ryan: that he began his cruise despite the warnings of an approaching storm, that he chose a course too close to land, that he did not take into account the westering current, that he carried too much sail, and that he did not adequately adjust his compass bearing despite the knowledge that the needle was off a full point ($11\frac{1}{2}°$). The Court also found that

Lieutenant Palmer, the navigation officer, made errors in navigation; and that "the deck officers on the night of her loss might have been at fault in not ascertaining the accuracy of the perpendicular soundings reported to them from time to time.

Ultimately, the Court's opinion placed overall blame on Commander Ryan's poor judgment of the situation. As always, the responsibility of a ship's loss falls upon her captain.

Contributing to the high percentage of fatalities after the *Huron* wrecked was the fact that, due to budget constraints, the life-saving stations were manned only between December 1 and April 30: the months when the weather was worst and when most strandings occurred. Since the *Huron* came to rest two hundred yards from shore, many people felt that more lives could have been saved by prompt action of life-saving crews who could have erected a breeches buoy before the masts fell and before the men were swept off the gunboat's decks. The sad case of the *Huron* had great repercussions in 1878, when Congress voted on a new bill for increased appropriations to the Life-Saving Service. The extra money permitted the operational season to be extended, and allowed for more stations to be built. (For more detail in this regard, see *Metropolis*.)

Life-Saving crews reported for work three days early. They ranged up and down the beaches dragging bodies out of the surf from as far north as fifteen miles from the wreck. The total of bodies recovered reached twenty-six; then another storm hit the coast, and dead sailors still lashed to the *Huron's* rigging were carried off forever to Davy Jones's locker.

After the weather moderated the beaches were littered with the dead. One dispatch noted that "coffins were useless. Some of the bodies were unrecognizable. All were bruised, discolored, swollen, and fast decomposing. The bodies have been picked up all along the shore from the wreck to within 10 miles of Cape Henry. Sixty-eight have been buried by citizens and the crews of the life-saving stations between Nos. 3 and 5, and no doubt intervening between those points others have been picked up and buried and not yet reported."

On December 1, divers from the *B. & J. Baker* examined the wreck. They reported that "all her wood-work is gone above the spar deck aft. The berth deck is carried away from the beams and floated up close under the spar deck, rendering it impossible for divers to reach the ward-room at present. The strong current and undertow operates against the divers, and to clear it away it will be necessary to blow up the spar. The vessel is no doubt hogged amidships or a little forward of that location. She lies in eight feet of water careened to port. It is hardly probable that any officers will be found in the ward-room, or men below."

A Signal Service observer at Kitty Hawk reported on December 3 that "Patrolman from North End states that one body came ashore at No. 5 Station, and the lower limbs of a man to-day." Bodies and body parts continued to come ashore for another week.

The job was gruesome, but necessary. On December 4 the wrecking crew blew up portions of the wreck in order to dislodge any bodies that may have been trapped inside, and to gain access to the paymaster's chest said to contain $10,000 in gold. They found one body.

When all was said and done, twenty-two men from both calamities were unaccounted for. Commander Ryan's body and those of other officers were taken to Norfolk for interment at the Naval Cemetary.

Lieutenant Walter Walton, Assistant Inspector of the Life-Saving Service on the North Carolina coast, conducted an investigation into the travesties committed by local residents. "It is shocking to record that out of 91 bodies found, (about 12 of whom were officers) not a single trinket, such as would be deemed a relic by the relatives of the dead, was found on their bodies. Watches and chains, money, and even finger-rings, had been stripped off by those who first found the bodies as they were washed up. Good evidence is found in the case of Lieut. Simons, whose third and fourth fingers of the left hand had been scratched and gouged by the body-robbers in their haste to secure their ill-gotten loot."

Furthermore, Evan O'Neill "knew where the keeper of Life-saving Station No. 7 lived, believed him to be at home, only two and a half miles distant, had a good boat, a free wind to go and return inside of Roanoke Island, would have reached Keeper Meeken's in 20 minutes, and yet remained silent and indifferent during three long hours of anguish and suffering. ... On his return to the beach O'Neill claimed to have saved one man who was very near the edge of the surf, but this is doubtful, as the evidence goes to show that Evan O'Neill's conduct on the beach was such as to cause general comment. One of the fishermen remarked, 'Look at Evan O'Neill; wouldn't you think he would try to save some of these men!' On the contrary, he seemed to be examining or inspecting fragments of drift-stuff as it washed up. He had very little to say, and kept apart from the crowd, and of the 22 witnesses, who were subsequently examined, was the only one who objected; and it was not until threatened with arrest that his appearance was secured."

By December 12, the wreck was "underwater, except a portion of the bow, at low water, and other parts here and there. The pivot gun is visible, and can be saved. The ship is hogged, and the whole starboard side ripped off. The sea is dashing in and over her."

Salvage was extensive. The Navy removed everything of value, and left the rusting hulk to its fate in the sea. Interestingly enough, *The Morning Star*, a Wilmington, North Carolina newspaper, reported in its July 22, 1881 edition that "Nag's Head's seventy guests are summoned to their meals by a bell from the wrecked *Huron*."

The hull of the gunboat sits upright on a bright sandy bottom, some two hundred yards offshore. It can be found by land ranges. A commemorative sign has been erected on the beach road inshore of the site. The bow of the wreck lies along a line drawn from the midpoint between the house with the yellow shutters (south and closer to the water) and the house with the red shutters (north and closer to the street), at the intersection with a line drawn from the end of the Nag's Head Pier. The stern of the wreck trends north.

Dynamic wave action keeps sand moving continually. All wrecks, beach wrecks especially, undergo periodic covering and uncovering. The *Huron* is no exception; features visible on one dive may not be exposed on another, and vice versa.

The *Huron's* bow is the most intact portion, standing ten to fifteen high. The hull is contiguous and noticeable above the sand all the way to the stern, where the port side is broken open and the relief is low. Objects inside are found largely to port due to the wreck's pronounced list upon grounding. Sections of wooden decking may be seen upon occasion, protruding at odd angles; no bulkheads or partitions still stand.

Oddly, one of the wreck's boilers has migrated from its bedplates amidships (where the other three boilers remain) to the bow, probably a result of explosives used during initial salvage and subsequent tidal action. Deck machinery is also visible in the bow.

Abaft the displaced boiler lies the fresh water tank, and abaft that the shell room, nearly amidships, where rifle cartridges and wooden shell boxes may be found. Just abaft the shell room are three boilers in a row, tucked to port. Beyond that should be the engine, but that structure is missing— salvaged long ago. The area is littered with brass pipes and copper tubing. The propeller shaft alley is straddled by the after hold storage areas; the shaft lies above the sand, extending from the engine area to where it exits the hull. If the propeller is still attached, it lies under the wreck. The rudder, sternpost, and steering quadrant are visible where the stern has broken down around them. The rudder is turned hard aport.

Divers should note that although the wreck is open for exploration by the public, a permit is required in order to recover anything from the site. The *Huron* has been nominated for the National Register of Historic Places partly because it is a trove of artifacts. According to the registration form, "Remains from the various ship's stores and other artifacts lie along the inside of the hull and are often concreted under a layer of rust and sand. Slates used for engine room duty rosters are stored on a half-buried shelf in the engine stores supply room. Ammunition and rifle parts may be seen concreted together along the sides where the shot locker once stood."

Artifacts recovered in the name of the State, in order to "prevent unauthorized recovery by relic collectors," include "silver plated eating utensils, ceramic plates, and wine bottles with cork and contents intact; pipes, fittings, and slate duty rosters from the engineering space; and ammunition stores, bayonets, and a fifty-caliber Remington rolling-block pistol." For further information, contact the North Carolina Department of Cultural Resources, Division of Archives and History, Fort Fisher Historic Site Museum, P.O. Box 58, Kure Beach, North Carolina, 28449.

Historians should note that the *Ranger*, the third sister of the *Alert*-class, survived in naval service until 1940. She was then transferred to the Merchant Marine Academy and used as a training ship and, later, as a museum. Although she was scrapped in 1958, her engines were saved and put on display at the American Merchant Marine Museum at Kings Point, Long Island, New York.

Political cartoonist Thomas Nast lampoons the *Huron* catastrophe. In the caption, Uncle Sam says: "I suppose I must spend a little on Life-saving Service, Life-boat Stations, Life-Boats, Surf-Boats, etc.; but it is too bad to be obliged to waste so much money." (From *Harper's Weekly*.)

KASSANDRA LOULOUDIS

Built: 1919
Previous names: *Bondowoso*
Gross tonnage: 5,106
Type of vessel: Freighter
Builder: W. Gray & Company, Ltd., West Hartlepool, England
Owner: Goulandris Brothers
Port of registry: Andros, Greece
Cause of sinking: Torpedoed by *U-124* (Kapitanleutnant Mohr)
Location: 26886.9

Sunk: March 17, 1942
Depth: 70 feet
Dimensions: 400′ × 52′ × 28′
Power: Oil-fired steam

40274.7

The *Kassandra Louloudis* was carrying as diverse a cargo as one could expect to find on a bill of lading: chain and hoist parts, monkey wrenches, pipe fittings, assorted hardware, conduit, turnbuckles, tires, cash registers, pneumatic tools and parts, brass rods, soap, a steel safe, and nine hundred rolls of roofing mat. She left New York on March 15, 1942, her destination Cristobal, Panama.

Courtesy of The Mariners Museum, Newport News, Virginia.

The evening of the seventeenth found the freighter in thick fog ten miles east of the Diamond Shoals. At 5:50 p.m., her radio crackled with an SOS from the tanker *Acme*: she had been torpedoed, a third of her men had been killed, and others were seriously injured. Navy planes dropped depth charges on a suspected target while the Coast Guard cutter *Dione* charged into the fracas.

Reasoning that the offending U-boat must have made a hasty retreat in light of such swift reprisals and military presence, Captain Themis Millas, master of the *Kassandra Louloudis*, changed course for the position of his fellow men of the merchant marine. Deviating from his routing instructions, Captain Millas steered a zigzag pattern "to pass Diamond Shoals Buoy on the port hand, very close to it." An hour later, within sight of the buoy, he spotted "the torpedoed tanker and its lifeboats full of men." Already, the *Dione* was taking on survivors.

Captain Millas did not count on Johann Mohr's tenacity of purpose. "Two freighters were coming up behind me about two or three miles away and one freighter was coming toward me, all passing through the Shoals . . . I saw one destroyer on my port hand about two miles distant, also the Coast Guard boat." All these ships lay within a radius of four miles.

Seeing that he was no longer needed, Captain Millas continued west in order to keep as close to land—and, ostensibly, to safety—as possible. He zigzagged at ten knots. As he "passed about three miles from the buoy on a westward course, a periscope suddenly came into view some one hundred yards off his port side and, almost simultaneously, he saw the frothing wake of a torpedo rushing toward his ship."

Captain Millas yelled for hard astarboard. As the *Kassandra Louloudis* veered to the right a torpedo passed twenty feet in front of the bow. There was not even time to breathe a sigh of relief before a second torpedo was spotted. Even as the gun crew brought out the two Italian machine guns with which the ship was armed, there was a tremendous explosion on the port side forward just below the water line between the No. 2 hold and the bunker hatch.

The engines continued to operate, but the steering gear was knocked out of commission. Radio Operator Eleftheriadis transmitted an SOS on an emergency antenna by hand-cranking a backup generator. As sea water poured into the gaping wound in the hull, the freighter careened over until she was listing forty degrees. It was time to abandon ship.

The engines were shut down, the freighter lost way, and lifeboats were launched. All thirty-five men escaped uninjured. Within forty-five minutes the *Dione* appeared out of the mist and took everyone aboard. The men from both the *Acme* and the *Kassandra Louloudis* were taken to Norfolk. Although sorely wounded, the *Acme* did not sink and was later towed into port, repaired, and returned to service.

The *Kassandra Louloudis* righted herself as she sank, and alighted on the bottom on an even keel with both masts and her funnel protruding from the water, and, at times, the upper level of the bridge. Because of the shallow depth, the wreck was marked with a quick flashing red buoy to warn off merchant shipping traveling through the area.

When the *Liberator* (q.v.) was sunk on the Outer Diamond Shoals only two days later, with her masts showing, there was some confusion for a while as to which wreck was which. Due to the large number of shallow water sinkings, the Diamond Shoals was beginning to look like a forest. In 1944, Navy divers positively identified the *Kassandra Louloudis* when they brought up parts of the wreck labeled *Bondowoso*, her original name.

The Navy report noted wryly that "disintegration was very rapid in the turbulent Cape Hatteras waters. The wreck had disappeared below the surface within a few months, and in the summer of 1944 when demolition operations were commenced, divers found the hull itself ripped apart with the cargo and wreckage spread over a considerable area." The *Kassandra Louloudis* was razed until a least depth of forty-five feet stood over the wreckage.

Today the wreck is completely broken up, but a pretty sight to see due to the profusion of coral growth and thick fish population. There is no bow structure at all, only the blunt beginning of wreckage that protrudes slightly out of the sand. The wreck is very wide due to the outward collapse of hull plates and supporting members. Moving aft, the first discernible feature other than twisted beams and half-buried chunks of steel are the boilers, nestled side by side and looming ten feet above the surrounding debris. Coral-encrusted pipes and lengths of tubing lie scattered about, as well as brass valves and flanges. China shards are found in the sand just forward of the boilers, where the remains of the wheelhouse and bridgeworks have settled.

The engine sits just abaft the boilers and at an elevation slightly less, as if the top had been lopped off. Abaft of this is the after cargo hold, now just a large pile of rubble. Coils of wire mixed in with the debris were probably part of the general freight. At the extreme stern one blade of the bronze propeller points up from inside the curve of the rudder post; the rudder is missing.

The *U-124* was lost with all hands west of Gibraltar on April 2–3, 1943; it was sunk by the HMS *Stonecrop* and the HMS *Black Swan*. See *Shipwrecks of North Carolina: from Hatteras Inlet South* for depredations against the *Esso Nashville*, *Naeco*, *Papoose*, and *W.E. Hutton*; and see *E.M. Clark* in this volume.

Above: the bridge of the *Kassandra Louloudis* is exposed in the trough of a big swell. Below: they may not be smiling, but the crew men are happy to be alive after losing their ship. (Both courtesy of the Naval Historical Center.)

Kyzickes as the *Paraguay*. (Courtesy of the Institute for Great Lakes Research.)

KYZICKES

Built: 1900

Previous names: *Paraguay*

Gross tonnage: 2,627

Type of vessel: Tanker

Builder: American Ship Building Company, Lorain, Ohio

Owner: Michel Aydia, Peter Paramythiotis, George Vouyoueles (all of Alexandria, Egypt)

Sunk: December 4, 1927

Depth: 15 feet

Dimensions: 292' × 42' × 23'

Power: Coal-fired steam

Port of registry: Greece

Cause of sinking: Washed ashore

Location: One mile north of Kill Devil Hills Coast Guard Station

On August 23, 1927, the United States Shipping Board approved the sale of the Sun Oil Company tanker *Paraguay* to foreign owners "on condition, however, that said vessel, subsequent to her first outward voyage from the United States, shall not engage in trade with ports of continental United States." Although her name was changed officially to *Kyzickes* by her owners, she was later erroneously reported as the *Paraguay*, probably because her nameboards had yet to be replaced.

On her first voyage under new ownership she carried crude oil from Baltimore bound for Seville, Spain. Only a day out of port she encountered gale-force winds that battered the aging steel hull hard enough to loosen rivets and shift hull plates. Because she sank heavily into the seas and returned slowly, solid waves of water swept across her rusty decks.

At 4:30 p.m. on December 3, the *Kyzickes* transmitted a pleading message of distress: "Leaking fore and aft badly. In need of assistance. Position latitude 36-35 north, Longitude 75-50 west. Unless you get to us quickly we may not be here. We tried to steer westward but drifting southward. Heavy seas running."

In response to the call for help a small fleet of ships changed course for the beleaguered tanker: the *Baron Harries, City of Atlanta, East Indian, Harvester, St. George,* and *Oxholm.* The Coast Guard cutter *Carrabassett* put out to sea from her base in Norfolk.

Water cascaded into the ruptured hull faster than the tanker's pumps could drain the bilges. The engines were choked off, and the ship went aimlessly adrift. At the mercy of the wind and waves, a huge wall of water hit the ship broadside and tore off her wireless. The *City of Atlanta* was near enough to keep transmitting the call for help.

Once the *Baron Harries* reached the reported position, and was standing by, the Coast Guard released the other rescue vessels from responsibility. But by that time the tanker had drifted so far that she could not be located. For hours a fruitless search was conducted.

During the night the predicament of the *Kyzickes* grew worse. She bobbed along like a submarine barely surfaced. As she buried her belly in the deep troughs, tremendous seas inundated her upper works. She sat so low in the water that waves continually battered her superstructure; most of her topside gear was washed away. In the darkness four men were swept off the ship, never to be seen again.

Dawn brought double-edged relief. The current drove the *Kyzickes* up on a shoal off Kill Devil Hills. Hard aground, she was no longer in danger of sinking; but the surf, whipped to a froth by the storm, pounded against the already stressed hull with telling effect. The ship was fast breaking up.

Life-savers from both the Kitty Hawk and Kill Devil Hills stations converged on the beach opposite the stranded tanker. A Coston flare signalled the *Kyzickes* that help was on the way. The twenty-four remaining crew men were huddled high in the ship's two masts, the only places of safety since most of the hull was submerged. The life-savers did their best to launch surf-boats, but every time were beat back by the power of the sea.

They finally resorted to the Lyle gun. With powder and shot they fired a messenger line over the rigging, attached the hawser, and set up the breeches buoy. Then began the harrowing hours of pulling in the survivors one at a time. Eventually, every man was brought to shore.

At the same time the men were being landed from the *Kyzickes* another drama was taking place off Hatteras. The Norwegian fruit steamer *Cibao* was driven ashore by seventy-mile-per-hour winds. Life-savers from the Hatteras and Creek Hill stations were involved in that rescue. (See *Shipwrecks of North Carolina: from Hatteras Inlet South.*) All in all, it was a busy day for the Life-Saving Service.

Almost added to this tragedy of ship losses was the *Carrabassett*. During her search at sea for the lost *Kyzickes* she ran into extremely violent weather. "High seas broke all over the vessel and one huge wave crushed her pilot house and partly flooded the ship." It was only by laying to until the waves subsided that the cutter managed to survive the storm.

On December 6 the bodies of two men believed to be from the *Kyzickes* washed ashore at Bodie Island, some twenty miles south of where the Greek tanker grounded. One body was partially dismembered; no positive identification was made.

The wreck of the *Kyzickes* lies on the outer shoal about a hundred yards offshore. At extreme low tide the waves can be seen breaking on wreckage visible from shore. All superstructure has long since been pounded into unidentifiable debris. The hull maintains its shape if not its integrity. The boilers and the propeller are exposed. Like all other wrecks that lie in the surf zone, its appearance changes from year to year.

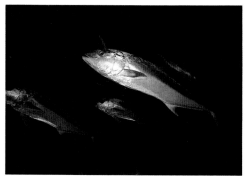

LANCING

Built: 1898   Sunk: April 7, 1942
Previous names: *Flackwell, Calanda, Omsk, Rio Tiete, Knight Errant*
Gross tonnage: 7,866   Dimensions: 470′ × 57′ × 31′
Type of vessel: Whaling factory   Power: Oil-fired steam
Builder: C. Connell & Company, Glasgow, Scotland   Depth: 160 feet
Owner: Hvalfanger A/S Globus (Melsom & Melsom, Mgrs.)
Port of registry: Larvik, Norway
Cause of sinking: Torpedoed by *U-552* (Oberleutnant zur See Topp)
Location: 26897.2   40182.3

The *Lancing* was an ancient ship but by no means senile. She was refitted first in 1926, and again in 1930. The dusty coal-burner was converted to run on fuel oil; her boilers supplied steam cleanly and efficiently to her triple expansion engine. She was designed as a whaling factory and carried whale oil in bulk, but during the war she transported fuel oil for the beleaguered British Isles. On this particular cruise her tanks were filled with 8,802 tons of pool marine fuel oil, which she was taking from Curacao to New York thence by convoy to England.

Because she traveled so much through U-boat infested waters, the *Lancing* was armed with a "4-inch gun mounted on the poop deck, one machine gun on the monkey bridge, two machine guns on the fore deck and two machine guns on the poop deck." She also kept an ample watch: six men including "two men on poop, two on the bridge, one on the monkey bridge, and one on the forecastle head."

As prepared as she was, though, Erich Topp managed to sneak through her defenses in the dark morning hours of April 7, 1942. He caught the 9-knot freighter with a single torpedo that struck the water line on the starboard side of the engine room. The blast peeled back the deck and opened a large hole leading to the machinery spaces.

Tons of water cascaded into the engine room so fast that fireman Emil Hansen had no chance to escape; he was drowned. The rest of the men on duty barely managed to climb out before the engine room was completely flooded. The engine ground to a stop. The *Lancing* lay helpless.

Topp remained an elusive target for the Norwegian sharpshooters, never even poking up his periscope where it could be shot off.

With his ship going down by the stern, Captain Johan Bjerkholt had no choice but to order her abandoned. The remaining forty-nine men got away in fifteen minutes. Luckily, there was no fire. The men hung around their ship for an hour and a half, watching her settle; "then she sank rapidly, the stern plunging first."

No outside help could be expected to come for them because the radio had been knocked out by the initial blast. The lifeboats drifted with the current. Fortune favored the men of the *Lancing*. Within five hours of the attack twenty-eight men were picked up by the tanker *Pan Rhode Island*; shortly thereafter, the remaining twenty-one were found by the British armed trawler HMS *Hertfordshire*.

Erich Topp had quite a successful patrol, sinking in all six vessels within the confines of the Eastern Sea Frontier; total tonnage amounted to 39,475. Further depredations of the *U-552* include the *Byron D. Benson* (q.v.), and three ships covered in *Shipwrecks of North Carolina: from Hatteras Inlet South: Atlas, British Splendour* (torpedoed just a few hours previous to the *Lancing*), and *Tamaulipas*. Topp is infamous for having torpedoed the U.S. destroyer *Reuben James* (DD-245) six weeks *before* Germany and the United States were at war. One hundred fifteen American sailors were killed because of Topp's premature aggression.

Topp relinquished control of the *U-552* to his successor on September 8, 1942. The U-boat survived the war only to be ignominiously scuttled by its crew upon Germany's capitulation.

The wreck of the *Lancing* lies almost perfectly inverted with a slight tilt to starboard; the keel rises some thirty feet off the bottom. The huge rudder and four-bladed bronze propeller present a spectacular sight. A washout under the stern dips as deep as 170 feet. The distinctive "whale door" just above the fantail ("above" because the wreck is upside down) is the feature that identifies the ship's original purpose. The 4-inch gun is buried, but one can swim under the main deck just forward of the poop and see bollards and mooring cleats and the mount for one of the machine guns.

The starboard side of the wreck is a vertical wall that cuts below the sand. A gigantic hole about fifty feet forward of the stern attests to the efficacy of German torpedoes.

The port gunwale stands some eight feet off the bottom, and it is along here that one can see wreckage spilled out of the interior. At least four boilers are visible where they have fallen from their bedplates and have tumbled halfway out of the hull. Close to midships is a giant gash that goes completely through the wreck but not up to the keel; it is big enough to drive a truck through. By swimming into the vast interior one can head aft into the forward boiler room.

The *Lancing* is known locally as the Slick Wreck.

Above: the *Lancing's* majestic profile. Left: Captain Johan Bjerkholt give details of the *Lancing's* loss to an intelligence officer. (Courtesy of the National Archives.)

Below: the *Liberator*. (Courtesy of Dallas La Crone.)
Right: only the *Liberator's* masts are exposed. (Courtesy of the National Archives.)

For photographs see page 109.

LIBERATOR

Built: 1918
Previous names: None
Gross tonnage: 7,720
Type of vessel: Freighter

Sunk: March 19, 1942
Depth: 90–120 feet
Dimensions: 410′ × 56′ × 29′
Power: Oil-fired steam

Builder: Bethlehem Ship Building Corporation, San Francisco, California
Owner: Lykes Brothers Steam Ship Company, New Orleans, Louisiana
Port of registry: Galveston, Texas
Cause of sinking: Torpedoed by *U-332* (Kapitanleutnant Liebe)
Location: 26888.7   40218.8

By mid-March 1942 not only was the east coast U-boat war in full swing, it was at the height of its destruction. From Maine to Florida the merchant fleet was in imminent peril. The Navy did its best to provide patrol craft but was woefully undermanned and short of warships. The only alternative was to arm tankers and freighters so they might defend themselves against the enemy. The Navy supplied both guns and gunners.

Because ships had been torpedoed off the Diamond Shoals every single night for the previous week, the *Liberator's* armed guard was understandably itchy. The entire gun crew camped at their gun post on the fantail and kept a sharp lookout for suspicious, low-lying vessels.

The *Liberator's* holds were filled with 11,000 tons of sulphur picked up in Galveston, Texas. The cargo was bound for New York. The heavily-laden freighter traveled independently, using the Number 5 Navy zigzag pattern by day and running blacked out after dark.

The night of March 18–19, 1942 was an exceptionally fiery one for vessels rounding Cape Hatteras. No less than three U-boats were operating in the vicinity at that time, and between them they tried to take out every ship that passed. First to take the plunge was the *Papoose*. Next was a running gun battle in which the *Mercury Sun* and *Gulf of Mexico* were shelled and set afire, although both escaped. Also before midnight a torpedo ripped into the hull of the *W.E. Hutton* and sent her to the bottom. (For accounts of the *Papoose* and the *W.E. Hutton* see *Shipwrecks of North Carolina: from Hatteras Inlet South*.)

Into this human-wrought cataclysm drove the *Liberator*. She ran the gauntlet fully alert and bristling for a fight.

About nine miles off Cape Lookout Light Buoy, Coxswain Frank

Camillo, captain of the Naval armed guard, spotted a "dark object" through his telescope. The long black hull and low superstructure matched perfectly the silhouette of a submarine. He called his crew to action as the unidentified vessel closed the distance between them.

Camillo took careful aim. He pulled the lanyard that sent a 4-inch projectile with deadly accuracy into the darkened "conning tower." The crew cheered exhultantly when they saw "a mass of sparks, flashes and flames." The second shot was as well-placed as the first.

The gun crew became confused when the target showed three lights over the "conning tower," and fired a flare toward the *Liberator*. Nevertheless, they were assured of the U-boat's complete destruction as they watched it "turn over on its starboard side and go down."

Unfortunately, the ship they fired upon was not a German U-boat but a U.S. destroyer. The USS *Dickerson* (DD-157) was looking for action, but not against an allied merchantman. Prowling for undersea raiders required stealth and speed—the reason why the *Dickerson* was blacked out and steaming fast. She was also there in case an intrepid U-boat commander found his mark; only two days before the *Dickerson* rescued survivors from the *E.M. Clark* (q.v.).

The official Navy report stated that "a shrapnel shell suddenly struck the starboard side of the *Dickerson's* bridge, passing through the railing on the wing of the bridge, the chart room, and finally exploding in the radio 'shack'. Three men on the *Dickerson* were killed outright, and seven persons were injured, including Lieutenant Commander J.K. Reybold, Commanding Officer, who later died, ten minutes before the ship docked at the Norfolk Navy Yard, Portsmouth, Virginia, at 1235. The *Liberator's* fire was not returned as it was believed by Lieutenant F.E. Wilson, Executive Officer, who had assumed command upon the injuries to the Commanding Officer, that the unidentified freighter was a friendly vessel."

Also killed were the radar man and the sound operator. Despite the observations of the *Liberator's* gun crew, the *Dickerson* did not sink. Her radio was destroyed, preventing communication. Because the gyro repeater was knocked out of step with the master gyro (it was eighty-five degrees off) Lieutenant Wilson got on course magnetically.

After this mistaken engagement the *Liberator* treaded water even more cautiously. Dawn found the freighter approaching the Diamond Shoals, the scene of so much activity just a few hours previous. Daylight brought good visibility. Just after 10:00 a.m. she passed the Diamond Shoals Lighted Buoy three miles to starboard—ships often cut inside the buoy in order to avoid the open sea and deep water where U-boats were more likely to lurk. Two other ships were within a quarter mile, offering herd security.

Johannes Liebe was no ordinary U-boat commander. Just as he did with the *Australia* (q.v.) three days before, he out-psyched Allied thinkers. Only this time he went one better. He brought his U-bost close in to the shoals and fired *outward*—and in broad daylight.

His torpedo ripped into the *Liberator's* port hull just as she changed course northward. The violent explosion demolished the engine room and the deck above, and converted one lifeboat into splinters. Five duty personnel were killed by the blast.

The freighter was instantly without power and out of control—a sitting target as she slowly lost way. Captain Albin Johnson ordered abandon ship. The radio operator transmitted a hasty SOS, but was forced to leave his post before receiving an acknowledgment. The captain quickly ditched the secret codes.

The *Liberator's* ever-alert gun crew saw no sign of the enemy, but a lookout on another ship did. "The *Chester Sun* was witness to the torpedoing of the U.S. cargo vessel *Liberator* ... She sighted the enemy U-boat, attempted to ram it and flashed an SOS on behalf of the fast-sinking *Liberator*, but was not herself damaged."

Meanwhile, thirty-five men got away in two lifeboats.

The *Chester Sun* and the tanker *Esso Baltimore* put on steam and got out of there before they suffered the same fate as the *Liberator*. The torpedoed freighter settled to the bottom twenty-five minutes after the attack. A half hour later the Navy tug *Umpqua* (ATF-25) arrived on the scene, took the survivors off their lifeboats, and transferred them to Morehead City.

The water was shallow enough that both the *Liberator's* masts stuck up out of the water. As late as September 1944 one mast was still standing. At that time "demolition of the wreck has not been requested by ComFive as it lies in water which is not navigable."

The wreck of the *Liberator* lies next to the breakers off the Outer Shoals coincidentally close to the *Australia*, also sunk by the *U-332*. The wreck is broken into three pieces that rest in deep washouts scoured by the constant swirling current. Although the surrounding sand level at the bow is 90 feet, the wreck sits 10 feet deeper in what appears to be a bathtub. The wreckage lies low. The first twenty or thirty feet is canted on its side, nose down, with the winches attached to the deck plates and one anchor in the high-side hawse pipe.

Farther aft lies the scattered wreckage of the forward part of the wheelhouse. At the stern the bathtub effect is the most pronounced, the sand sloping steeply from 100 feet to 120 feet. The wreck is severely damaged by storm and wave action. Lumps of yellow sulphur are evident on the bottom, and are safe to collect as souvenirs.

The wreck was positively identified when Dallas LaCrone recovered some of the brass letters from the bow.

Oberleutnant zur See Eberhard Huttemann replaced Liebe as captain of the *U-332* on January 27, 1943. Under his command the *U-332* was lost with all hands on May 2 or 6, 1943, in the Bay of Biscay. Credited with the kill was RAAF Squadron 461.

MAGNOLIA

Built: 1852
Previous names: *Augusta*, USS *Augusta*
Gross tonnage: 1,310
Type of vessel: Wood hulled side-wheeler
Builder: William H. Webb, New York
Owner: Ocean Steamship Company, Savannah, Georgia
Port of registry: Savannah, Georgia
Cause of sinking: Foundered
Location: Off Cape Hatteras

Sunk: September 30, 1877
Depth: Unknown
Dimensions: 220′ × 35′ × 21′
Power: Coal-fired steam

The *Magnolia* began her career as the *Augusta*, owned by the New York & Savannah Steam Navigation Company, and ran regular service between those two ports. In those pre-inflation times the one-way passenger fare was $25. The *Augusta* kept her route for nine years, until the outbreak of the Civil War.

On August 1, 1861 she was sold to the Federal government for $96,940, and was commissioned in the U.S. Navy on September 28. As part of the South Atlantic Blockading Squadron the USS *Augusta* saw quite a bit of action. On November 7 she participated in attacks on Fort Beauregard and Fort Walker and helped drive off Confederate vessels, leading to the capture of Port Royal that afternoon. On December 6 she "assisted in the capture of the British schooner *Cheshire* off Savannah. The blockade runner had a cargo of blankets from Liverpool for the Confederate Army." On the last day of the year she "captured the British schooner *Island Belle* off Bull's Island, S.C. from Cuba with molasses and sugar."

She continued on blockade duty for the remainder of the war. With armament consisting of "six 8-inch guns, one 100-pound Parrott rifle and two 30-pound rifles, and a 12-pound howitzer" she fought off the Confederate rams CSS *Chicora* and CSS *Palmetto State*. The *Augusta* was decommissioned on June 6, 1865, but recommissioned the following year on May 6. She then towed the monitor *Miantonomoh* from New York to Russia, visiting many ports on the way there and back. After that a year long cruise took her to the Mediterranean.

On December 26, 1868 the Navy put up the *Augusta* for auction. She went for $20,700 to C.K. Garrison, who had her completely reconditioned and renamed *Magnolia*. She then ran passenger and freight service from New York to Charleston and Florida ports, even after she was sold to the Central of Georgia Railway and Banking Company. In 1874 the C.G.R.B. Co. transferred all its steamships to a subsidiary company called the Ocean Steamship Company.

On September 27, 1877 the *Magnolia* left Savannah for New York with forty-two officers and crew and three passengers. Her cargo, worth $75,000, consisted of "929 bales of Upland cotton, 9 bales of Sea Island cotton, 120 bales of domestics and yarns, 45 casks of rice, 8 barrels of spirits of turpentine, 456 barrels of resin, 176 sacks of rice chaff, 100 coils of rope, 33,000 feet of lumber, and general merchandise."

A succinct account of the *Magnolia's* loss was given by her captain, E.H. Daggett. "Left Savannah 27th at 12 M.; wind northeast, moderate, and some rain squalls toward evening; 28th, took heavy squalls from north-northwest; took in sail and steamed; 29th, moderate wind, northeast; at 3 P.M. wind increasing, northeast and squally; took soundings on Hatteras Shoals; 30th, 4 A.M., discovered vessel was leaking; started pumps, but could not gain any; about 5 A.M. fire-room floor gave way; at 8 A.M. water put out fires; then started a gang of men on each side with buckets, bailing—pumps being choked and water gaining all the time; at 12 M. called officers and decided that it was impossible to save the ship; at 2 P.M. prepared to abandon; at 3 P.M. first boat left; at 4:45 Captain left the ship, with 12 feet of water in her and gaining fast; at 6 P.M. all hands safe on board the bark *Stralsund*, Captain Oehlberg, Baltimore to Baltic, who . . . transferred all to pilot boat *E.C. Knight*, which landed us at Lewes with nothing but what we stood in. Officers and crew desire to express thanks to Capt. Oehlberg for his kind attention."

Captain Daggett left out a few salient details. The *Stralsund* did not happen to be standing alongside when the *Magnolia* was abandoned, but was twelve miles away. "One boat, containing seven men, was swamped shortly after leaving the *Magnolia*, and everything in it was swept overboard, the boat being buffeted about for three hours. The men, having no oars, hung on to the sides of the boat until they were rescued by their comrades. The transfer occupied four or five hours' time. The sea ran very high, and five trips were made between the ships." Because the *Stralsund* was to leeward of the *Magnolia* it was difficult for her to beat against the wind in order to close the distance.

In the true tradition of the sea, Captain Daggett was the last person to leave his ship. Then, he and the men in the last lifeboat were nearly left behind. When the *Magnolia* was seen to disappear beneath the waves, those on the *Stralsund* assumed that the others had been lost. It was only because the *Magnolia's* second officer was so insistent upon searching for his captain that Captain Oehlberg sent back another boat in search of the lost men, and rescued Captain Daggett and the others. Only by such heroic exertions were no lives lost.

It would seem that if Captain Daggett took soundings on Hatteras Shoals on the twenty-ninth, and the *Magnolia* was headed north, the wreck should lie somewhere north of there.

The majestic manta.

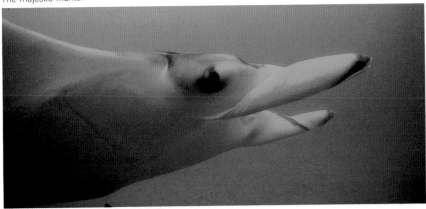

This picture was taken the day before the *Marore* was sunk. (Courtesy of the National Archives.)

MARORE

Built: 1922
Previous names: None
Gross tonnage: 8,215
Type of vessel: Bulk ore carrier
Builder: Bethlehem Ship Building Corporation, Sparrows Point, Maryland
Owner: Ore Steam Ship Corporation
Port of registry: New York
Cause of sinking: Torpedoed by *U-432* (Kapitanleutnant Schultze)
Location: 26885.2

Sunk: February 27, 1942
Depth: 130 feet
Dimensions: 550' × 72' × 44'
Power: Oil-fired steam turbines

40504.2

For Captain Charles Nash, master of the *Marore*, the passage between Cruz Grande, Chile and Baltimore, Maryland was a milk-run. The only differences between this and previous voyages were the course instructions provided by the Naval Routing Officer at Balboa, Canal Zone, and the removal of two suspicious-acting crew members.

With all the U-boat activity occurring off the American east coast, Captain Nash dismissed deck engineer John Ryan and wiper Henry Jackson because they were "great talkers, continually frightening the crew." Both men were discharged at Balboa, journeyed overland, and inexplicably permitted to rejoin the ship at Colon.

After leaving the Panama Canal, the *Marore* crossed the Caribbean Sea, passed between Cuba and Florida, then headed north hugging the coast. The unarmed vessel traveled independently, did not zigzag, but did run blacked out at night. Burdened with 23,000 tons of iron ore, her speed was a steady ten-and-a-half knots.

Along the way the radio crackled with U-boat sightings; the constant menace was ever just over the horizon. After nearly four weeks on route the *Marore* passed the Diamond Shoals, on the night of February 26. The sea was moderate, and visibility was about five miles.

When Captain Nash spotted the running lights of an approaching ship, he switched on his own navigation lights in order to announce his presence and avoid a collision. Unfortunately, a lurking U-boat was lying in wait for just such an occurrence. About thirty minutes past midnight "the starboard lookout detected a loud buzzing sound, similar to a plane noise. A fraction of a second later, everyone aboard the *Marore* heard a sharp, extremely loud explosion just aft of amidships on the starboard side. Moments later the big ore-carrier took a definite list to starboard."

A column of black smoke accompanied the blast, followed by the raucous ringing of the ship's automatic alarm bell. The radio shack was largely demolished, with its antenna grounded, its transmitter ripped off the bulkhead, and the power lines severed. In the engine room the assistant engineer on duty, E.B. Stahl, was knocked off his feet, but immediately jumped up and, following the captain's prearranged instructions, reversed the engines and brought the ship to a stop.

All the men but nine were in their bunks at the time, but were quickly roused by the clamoring alarm. Captain Nash ordered abandon ship. As the men gathered in an orderly fashion at their lifeboat stations a head count revealed that no one was missing or even injured. The entire crew pulled away in three lifeboats.

According to official Naval documents, "Ten to fifteen minutes later, with all boats clear of the *Marore*, two, or possibly three submarines began shelling the vessel from three different points. This fact gave credulence to the belief that Axis U-boats were operating in a 'pack' formation. From very close range the submarines poured tracer shells into the sinking vessel at intervals of 20 seconds. The Captain said approximately 100 rounds were fired, and he was forced to admit that the marksmanship displayed was excellent. 'I don't think they missed a single shot.'"

In a more poetic moment Captain Nash claimed, "All three intermittently fired tracers. They hit the water, bounced like crazy tennis balls and lit up the whole area, giving the gunners a perfect target."

Radio Operator Christopher Core described the tracer shells as "a beautiful display of fireworks. They looked like Roman candles, but we couldn't enjoy it."

Despite the testimony of witnesses, German records credit only Kapitanleutnant Heinz-Otto Schultze and the *U-432* with the kill. In fact, this was Schultze's last attack before returning home; it is very likely that his shelling of the *Marore* was precipitated by the expenditure of his last torpedo.

Captain Nash last saw his ship "down by the stern and capsized so that only a blister of the bilge remained visible above the water."

The U-boat (or U-boats) disappeared in the darkness. The men sat quietly in their lifeboats throughout the night. Fine weather continued after dawn, and the sun added its warmth. Captain Nash and the thirteen men in his boat rigged the sail and headed west. "At approximately 1100 the morning after they were attacked, twenty-five of the men, in two of the three lifeboats were picked up by the Atlantic Refining Company tanker SS

John D. Gill. The *John D. Gill* was unable to reach the third boat because it was in too shallow water." (Three weeks later the *John D. Gill* was torpedoed and sunk off Wilmington, North Carolina. See *Shipwrecks of North Carolina: from Hatteras Inlet South* for details.) The men were transferred to the *YP-27*, which took them to the Naval Operating Base at Norfolk.

The captain's boat was sighted by lookouts from the Big Kinnakeet Coast Guard Station. Motor surf boat No. 3843 was promptly manned and launched. As usual, the Coast Guard report was succcinct and without histrionics. "Found 14 of crew in lifeboat, took 7 in surfboat through surf to shore, returned and took the remaining seven to shore, towed in lifeboat. Sea was rough." A Coast Guard truck then took them to Norfolk where they were reunited with the rest of the crew.

On the same patrol the *U-432* also sank the *Olinda, Azalea City, Norlavore* (q.v.), and *Buarque* (q.v.). It returned to the American coast in June 1942, but sank only two small fishing boats. It was sunk in the North Atlantic on March 11, 1943, with twenty-six crewmen killed and twenty captured.

During interrogation Captain Nash claimed that the *Marore* sank three miles east of Wimble Shoals buoy. A survey conducted in 1944 located a sunken ship in that approximate position. "Underwater photographs show that the wreck is definitely not the *Mirlo*, and is probably definitely the *Marore*. The wreck lies on its side, is of modern welded plate construction, and has king posts similar to those of the *Marore*, and does not appear to be heavily enough fouled to have been sunk as long ago as the *Mirlo* was. . . . A plot of Sonar target widths indicates the wreck to be of approximately the same length as the *Marore* (550 feet)." (See *Mirlo* for a discussion of those references.)

Despite the above description, the hull of the *Marore* is upside down today. If one presumes that Captain Nash defined "capsized" as "rolled over" but not necessarily perfectly inverted, and that the Navy survey report defined "on its side" as being any position within 45° of the horizontal, than one can imagine the wreck originally lying hard over and resting on its kingposts; when the kingposts bent from the sustained weight of a ship they were not meant to support, or lost their structural integrity as the metal began to rust, then the hull could have rolled over as the sand was scoured from under it.

To further stretch the imagination, the 1944 survey report claimed that "the fathometer indicated depths of 93–96 feet in the immediate vicinity of the wreck, and the least depth recorded over the wreck was 41.5 feet at M.L.W." (Mean low water.) Today the depth is 130 feet.

The wreck is so nearly intact that entrance to the vast interior is severely limited. The engine room is accessible through truck-sized damage holes, although very little exploration has been conducted inside. Most of the wreck is an impenetrable steel vault, looking rather like an inverted submarine.

There is no noticeable debris field largely due to an unusual bottom feature: completely surrounding the wreck is a large expanse of white fluff that is stirred up by even the most careful fin kick. The result is an underwater snowstorm that worsens the normally poor visibility. This occurs because the wreck lies in a slough in which silt has accumulated over the years.

The propellers were blown off and recovered by salvors.

The *Marore's* survivors.

MERAK

Built: 1910
Previous names: None
Gross tonnage: 3,024
Type of vessel: Freighter
Builder: Rotterdam Droogd. Maat, Rotterdam, the Netherlands
Owner: United States Shipping Board (Emergency Fleet Corporation)
Port of registry: United States
Cause of sinking: Shelled by *U-140* (Korvettenkapitan Kophamel)
Location: 35-13-43N

Sunk: August 6, 1918
Depth: Unknown
Dimensions: 325′ × 47′ × 20′
Power: Coal-fired steam

75-12-06W

The *Merak* was on her way from Norfolk to South America with 4,000 tons of coal when she ran afoul of the *U-140* off the Diamond Shoals. Said Second Mate Salvatano Monti:

"We were traveling along smoothly at a speed of about eight miles an hour, the weather was fine and the sea calm. We were not far from the *Diamond Shoal* Lightship, there were two ships in the distance and we were just about to change our course, when without warning a shot whizzed past the bridge. Several other reports followed but I was unable to make out a submarine, all I could see were flashes in the distance."

Although the U-boat was not visible from the bridge of the *Merak*, the crew of the *Diamond Shoals* lightship (q.v.) saw it clearly on the horizon. The lightship sent out an SOS, as did the *Merak's* Third Class Radio Electrician, Enoch Payne Hardy; neither received acknowledgment.

According to one report, the *Merak* zigzagged in an attempt to avoid the deadly shells, and ran aground in the process. Korvettenkapitan Kophamel, seeing that the steamer was helpless, altered course for the lightship in order to silence her radio. He fired six shells that came close

The *Alcaid* is a sister ship of the *Merak*. (Courtesy of the Vereeniging Nederlandsch Historisch Scheepvaart Museum.)

enough to inundate the lightship's deck with water and scare off the crew, who got away in a lifeboat.

Now Kophamel returned to his sitting duck. Monti: "We had no guns to return the submarine's fire, and as a result, the submarine came steadily toward the ship, firing at intervals. After about 30 shots were fired, we decided to abandon the ship . . . in two boats and started towards the shore. We were some distance from the boat when the submarine went up to the ship and placed a bomb aboard which sunk the ship. . . . After this the submarine steamed towards the boat in which the Captain was and" interrogated him.

After ascertaining the name of the vessel, her nationality, cargo, tonnage, and ports of call, Kophamel said (according to Monti, and verified by Second Assistant Enginer Richard William Ritchie, Jr.), "Have you a sail? You are about ten miles off shore and I don't think you will have any trouble in getting there. Thank you."

Monti continued, "The submarine then steamed away in the direction of the Lightship and opened fire on same. I did not see the Lightship sink." The boats hauled sail. "We lost sight of the boat containing the Captain and other members of the crew. When we landed on the beach, we built a fire, and thereby tried to attract the attention of the other boat. Not long afterwards men from Station 181 of the Coast Guard came to our rescue and took charge of the boat." These twenty men were taken to Elizabeth City.

Captain Charles Gerlach and the other twenty-two men from the *Merak* spent the night at sea. The next day they were picked up by the steamship *Adonis*, and taken to Norfolk.

The wreck of the *Merak* has not been positively identified. Contemporary Naval documents gave the *Merak's* position as 35-57N/75-40W. This spot is some twenty-five miles southwest of the *Diamond Shoals* lightship: not in keeping with the lightship crew's testimony, and out of sight of lookouts. It can certainly be discounted.

The Navy Wreck List of 1954 cited Coast Guard records that plotted the final resting place at 35-13-48N/75-11-13W. This was updated by the Navy Wreck List of 1957, which replotted the position as 35-13-43N/75-12-06W. Also, in the latter list an unknown source was credited with the claim that the wreck had been located on April 1, 1923 and wired-dragged to a least depth of 73 feet. Was this an overlooked truth or a cruel April Fool's joke?

Both the latter positions are consistent with eyewitness accounts given by the crew of the *Diamond Shoals* lightship, but neither position is on a shoal. Nor could a ship that ran aground be expected to lie at a depth that could be wire-dragged to 73 feet.

Uwe Lovas has spent considerable energy exploring the possible whereabouts of the *Merak's* remains. He discounts the report that the *Merak* grounded. (Monti made no mention of grounding in his interrogation.) Lovas found a wreck at the Navy's 1957 position, but wrote "there is insufficient metal mass at that location to constitute the remains of an entire steamship with a displacement of 3,000 tons. The magnetic anomaly caused by the wreckage is weak, poorly defined and limited to a small area. During 1989, I made two dives at this site. The few debris that were visible about the sand consisted mainly of hull plates." The loran coordinates are 26857.1/40340.1.

A better prospect, he believes, is 26869.7/40273.1: a spot that is four and a half miles northeast of the former location of the *Diamond Shoals* lightship and one and a half miles southeast of the Diamond Tower. In 145 feet of water he found the wreck of an unidentified steamer "similar in size to the *Merak*. Lying upside down, the hull is broken into at least two separate pieces. ... Over the course of several dives, I have closely examined the bow wreckage, looking for artifacts that could help identify the ship. Unfortunately, nothing has been spotted. Nor did I see any sign of the coal cargo, but this would not be surprising. Coal is almost neutral in water, and the swift Gulf Stream current would have carried much of it away. One mast is visible in the sand on the northern side of the bow section. Swimming past the break of the bow wreckage, the center portion of the hull is encountered 75 feet or so away, laying perpendicular to the bow section. During all my dives on this wreck, I have never swum further astern than amidships. Speaking with someone who has dove on the stern, he told me that it is also resting upside down, a single propeller visible."

Lovas cautions that "the wreck is located near the Gulf Stream. Current velocity is usually two knots or higher. To make matters worse, because the wreck is upside down, the grapnel almost always catches the marine growth on the side of the hull, and is held to it by the current. Not a reassuring purchase, as the hook tends to slowly ride up the hull during the course of a dive."

The mystery surrounding resting place of the *Merak* awaits unraveling. For now it lies serenely hidden by the murk of time.

For the final disposition fo the *U-140*, read the last two paragraphs of the *Diamond Shoals*.

Toadfish.

METROPOLIS

Built: 1861

Previous names: USS *Stars and Stripes*

Gross tonnage: 879 tons

Type of vessel: Passenger-freighter

Builder: Charles Mallory, Mystic Connecticut

Owner: M.H. Simpson, C.W. Copeland, and the Lunt Brothers

Port of registry: New York

Cause of sinking: Ran aground

Location: Three miles south of Currituck Beach Light

Sunk: January 31, 1878

Depth: 15 feet

Dimensions: 198′ × 34′ × 16′

Power: Coal-fired steam

According to U.S. Navy records the *Stars and Stripes* was built "as a speculation for C.S. Bushnell—was purchased by the Navy at New York City from C.S. Bushnell on 27 July 1861; was fitted out for naval service at the New York Navy Yard and was commissioned there on 19 September 1861, Lt. Reed Werden in command."

As originally constructed she was 124′ long; her tonnage was given as 407, but the Navy used displacement tonnage instead of gross tonnage given by Lloyd's Register of Shipping. Her hull was wood. The ship was propelled by a direct-acting engine and a single screw; her two masts were square-rigged. The Navy bought the *Stars and Stripes* for $55,000, then armed her with four 8-inch smoothbore cannons and one 20-pounder rifle.

Due to the outbreak of the Civil War the *Stars and Stripes* was assigned to the Atlantic Blockade Squadron. With a complement of ninety-four sailors and marines she patrolled the east coast, where she captured the Confederate schooner *Charity* loaded with cotton. During January and February of 1862 she was part of the Burnside Expedition (see *Pocahontas*), and participated in the attack on Roanoke Island and in the capture of New Bern. Later, she helped destroy the blockade runner *Modern Greece*, ashore near Wilmington, North Carolina. After a refit the *Stars and Stripes* operated in the Gulf of Mexico for the remainder of the war; she was constantly in the thick of the action.

After the cessation of hostilities the *Stars and Stripes* was decommissioned (June 30, 1865). On August 10 she was sold at public auction for $30,000 to Thomas Watson & Sons of New York. She was reconditioned for the freight and passenger trade, and her name was changed to *Metropolis*. For five years she ran between New York and Havana. She was sold in 1870 to a Boston company, and again in 1871 to M.H. Simpson, C.W. Copeland, and the Lunt Brothers. .

Her new owners had the ship lengthened at Newburyport, Massachusetts, and "at the same time compounded her original engine by adding small cylinders to each existing cylinder." The *Metropolis* steamed from New York to various east coast, Caribbean, and South American ports. Through years of hard service the once-staunch ship fell into disrepair. Chartered to a railroad company to transport cotton from Wilmington, North Carolina, she left New York on December 2, 1877 and "limped into Hampton Roads two days later with six inches of water in the engine room from a serious leak. She was towed to a berth and patched up. The railroad company however cancelled the charter by reason of the steamer's unsuitable and unseaworthy condition."

The ship was sent to New York for repairs. In addition to having her shaft replaced, her bottom was stripped and caulked and her hull was painted. However, the sheathing was not put back on. Assistant Inspector Craft signed a certificate of inspection after testing the vessel and finding her fit and seaworthy.

In January the *Metropolis* was chartered to the Pennsylvania Railroad Company, which was then building the Madeira and Mamore Railroad in South America. (The Mamore River runs into the Madeira River, which runs into the Amazon.) In addition to transporting 500 tons of iron railroad material, 220 laborers under three-year contracts were scheduled to leave Philadelphia for the voyage, via St. Thomas, to Para, Brazil.

In order to accomodate so many people, the *Metropolis* "had on board a novel apparatus by which the cooking of the steerage passengers was to be done with ease and rapidity. The arrangement consisted of four wooden tanks in the steerage kitchen, into each of which ran a pipe connected with the boiler and extending from the top of the tank to the bottom. Into these tanks, whose aggregate capacity was about six barrels, was placed the food to be cooked, and then steam from the boiler forced through communicating pipes. By this means it is said meat, vegetables, coffee, &c., in large quantities could be properly prepared for the table in from 20 to 30 minutes.''

The *Metropolis* pulled out of Philadelphia at 9 a.m. on January 29, 1878. Along with her crew, laborers, and fourteen cabin class passengers, she carried 258 souls. The ship reached the Delaware breakwater an hour before midnight, and duly discharged the pilot. When she poked her bowsprit into the Atlantic and turned south she encountered heavy weather that worked the ship like a corkscrew. Her wooden hull creaked and groaned, the wind whistled through her rigging in a wild, bone-chilling screech. The apparatus by which so much food could be cooked lay cold and unused while seasick passengers heaved previous meals in the reverse direction.

During the night Chief Engineer Joseph Lovell discovered four feet of water in the shaft alley. He ''asked for the aid of a carpenter. With him and the chief mate we went through the shaft alley, where the water was up beyond our waists, and we discovered the leak in the stern of the ship, coming through the dead wood in all parts of her. I immediately reported to the Captain, telling him that we could never make our destination in that condition.''

Captain J.H. Anker turned his ship toward the Virginia Capes. He ordered all hands to the pumps, and kept the donkey-engine running full time. Some of the crew was detailed to lighten the load by hauling coal from the bunkers and heaving it overboard. Alerted by the hustle and bustle, several passengers volunteered their services as coal passers. ''At midnight the circulating pump broke down and the water poured in much faster than it could be pumped out. A few hours later a heavy sea struck the vessel, carrying away her smokestack, boats, engine-room (bulkhead), and the doors of the forward saloon, letting in a large quantity of water.'' The fifty tons of discarded coal did not come close to offsetting the amount of sea water already shipped.

Lovell: ''The lights were all put out by the heavy seas. I secured a lantern from one of the passengers; my assistant engineers were all at their posts, but were in utter darkness. ... The first assistant engineer reported that the fire-room was full of water, and that the men were afraid to go down below. I told the men to come with me, for if we could keep steam up we might save the ship. A barrel of tallow was then thrown in the furnaces, as well as all the wood that could be found.''

The beleaguered steamer was now engulfed in a howling snowstorm. The cold was numbing. Life preservers were passed out to anxious passengers while crew members tried valiantly to plug the leaks in the after steerage where the icy sea made its greatest incursion. Any who were not too sick to work joined the bucket brigade, passing water filled buckets from one to the other and out the hatchways.

The *Metropolis* was driven along helplessly by the force of a full gale. When her stern post was carried away she was almost completely at the mercy of the elements. The only chance for survival was to beach the ship. The engines kept up their revolutions at one-third speed, and hastily-rigged canvas provided a semblance of control.

The ship took such a pounding from the waves that her upperworks began breaking up. All the lifeboats but one were dashed to pieces. Water partially doused the flames under the boilers. The ship wallowed sickeningly in the troughs. Dawn found breakers ahead.

At 6:45 a.m. the ship struck the beach head on. By that time all the head sails had been set in order to drive the vessel high upon the beach but, because the *Metropolis* was weighed down by so much water, she could not rise above the shoals to reach shallower depths. She stranded a hundred yards from the crashing surf.

"The sea broke over the decks of the ship with great violence, and many of those on board who had rushed on deck were swept away. Their cries for help were agonizing, but all were powerless to help them."

First Mate Charles Dickman adds detail: "After striking, the ship was washed with immense seas, which swept away completely the after part of the hurricane deck, and the people who had clustered there were forced to take to the fore-rigging and top-gallant forecastle for greater safety. Occasionally, three or four would jump overboard and swim for the shore. One of the ladies, Mrs. Myers, wife of one of the foremen of laborers, was washed out of the pilot-house, knocked senseless against the rail, and was drowned, her husband standing by her at the time. A moment after he jumped overboard and he also was drowned."

The ship's bell was rung continuously. Two rare passersby, N.E.K. Jones and James Capps, heard the pitiful peal. Peering through the clinging mist they caught a glimpse of the wreck and discerned people crowded on the barely protected bow. Capps immediately ran for the house of Swepson Brock, half a mile away, and told him of the wreck. Brock wasted no time in sadling his horse and galloping for the Life-Saving station five miles away.

According to the report of Captain James Merryman, Inspector of Life-Saving Stations, "Jones discovered several persons struggling in the water near by, and one or two further up the beach among the debris of the wreck, already breaking up, although stranded but little more than an hour. Jones at once engaged in hauling persons out of the surf, and had thus brought out six or eight of them when Mr. Brock rode by on his way to the station."

The Life-Saving crew was galvanized into action. While the surfmen loaded the hand-cart with the life-saving apparatus, station keeper John Chappell went ahead with Brock to the scene of the catastrophe. Chappell carried a medicine chest on his back, and with its stimulants brought back to consciousness many people who otherwise may have died.

Merryman: "Station 4 is situated on a portion of the coast so flat that for nearly a mile inland, and so slightly above ordinary high water, that the storm-tides sweep over it, and, surrounding the station, cover the sandy plain to a depth of several inches, and this had occurred the night before, making the sand so soft and yielding that the wheels of the cart, with their broad tires, five inches wide, cut four or five inches below the surface, while the feet of the men, as they labored with their load, sank in the sand at every step; consequently, the party could make but slow progress. The cart contained the mortar, three balls, the whip-line and block, the breeches-buoy, a tackle, powder-flask, quick-matches, match-rope, and line-stock, line-box, and a Merriman life-saving suit, which, with the cart, made a dead weight of more than 1,000 pounds." Already weakened by nighttime patrols as long as thirty-two miles, the six stalwart surfmen strained at the braces. They struggled for a mile and a half before being overtaken by John Dunton, who offered to hitch his horse to the cart.

Not until nearly six hours after the ship came ashore was the first shot fired. The strong wind blowing from the south bowed the line, causing it to miss the wreck to leeward. Chappell compensated for the windage and laid the second shot across the foretop-sail yardarm. The second mate climbed the swaying mast, "got the shot-line from the yard-arm and carried it into the slings of the yard, when he hauled in the slack from shoreward on the starboard side of the hurricane deck, their only remaining foot-hold, as the after part of the vessel, together with a great portion of the port side, was already gone, while the extreme forward port of the vessel was seen to be moving independently of the remaining portion. The whip-line was at once made fast to the shot-line by the life-saving men and was hauled toward the ship."

Then came a cruel stroke. As the survivors huddled on the forward end of the *Metropolis* waiting for rescue by breeches buoy, the line chafed over the iron wires of the jib-stay, and parted. As Merryman later reported, "This is the first instance in the history of the service that a shot-line has parted after reaching a wreck. The line used was a new one, of Italian hemp, braided after the style of the patent sash-cord of the Silver Lake Company. It is always free from turns, however coiled, and very rarely kinks when flying from its faking-box." What was worse, there was no more powder on hand for the mortar.

Brock again put his valiant steed to work; he raced back to the station for more powder. As soon as he returned, Chappell fired the third shot. This time the ball separated from the line and fell far out to sea. Blame was placed on the thrice-used whip-line being wet and full of sand, and therefore too heavy for the connecting wire. The fourth and last shot went the same way. Now the life-savers were out of balls and line. With no hope of rigging a breeches buoy, there was nothing they could do to succor those aboard the ship other than drag struggling people out of the surf as they came ashore on their own.

Said passenger Charles Connelly, "At this time the whole afterpart of the ship, with the mizzen mast, was carried off, and nearly all of the hurricane deck had gone. The pilot-house and Captain's office were carried off. The bows commenced to separate, and presently the whole forecastle almost entirely parted from the ship."

The *Metropolis* was disintegrating rapidly.

Chappell "put on the Merriman life-saving dress and attempted to reach the wreck with a line, but, greatly fatigued by his march and labor, he was unable to stem the strong current and force his way beyond the breakers, and after two praiseworthy efforts was compelled to abandon the endeavor exhausted."

The only remaining lifeboat made it through the waves carrying a few stalwart crewmen. Quartermaster James Poland tried three times to swim a line to shore only to be dragged back by the incredible undertow; he was finally forced to let go the line in order to gain the beach alive. Lovell "succeeded in reaching the shore on a cabin door."

Merryman: "When the hapless people remaining on the wreck realized that no further effort could be made for their rescue from the fast-crumbling remains of the doomed *Metropolis*, they accepted their last alternative, and singly and sometimes in groups plunged overboard, trusting their lives to the treacherous waves. The surf by this time was running high, and the waters were laden with floating fragments of the wreck, amid which, sorely and in some cases fatally injured, drifting northward and driven by the rolling breakers shoreward, came the struggling, drowning people, to be received in the welcome arms of their rescuers, who, with precarious foot-hold, strove in their work waist-deep in the inner breakers and undertow."

Chappell and his surfmen were aided by local residents in their heroic rescue efforts. "Even a noble Newfoundland dog, owned by Mr. Brock, incited by the example before him, joined in the work, and plunging into the surf safely brought to shore a half-drowned man. In a word, all present were engaged either in hauling the people out of the surf or receiving them from others and assisting them to the fires kept burning near the sand-hills.

"The labors of the rescuers in the surf were unceasing, but their greatest exertions were required when the vessel finally broke up, toward sunset, and the surf was thick with people and fragments. The rescuers, without exception, were battered and bruised by the wreckage while extricating the drowning people from the masses of floating rubbish." Commendation should also be given to Brock's unnamed horse, which did more than its share of work that day.

Captain Ankers remained aboard his ship until there was nothing left to stay on; then he struck out for land. He "was seen struggling in the surf, clad in a rubber-swimming or life-saving suit. He was hopelessly tossed about in the sea, utterly unable to help himself. Observing this, Keeper Chappell went further into the breakers, followed by Surfman Piggott Gillikin and Mr. Brock, and seizing the captain brought him, aided by his companions, safely ashore, much exhausted, and with his rubber dress, from some unexplained cause, nearly filled with water.''

By evening the beach was strewn for miles around with flotsam, broken timbers, and the bodies of the dead. The final death toll was first recorded as ninety-eight, later adjusted to ninety-one, and finally accepted as eighty-five.

The living were whisked off to private homes and cared for by the locals. ''The citizens fed and clothed them to the full extent of their means, and their generous hospitality is worthy of all praise.'' Meanwhile, temporary graves were dug for the deceased. The United States Revenue Marine Hospital Service sent doctors and nurses aboard the steamer *J.W. Haring* loaded with clothing, medicines, and provisions. The steamer *Cygnet* was dispatched to bring home the survivors. Captain Ankers made his way to Norfolk by buggy.

By the next day only ''the boilers and a part of the engines were visible from the beach on Currituck light, and a part of the vessel's bow, evidently held against the sand by some heavy weight, was swinging to and fro in the waves. The ragged ends of the stern and quarter frames are exposed by each succeeding roll of the sea.''

Norfolk's Deputy Postmaster arrived to see about salvaging the large shipment of business letters consigned to Brazil. ''The Purser's room, containing the mail, was washed ashore, and the mail-bags were found along the beach. . . . of the 11 bags containing mail matter on board 10 were washed ashore, but he only succeeded in recovering two—one intact, and the other was being used as a tobacco bag by one of the survivors. The contents were missing of the letters, and nothing could be found of the other bags or their contents. Parties on the beach say the bags were cut open and rifled of their contents. The letters, after being opened, were strewn along the beach.''

In Philadelphia, merchants and business men held an impromptu meeting in order to initiate a relief fund for the families of the husbands and fathers who had died on the wreck. Most of the railroad workers left behind wives and children who suffered not only the loss of their loved ones but the loss of support. Citizens were encouraged to contribute as much as they could afford.

As in the case of the *Huron* (q.v.) desecration of the dead ran rampant. William Harrison: ''Up to this morning I have taken up 50 bodies. The only things I have been able to recover on the bodies up to this time are a pocket-knife and a bunch of keys on one, a pass-book and brass-handled knife on another, and a pair of spectacles. The bodies, without any exception, have been robbed of all things whereby I could possibly identify them.''

A week later, as bodies continued to wash up on the beach, surviving railroad workers demonstrated their willingness to re-embark for Brazil on the next available steamer by crowding into corporate headquarters in Philadelphia. Most were still wearing donated clothes.

Recriminations came quickly. Captain Ankers was absolved from all blame, and even became the hero of the moment due to the praise of surviving passengers who lionized his cool handling of the situation.

Voices raised in protest about the vessel's unseaworthiness were challenged by a statement signed by Joseph Rooney and concurred with by Lloyd's Surveyor James Leary: "By direction of the inspectors of the underwriters I stripped the metal from the vessel, thoroughly recaulking her bottom and top sides, and doing everything as directed and thought necessary by the inspectors, the owners freely acquiescing in all they suggested, and ordering the ship put in complete and thorough condition. I have seen the timbers of the ship exposed both upon the inside and outside, and to my certain knowledge they were perfectly and thoroughly sound. While upon the dock the rudder was unshipped, the casing recaulked and releaded, stern-post removed and replaced in a thorough and substantial manner. I do not know of anything more that could be done to render the ship more seaworthy than she was."

Yet, Captain Merryman recovered pieces of wreckage and found that while planking from the newly-added midship section was strong, wood from the foreward and after sections was "as rotten as punk." Furthermore, at an inquiry ordered by Secretary Sherman, Captain Thomas Monroe, Surveyor of the Board of Underwriters, testified that "from the appearance of the lower hold amidships it was a very bad show to put 400 tons of iron there, because if she got to sea with that weight in her she would be likely to spring, and open the butts and scarfs of the keel. She was diagonally strapped between the knees in the lower hold fore and aft, and an evidence of weakness was apparent between decks. Fore and aft she was strengthened by five or six stringers, and also iron diagonally braced between the knees, and by an iron belt extending nearly the length of the vessel, which was another evidence of weakness."

George Lunt countered by stating that he had spent nearly $100,000 on maintenance and additional bracing not because the ship was inherently weak, but to ensure the hull's staunchness.

The real bombshell came from Eben Manson, master carpenter and contractor. His affidavit reads: "In May, 1871, I contracted with the Lunt Brothers, of New York, to cut open the steamer *Stars and Stripes*, and lengthen her out 56 feet. After the steamer had been cut open I noticed many rotten timbers in her bow and stern. I told George D. Lunt, who superintended the work, that the stern should be taken out, as it was decayed and not suitable to remain in her. Mr. Lunt objected, and directed me to put in new pieces to cover up the rotten wood, which was done. New pieces were also put in the decayed timber across the air streak, so that the Inspector could not detect the rotton wood underneath. Fifteen or twenty carpenters, who were at work for me on the vessel, will testify to the above facts if required so to do."

Subsequent investigation by the United States Inspectors of Hulls and Boilers also revealed that "the vessel was badly stowed and the leak was caused by the shifting of the railroad irons." Also, despite the 270 life preservers carried by the *Metropolis*, the Inspectors thought there was "little or no life-saving apparatus on board."

As damaging as the evidence appeared against George Lunt, Solicitor Raynor of the Treasury Department was not one to jump to conclusions. "The loss of the vessel was undoubtedly caused by the leak at the rudder-post, which was the result of imperfect repairs, and the general unsea-worthiness of the vessel; but it remains to be shown whether the owner of the vessel is guilty of a knowledge of this fact."

Wondering why Manson "should confess that he is guilty of manslaughter in doing that which he says caused the wreck of the *Metropolis* and the loss of 91 lives," Raynor investigated the accuser and discovered that he harbored ill-feelings toward the Lunt Brothers over monetary matters. Manson was discredited. Besides, Lunt made no attempt to sell the supposedly unseaworthy vessel, or to overinsure it. And lastly, the Board of Inspectors did not think that a wooden facade could adequately cover up a badly deteriorated hull; an experienced inspector would have noticed it.

Ultimately, principal owner George Lunt was exonerated of blame.

The Life-Saving Service came under sharp censure due to the tardiness of the help offered and the inefficiency with which it worked. In its defense were facts unknown to those survivors who voiced their complaints: the wreck came ashore thirty minutes after a patrol had passed the spot; no horses were available so that men had to haul the mortar and ammunition cart (weighing 1,000 pounds) through five miles of soft sand; sixty-mile-per-hour winds seriously hampered rescue operations; strong current, not incompetence, broke the messenger line; more powder and shot was stored at the station but had to be carried by man-power alone (by the time they returned the foremast had fallen).

To their inestimable credit, life-saving personnel were responsible for dragging many survivors from the water despite being pummeled by crashing debris, and suffered many injuries and much exposure for their efforts. They even resuscitated several people thought to be dead. In the final analysis, the life-savers performed heroically considering the conditions and the limited equipment at their disposal.

Yet, despite his intrepidity, John Chappell was reluctantly relieved of his position as Keeper. Merryman: "His conduct of operations at the wreck was in all respects satisfactory. ... When the last hope of renewing the broken connection with the wreck had to be abandoned, he put on the life-saving suit and made two desperate and hazardous efforts to force his way out with a line to the vessel through the tumbling fragments and the fierce current. In the struggle of the last three hours in the breakers, he was foremost and indefatigable, braving every danger, and saving many persons, including the captain, whom he was the first to seize in the surf. He was repeatedly struck down in the undertow by whirling timbers and bruised and battered by the wreckage, but he stood to his work to the very last moment, constantly at the hazard of his life. It was impossible that conduct such as this could fail of its due appreciation; yet it could not be overlooked that to the circumstance of his powder-flask not being full the cessation of effort to rescue the people upon the wreck by the life-saving appliances was due, and in view of this fresh evidence of dangerous defect in an otherwise stout and manly character, the recommendation of a more careful man for keeper could not but be made.''

As the *New York Maritime Register* so wryly noted, if any fault was to be found in saving lives, ''the blame here should be attached to the false economy which prevents the establishment of additional stations on the more exposed parts of the coast.'' Appropriations were such that the stations bracketing the site of the *Metropolis* were thirteen miles apart. In the General Superintendant's report for 1876, he stated, ''The distance between the stations averages 10 miles, which is too great to admit of their complete surveillance by the patrol. The number and serious character of the disasters which have occurred thereon clearly indicate the need of an additional number.'' This was amended in 1877 to read, ''The distance is so great as to materially impair the chances of reaching vessels in time to effect rescue, and recommends that authority be given for establishing additional stations at intermediate points between those existing.''

Together with the great loss of life on the *Huron* only two months before, the hue and cry over the inadequacy of the Life-Saving Service finally fell upon hearkened ears. Mr. Cox introduced a bill in Congress that was the only one to pass during 1878's second session. It increased funding for the Service in order to allow for more stations, a longer operating season, and higher wages for keepers and surfmen.

A valuable lesson had been learned—but at a high cost in human lives. Fortunately, it was a lesson that was not forgotten.

The *Metropolis* is known today as the Horsehead Wreck.

Mendocino is a sister ship of the *Mirlo*. (Courtesy of the Steamship Historical Society of America.)

MIRLO

Built: 1917

Previous names: None

Gross tonnage: 6,978

Type of vessel: Tanker

Builder: Sir J. Laing & Sons, Ltd., Sunderland, England

Owner: H.E. Moss Company, Liverpool, England

Port of registry: London, England

Cause of sinking: Mined by *U-117* (Kapitanleutnant Droscher)

Location: 26847.0

Sunk: August 16, 1918

Depth: 110 feet

Dimensions: 425′ × 57′ × 33′

Power: Oil-fired steam

40450.8

By August the U-boat war was in full swing, and ship masters were ever on the lookout for tell-tale periscopes and torpedo wakes. Coastal traffic hugged the shore, ready at a moment's notice to veer for shoal water should the enemy makes its presence known. Lookouts stood extra duty. And, since British vessels had long been armed, on board the *Mirlo* a gunner maintained a constant vigil from his station at the 4-inch gun aft.

The tanker left New Orleans on August 9 with 9,250 tons of gasoline and refined oil carried in bulk. She planned to refuel in Norfolk before making the Atlantic crossing for Thameshaven, England. The weather was clear, the sea moderate, visibility good, and spirits high. The *Mirlo* steamed due north at eight and a half knots until she passed Wimble Shoals.

There was no warning as a tremendous explosion ripped through the *Mirlo's* No. 2 tank. A huge column of water spouted into the air, tearing up deck plates like they were tissue paper. The concussion blew out the electrical system and plunged the ship into darkness.

Down in the stokehold, Fireman John Griffiths said he "could not see anything but steam and dust." Bulkheads were twisted and jambs warped.

Griffiths called out to his companions but got no answer. Trying to escape, he found the engine room door jammed. He crawled through the blackness, located a hammer, and was beating against a door when a second explosion buckled the plates in the fireroom and ignited a fire. Fortunately for Griffiths, the door sprung enough for him to squeeze through and make good his escape up the engine room ladder.

The second explosion hit at the bulkhead between No. 1 tank and the stokehold. (The tanks were numbered from aft to fore.)

Captain W.R. Williams noted that the explosions caused "the dynamos to be put out of commission, also breaking engine and destroying telegraph, and putting wireless gear out of commission." Captain Williams noted another steamship to the northwest (toward shore) and blew his steam whistle: his only way of calling for help. The steamer responded by taking off on a zigzag course, her captain undoubtedly thinking, as did Captain Williams, that the *Mirlo* had been torpedoed and that a quick retreat was in order.

The tanker's plight was observed by the lookout from Life-Saving Station No. 179, who saw "a great mass of water shoot up in the air which seemed to cover the after part of the steamer."

The *Mirlo* took on a starboard list that was quickly increasing. Flames licked out through cracked hull plates and decking aft. Captain Williams ordered abandon ship. While the boats were prepared for launching, Captain Williams threw overboard a weighted bag containing the ship's confidential documents.

Williams: "The starboard lifeboat was lowered first, which got away from the ship. The port lifeboat was then lowered and entered the water all right, when it was noticed that the tiller fouled the after falls, causing the boat to shear off from the ship and capsize. All the men that were in her were thrown into the water. At the same time the boat capsized she cleared herself from the ship. The starboard boat tried to go to the rescue. Then the orders were given to clear the after boats and lower same."

According to another statement signed by First Officer F.J. Campbell and eight others, "The men in the water grabbed the overturned boat and drifted clear of the ship. Two men climbed aboard over the falls. The Steward helped them aboard. The after boats could not be reached at first on account of the flames, but the Captain put the helm over and caused the flames to shift to the starboard side, making it possible to man the after boats."

Captain Williams stayed on the bridge until only one boat remained. "After ascertaining that all hands were off the ship we lowered away. During these operations the boats falls caught fire, and it was with great difficulty that we succeeded in pulling away from the vessel. In a few minutes after leaving the ship, the ship exploded with terrific force fore and aft, at the same time catching fire fore and aft. It was with great difficulty that we managed to clear the fire and smoke that was floating on the water, caused by the ship bursting and all the cargo coming out." The *Mirlo* came apart at the seams, and appeared to split in two.

The men pulled desperately at the oars as the oil spread in a gigantic rainbow slick, with a raging conflagration not far behind. Ten of those dumped from the overturned lifeboat could not get away in time and were either drowned or consumed by the blaze. "Flames separated the two remaining boats. After pulling two hours, the port after boat met the Life Saving Boat. The Captain, who was in the boat, told the officer in charge of the life saving boat that he better go out and see if he could pick up anyone from the other two boats."

By this time the *Mirlo* was gone. The ocean was afire: a field of debris fed by the cargo of gasoline and oil rising from the ship's ruptured tanks. Life-Saving Station Keeper John Midgett gave the following account:

"The lifeboat then headed to the burning mass of wreckage and oil. Upon arrival the sea was found to be covered with blazing gas and oil. There appeared to be great volumes of flames about 100 yards apart, and the ocean for hundreds of yards covered with flame. In between the two large bodies of flame, at times when the smoke lifted, a boat would be seen bottom up with six men clinging to it and a heavy swell washing over it. With extreme difficulty the coast guard boat ran through the smoke and floating wreckage and rescued the six men from the upturned boat. The rescued men stated that many times they had been compelled to dive under the water to save themselves from being burned to death. All had burns, but none was in a very serious condition. They also stated that they had seen some of their crew sink and disappear in the burning sea. The life-savers continued their search in the vicinity, but no more men could be found. As one boat was still missing, the lifeboat headed before the wind and sea and in a short time the third boat, with nineteen men, was sighted. It was found to be overloaded and so much crowded that the men in it could not row and were drifting helplessly with the wind and sea about nine miles southeast of the station. The lifeboat ran alongside and took the steamer's boat in tow."

Mirlo's crew's statement: "The life boat returned to the port after boat in about an hour and a half with the starboard forward boat in tow, and six men in the life boat picked up from the capsized boat, took the port after boat also in tow and landed the party on the beach."

Altogether, forty-one men were saved. This was certainly one of the Life-Saving Service's more heroic rescues.

Despite the fact that neither a U-boat nor a torpedo's wake had been spotted, the captain and crew of the *Mirlo* believed the ship had been torpedoed. An examination of the area conducted the followed day proved otherwise, when the U.S. destroyer *Taylor* (DD-94) radioed an urgent message to the Office of Naval Intelligence (ONI): "Sighted floating mine one mile east of wreck. Due to shallow water vicinity of wreck probably mined with submerged anchored mine. Recommend that ships be warned and vicinity wreck swept by mine sweepers."

The minesweeper *Teal* spent the next two weeks combing the area around Wimble Shoals. She swept up two enemy mines on August 18, two on the twenty-fifth, two on the thirtieth, and three on September 5. Counting the two that detonated under the *Mirlo*, this accounted for eleven of the ten mines the Germans claimed to have laid. Obviously, someone's figures were off.

The minelaying culprit was the *U-117*, also responsible for laying mine fields off Winter Quarter Shoals (Virginia), Fenwick Island Shoals (Maryland), and Barnegat Inlet (New Jersey). The *U-117* returned to the United States after the war, sailing under an American crew and commissioned in the U.S. Navy. It did its bit for the Victory Loan campaign, then was sunk off the Virginia Capes as a test target, in 1921. (See the Special Report in *Shipwrecks of Virginia* for complete details.)

Oddly enough, the wreck of the *Mirlo* is not known today. It seems impossible that a 425-foot-long ship could be hiding in shallow water close to shore without divers and fishermen knowing about it.

First Officer Campbell thought that at the time of the explosion (not the sinking) the *Mirlo* was "just inside of Wimble Shoal Buoy," while Captain Williams placed the attack position as "off Wimble Shoal Buoy, bearing north by west half a mile distance."

An examination of the various official reports reveals quite a difference of opinion on where the *Mirlo* came to rest. The USS *Taylor* located the wreck "22 one half miles 27 degrees true from Cape Hatteras." The Report of Submarine Attack issued by the Office of Aid For Information (Commandant, Fifth Naval District) placed it "in about 6 fathoms of water on northeast end of Wimble Shoal," with the "Wimble Shoal Buoy bearing S × W ½ mile distant." Next to "direction and distance from the station," Midgett wrote in his Coast Guard report, "Wimble Shoals Light Buoy, NE by E 12 miles."

A post-war analysis made by the U.S. Navy placed the wreck at 35-30 N/75-18 W. Modern charts show no wreck symbol in that position. In 1923, the Navy claimed to have located the *Mirlo* at 35-42 N/75-25-30 W. The charts show a wire-drag symbol there, but the spot is less than three miles off the beach.

During a 1944 wreck survey the USCG *Gentian* photographed a wreck at 35-32.6 N/75-14.7 W. This closely approximates the *Taylor's* original position. Although the reviewers of that survey were aware of the *Mirlo's* proximity (in the historical context), they determined the wreck to be the *Marore* (q.v.). "The wreck lies on its side, is of modern welded plate construction, and has king posts similar to those of the *Marore*, and does not appear to be heavily enough fouled to have been sunk as long ago as the *Mirlo* was." The latest charts still show a wreck symbol there, and it is still assumed to be that of the *Marore*. How, you may ask, did the *Taylor* locate in 1918 the remains of a ship that did not sink until 1942?

To add more confusion, although the 1986 navigational chart shows the same wreck symbol as the 1972 chart, the AWOIS listing that backs it up claims the position came from a hang number first given in 1979. What generated that same position prior to 1979?

So the question remains: exactly where is the *Mirlo*?

To this researcher, with the information presently available, it appears to be a wreck known locally as the *Ciltvaira* (q.v.). That the wreck at loran coordinates 26847.0/40450.8 is *not* the *Ciltvaira* is obvious. The wreck at that location has a deck gun on its stern, while a cursory glance at the photograph of the *Ciltvaira* under tow after being torpedoed clearly shows no such gun. The *Mirlo* carried a gun.

After conducting my first survey I estimated that the wreck was approximately four hundred feet long. The stern section is intact and lists to starboard about 45°, and rises some twenty feet off the bottom. The gun is prominent on top. The interior is readily accessible from where the hull is broken open some thirty feet forward of the fantail; the rough coral protrusions can tear a wetsuit with ease. Forward of that the engine and boilers are exposed because the hull plates have collapsed outward. Then comes a long, long expanse of breakdown with very little recognizable structure, and with a relief of less than eight feet.

The wreck is likely British can be inferred from the manufacturer's plaque recovered by Billy Palmer; it was made in Glasgow, Scotland, as was a gunsight removed from the deck gun. Confusing the matter, however, is the existance of a gigantic bronze bell some three feet across at the base, with the inscription in raised letters read by Danny Bressette as "U.S.L.H.S." (United States Light House Service?) What was a Light House Service bell doing on a British vessel?

Only further exploration will determine whether or not this is indeed the wreck of the *Mirlo*.

MORMACKITE

Built: 1945
Previous names: *Wild Rover*
Gross tonnage: 6,214
Type of vessel: Freighter
Builder: Moore Dry Dock Company, Oakland, California
Owner: Moore-McCormack Lines, Inc.
Port of registry: New York
Cause of sinking: Foundered
Location: 150 miles east-southeast of Cape Henry, Virginia

Sunk: October 7, 1954
Depth: Unknown
Dimensions: 438' × 63' × 27'
Power: Twin oil-fired steam turbines

The *Mormackite* was a C-2 bulk cargo carrier specifically designed for the ore trade in which she was engaged. In Victoria, Brazil huge conveyor belts dumped 9,000 tons of magnesium ore onto chutes which spread the rock into the ship's holds pyramid fashion; the load was not flattened by hand trimming, nor was such a method common practice. With the addition of 500 bags of cocoa beans, the *Mormackite* was ready to leave for Baltimore.

The voyage was uneventful until the ship arrived off the coast of North Carolina, where she encountered fierce, gale-force winds and high seas. The freighter, and those like her, had weathered many such storms, so there was no reason for the crew to worry about her condition.

Waves pounding constantly against the hull caused the ship to roll with a motion that was sickening even to the most hardened seamen. Then came a deep, grating sound as the topmost portion of the ore slid suddenly to port. The rushing rockslide upset the ship's balance, causing the *Mormackite* to heel over until the upper deck touched the surface of the sea. The ship hung at a thirty degree list for perhaps five minutes, then gradually settled back to about twenty degrees.

It did not take long for all hands to get on deck. Several donned life preservers simply as a precaution; others stood by lifeboats awaiting the order to launch. But the ship's officers had other plans. Since the ship had started to right on her own, it might be possible to restore her to an even keel. Chief Mate Harold Richardson and Chief Engineer Edward Wall stuck fire hoses into a starboard deck opening and poured in tons of water to counterbalance the uneven weight of the ore. The officers demonstrated confidence that the ship could be saved.

Despite all efforts, the *Mormackite* continued her slow roll. No official order was given to abandon ship, but thirty minutes after the first portside plunge, when the stack began to ship water, Captain Patrick McMahon shouted, "Okay, let's go."

Courtesy of the Steamship Historical Society of America.

The freighter capsized quickly, throwing forty-eight men into the water before the lifeboats could be released from their chocks. The ship sank like a rock. Nothing was left but flotsam and men struggling in the storm-tossed sea. Most of the crew were not wearing life preservers, and were promptly drowned. Those who managed to stay afloat grabbed onto pieces of wreckage for support. Radio Operator Marvin Knieger, thrown against messman Thomas Leamy, claimed he got out a wire, "but I didn't have time to give the location."

No SOS was received; no one ashore or on ships at sea were aware that the *Mormackite* was gone. It was early in the morning of a long day.

The last radio contact the Moore-McCormack Line had with the *Mormackite* was on the evening of October 6. At that time Captain McMahon informed the company that he planned to reach Cape Henry by 2 p.m. the next day, and arrive at Quarantine off Baltimore in time to dock the morning after. When the *Mormackite* did not appear at her berth on schedule, company officials contacted the tug company responsible for pushing the ship into her slip, then the Cape Henry pilot. No one had seen the ore carrier. By that time, the ship had been underwater for more than twenty-four hours.

Telephone lines buzzed all day, radio communications were checked, and ships traveling the *Mormackite's* proposed route were asked for sighting reports; all proved negative. Finally, at 4 p.m., the Coast Guard was asked to conduct a search. It was so late in the day, though, that effective scanning over such a broad reach of ocean was impossible. Not until dawn, over forty-eight hours after the disappearance of the *Mormackite*, was an intensive search mounted.

Twelve Coast Guard planes flew patterns offshore, while Coast Guard cutters, merchant ships, and three destroyer escorts combed the ocean for signs of the lost freighter. It was not long before one of the planes spotted a body in the water. A radio call put the Greek freighter *Macedonia* on the right bearing, and in short order Chief Steward Miguel Hernandez was pulled alive from the sea.

Another plane located the debris field and by following the direction of drift discovered other survivors clinging to make-shift rafts, pieces of driftwood, or simply floating free in life jackets. Rafts were dropped to the beleaguered seamen, but most were so weak they did not have the strength to climb aboard. Pilots watched helplessly as sharks tore into both the living and the dead for their grisly morsels of flesh. Float lights dropped to the survivors marked their position until rescue craft could arrive.

Those who lived related horrible stories of the struggle to stay afloat amid schools of roving sharks. "I kept kicking my feet to keep them away," said John Davis. "I saw a man just a few yards away when the sharks" attacked and killed him. Tadio Del Valle said there were "plenty of visitors, twelve, fourteen and sixteen feet long."

The men had had no food or water during all that time. Del Valle was on a raft with two other men. "On the last day we started to think how we could take our lives away the easiest. When you're drinking salt water and taking it into your lungs, it is terrible. Yesterday morning the three of us on the raft decided to do it. Then we saw a Navy carrier and then there were planes. Another hour and we would have been dead." (He must have mistaken one of the destroyer escorts for a carrier.)

By the time rescue operations were called off for the night only eleven of the *Mormackite's* crew had been picked up; all suffered from exposure to wind, sun, and salt water. Twelve bodies were recovered, leaving twenty-five men unaccounted for. None of the ship's officers survived the ordeal.

The unknown grave of the *Mormackite* serves as a reminder that the forces of nature are greater than any of man's paltry contrivances.

NEW JERSEY

Commissioned: May 12, 1906
Previous names: None
Displacement tonnage: 14,948
Type of vessel: Battleship
Builder: Fore River Shipbuilding Company, Quincy, Massachussetts
Owner: U. S. Navy
Armament: Four 12-inch guns, eight 8-inch guns, twelve 6-inch guns,
          four 21-inch torpedo tubes
Cause of sinking: Aerial bomb test
Location: 26864.9

Sunk: September 5, 1923
Depth: 330 feet
Dimensions: 441' × 76' × 23'
Power: Coal-fired steam
Official designation: BB-16

40217.4

VIRGINIA

Commissioned: May 7, 1906
Previous names: None
Displacement tonnage: 14,980
Type of vessel: Battleship
Builder: Newport News Shipbuilding and Dry Dock Company, Virginia
Owner: U.S. Navy
Armament: Four 12-inch guns, eight 8-inch guns, twelve 6-inch guns,
          twelve 3-inch guns, twenty-four 1-pounders, four .30-caliber
          Colt machine guns, four 21-inch torpedo tubes
Cause of sinking: Aerial bomb test
Location: 26863.4

Sunk: September 5, 1923
Depth: 350 feet
Dimensions: 441' × 76' × 23'
Power: Coal-fired steam
Official designation: BB-13

40212.0

The careers of the *New Jersey* and the *Virginia* were inextricably intertwined. They were sister ships despite being built at different shipyards, and entered service at the same time. Following summer shake down cruises, both ships rendezvoused in Oyster Bay, Long Island for a Presidential review; they anchored off Teddy Roosevelt's home.

Immediately afterward they were sent to Cuba where "a revolution had broken out against the government of President T. Estrada Palma. The disaffection ... grew in the early autumn to the point where President Palma had no recourse but to appeal to the United States for intervention. By mid-September, it had become apparent that the small Cuban constabulary (3,000 rural guards) was unable to protect foreign interests." The sister battleships did not engage in hostilities.

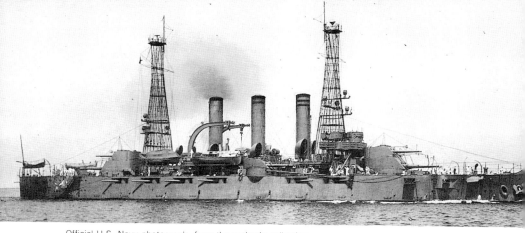

The highlight of the following year of service was participation in the Jamestown Tricentennial Exposition at Hampton Roads, Virginia. After that, the *New Jersey* and the *Virginia* joined fourteen other battleships and six destroyers on a cruise around the world that lasted for fourteen months: from December 6, 1907 to February 22, 1909. Roosevelt's motto was: "Speak softly, but carry a big stick." While Roosevelt spoke softly to the nations of the world, the twenty-two warships (his "big stick") called on foreign ports to announce America's military ascendancy and potential naval supremacy.

This circumnavigation of the globe was the greatest demonstration of peacetime sea power in U.S. Naval history—remembered today as the cruise of the Great White Fleet. (So named because the ships' hulls and superstructures were painted white, for high visibility.) The fleet headed south through the Caribbean, rounded Cape Horn, then crusied north to San Francisco; all along the way it stopped at coastal communities to make its presence known. The fleet then crossed the Pacific, put in at Hawaii, and made way for Australia. "Each city seemed to offer a more enthusiastic reception for the American sailors and their powerful ships than had the last."

The crux of the cruise was the visit to Japan. Strong tensions existed between Uncle Sam and the land of the Rising Sun. In 1905, the Japanese fleet trounced the Russian navy in a decisive battle in the Straits of Tsushima. Japan followed this dramatic victory by defeating the Russian army. President Roosevelt helped negotiate a peace treaty between the two warring nations. The result was the precipitation of the Russian revolution, and the emergence of Japan as a world power not to be taken lightly.

Underground rumor bespoke a hostile reception for the U.S. Navy. But when the Great White Fleet entered Yokohama, in Tokyo Bay, it was met with great "expression of friendship, both through elaborately planned entertainment and spontaneous demonstration." Tensions evaporated. "Not only was a threatened conflict with Japan averted, but notice was served on the world that the United States had come of age, and was an international power which could make its influence felt in any part of the world."

The Great White Fleet then cast anchor at the Philippines, China, and Ceylon, passed through the Suez Canal, and made stopovers at many Mediterranean ports before crossing the Atlantic and returning to Hampton Roads. The cruise was a triumph of diplomacy for the United States government, and an extravagant exhibition of military might for the U.S. Navy.

Although the sisters sometimes went their separate ways during the next five years, both were involved in the the Mexican insult in 1914. Subsequently, each spent time in reserve because their services were not needed. The outbreak of war in Europe was the impetus for much-needed overhaul. Neither ship saw action; they were principally engaged in coastal protection and convoy duty. It was during this time that the sisters worked perhaps too closely together; so close, in fact, that they collided with each other.

After the signing of the Armistice, the *New Jersey* and the *Virginia* were fitted "with additional messing and berthing facilities" in order to bring back "doughboys" from the front. Together they returned more than 11,000 fighting men, the *New Jersey* making five trips and the *Virginia* six.

The *New Jersey* was decommissioned on August 6, 1920; the *Virginia* one week later. Both needed extensive repair and modernization that was not economically feasible considering the advances in technology and naval strategy brought about by the war. As battleships, some considered them obsolete. There was talk of using them as coaling hulks, but the idea was

Official U.S. Navy photograph, from the author's collection.

rejected by the terms of the Naval Limitation Treaty then being ratified by the world's major powers.

Although their assessed replacement value was $5 million each, their appraised value for sale as hulks for scrapping was only $83,000 each. This was *after* the "removal of ordnance, navigational material, boats, anchors, chains, machine tools, miscellaneous motors or auxiliaries, pumps, winches, vent sets, ammunition hoist motors, crane motors, laundry outfit, etc., also after removal of fittings that can be used to improve merchant type vessels such as metal furniture, joiner metal doors, wire mesh, partitions, metal bins, shelves, etc., pantry and galley fittings, watertight doors, hatches, manholes, air ports, deck scuttles, ventilation terminals, awning stanchions, hatch ladders, accomodation ladders, boat davits, boat cradles, coaling booms, etc."

The *New Jersey's* steering stand was removed for emplacement on the USS *Utah* (BB-31), then under construction. The *Virginia's* silver service was given to the USS *Richmond* (CL-9) with the proviso that it be placed upon another *Virginia* should one be built. All except the 12-inch guns were removed (although the turrets for the 8-inch guns were left onboard). Thus the battleships were stripped of all adornment, armament, and usable items. A memorandum from the Bureau of Construction and Repair noted that "the subject named vessels have been largely depleted as regards portable articles. However there yet remain miscellaneous articles of furniture, such as chiffoniers, silver cabinets, library cabinets, plumbing fixtures, auxiliary machinery, etc, the condition being fair to poor."

The Bureau also noted that "the watertight integrity of the ships has been very materially disturbed by the removal of watertight doors, watertight hatches, manholes, etc, and in many cases the drop bolts have been removed and the covers remain. There are a great number of holes of all sizes left in the decks and bulkheads due to the removal of deck fittings, piping, stuffing boxes, etc. The removal of these articles makes it impracticable to secure reasonable watertight integrity for the inner hull, bulkheads, decks, etc, without the expenditure of an unwarranted amount of money."

Nevertheless, there was strong opposition to scrapping the ships totally. Acting Secretary of War M.S. Davis wrote, "The Department must find the subject battleships unfit for further Naval service as necessary primary consideration before steps can be taken looking to the disposal of these craft. . . . With the uncertainty as to the final ratification of the Naval treaties by all the contracting powers it would appear inadvisable at this time to dispose of ships which are not obsolete and which would not even be considered for disposal except for the existence of these treaties. Consequently, the matter appears to be one of decision of public policy alone." The claim was put forth that both ships could still serve well in home waters if not at sea.

At the center of this fracas was U.S. Army General Billy Mitchell, retrospectively described as "founder of our air force and prophet without honor." At a time when sea power and a strong navy were every country's ideal of omnipotent sovereignty, Mitchell was building a fledgling air corps and training pilots to accurately bombard, not stationary land targets, but capital ships at sea. He claimed that his biplane "gnats" could easily drop bombs on an invading fleet and escape harm through superior speed: a coastal defense that was more effective and less expensive than sustaining a perimeter of picket boats. He also claimed that a modern air force could make obsolete not just a few outdated warships, but the entire concept of naval engagement. Naturally, Naval personnel steeped in centuries of tradition objected strongly to arguments contrary to established protocol.

The controversy that sprang from these diametrically opposed strategic opinions placed Mitchell in the line of fire by proponents of a larger and more powerful Navy. He was constantly broadsided by obstinent and near-sighted career officers whose sense of security was more closely entwined with the future of their jobs than with the defense of their country. Billy Mitchell wanted to use the *New Jersey* and the *Virginia* as full-scale target ships to demonstrate again the efficacy of aerial bombardment against thickly armored battleships. I say "again" because he had already proven his point in 1921, when he sank with bombs four ex-German warships in the Southern Drill Grounds east of Cape Henry. To fully appreciate Mitchell's role in that devastatingly portentous campaign, the reader is referred to the Special Report in *Shipwrecks of Virginia*, by this author.

Davis expostulated disparagingly, "The bombing tests will destroy two battleships with no differentiation between the stripped *Virginia* and *New Jersey* and a latter type with all the characteristics of the modern battleship class, like the *Maryland*. It has already been proved that undefended battleships may be destroyed by bombs dropped from aircraft. There is much loose talk about the waving value of the ships of the line and much of this opinion has weight in quarters that should be better informed of what constitutes sea power. The destruction of the *New Jersey* and the *Virginia* by bombs will add nothing to knowledge and by misconstrued results to the Navy and the best interests for the defense of the country harm."

Rear Admiral W.A. Moffett, Chief of the Bureau of Aeronautics, agreed, but with a different rationale, complaining that consequent news-paper converage would "boost Army Aviation at the expense of the Navy." Competition between the departments of defense is an old story.

Billy Mitchell won his battle: against entrenched bureaucracy as well as in the air and on the sea. The *New Jersey* and the *Virginia* were released for the test on the condition that they were sunk beyond the fifty fathom curve, in order to meet the terms of the Naval Limitation Treaty. Mitchell chose Cape Hatteras as the test site because, as he wrote, "First, the fifty fathom curve is nearest to the Atlantic Seaboard in the vicinity of Cape Cod and Cape Hatteras; and, second, by conducting the tests off Cape Hatteras we could instruct our personnel in the establishment of emergency airdromes and in operating from a base where they would be entirely dependent upon supplies forwarded from the back area."

By the end of August 1923 the die was cast. The two battleships were towed from Boston by the USS *Contocook* (AT-36) and the USS *Rail* (AM-26) with explicit orders that the targets be anchored "about 22 miles east by south from Cape Hatteras off the Diamond Shoals Lightship. It is requested that instructions relative to the exact location of these two (2) battleships at their final anchorage be such as to place the USS *Virginia*, about 3 miles south of the Diamond Shoals Lightship, and the USS *New Jersey*, about 2 miles south of the Diamond Shoals Lightship. Both battleships should, of course, be in 50 fathoms of water and if the above exact location does not permit of their being anchored in this depth, then it is requested that they be anchored a mile apart in as near these positions as possible consistent with placing them in 50 fathoms of water."

Assigned as an observation vessel for more than a hundred Army and Navy officers, government officials, the press, and foreign military attaches, was the *St. Mihiel*, a U.S. Army troop transport. Among those aboard were General Pershing and Admiral Shoemaker. "A destroyer flotilla consisting

The Cape Hatteras Airdrome, photographed on July 16, 1923. (From the author's collection.)

LANDING DOCKS

of five destroyers is stationed at regular intervals on a line drawn directly from the temporary airdrome at Hatteras to the battleships, for patrolling, observation, and rescue purposes. The board of Air Service Observers with Officers from the Ordnance Department, Coast Artillery Corps, and Chemical Warfare Service are on the mine planter *John Henry* and *Schofield* stationed in vicinity of battleships.''

Arrangements were also made for the big splash to be captured on film: "Four civilian motion picture photographers, representing Pathe, International, Fox and Kinograms News Reels, and one from McCook Field, are to photograph the bombing from the air. Under instructions from the Information Division, O.C.A.S. the civilian photographers have agreed to furnish the Chief of Air Service with complete copies of everything made by them. Oblique photographs are to be made by two photographic planes with a third plane standing by. The planes are to operate in relays so that a photographic plane is near the target at all times. Arrangements have been made for a photographer with oblique camera to board the blimp *TC-2*. Also a still photographer will be aboard the mine planter *Joseph Henry*, and another still photographer will be on the ground at the Hatteras Airdrome at all times.'' In addition, "the 2nd and 20th Photographic Sections will secure photographs of all phases of the attack.'' This was one event that was going to be well covered, for whatever it was worth.

The rules of engagement were based on the assumption that "our pursuit aviation has gained temporary superiority of the air and that our attack aviation has successfully completed their attacks at low level altitude against the personnel of these battleships.''

The test took place on September 5, 1923. The first flight consisted of six Martin bombers, each carrying four 600-pound bombs. The planes left Langley Field, Virginia in dense rain and fog that persisted most of the way to the target area, 135 miles away. They arrived at 8:40 a.m., and dropped their bombs on the northernmost battleship (the *New Jersey*) from an altitude of 11,200 feet; one plane made three runs. The planes then landed at the temporary airdrome at Hatteras for refueling and rearming.

Lieutenant Commander H.B. Grow, a Naval observer, reported that "The three 600-lb. bombs which hit the *New Jersey* caused very little real damage. It was possible from our position, with high-power glasses, to observe in detail the effect of these hits, and it appeared that nothing happened excepting a slight rupture of the side plating and superstructure, riddling of ventilators with fragments, and other superficial damage to the upper works. Naturally, any exposed personnel in the vicinity would have been killed, but the fighting efficiency of the ship as a whole would have remained undamaged.''

The second flight closed in on the *New Jersey*: seven planes carrying one 2,000-pound bomb each, and one plane, "which had not arrived in time for the first attack,'' carrying four 600-pound bombs. Unfortunately, none of these bombs hit the target. Mitchell lamented, "The two thousand pound bombs were dropped sufficiently close to the ship to have sunk it had they functioned as well as in 1921. Two things were obvious on this attack: First, the bombs were sticking in the traps, and, second, either the fuses had deteriorated, or the bombs were not exploded at a proper depth."

The third flight went after the *Virginia*, this time with 1,100-pound bombs of which each plane carried two. Mitchell: "The attack began at 11:53 and was ended at 12:07. Fourteen eleven hundred pound bombs had been dropped which literally tore the ship to pieces." Even Naval observer Grow was impressed. "One 1100-lb. bomb detonating beneath the deck completely demolished the ship as such. Both masts, the bridge, all three smokestacks, and the upper works disappeared with the explosion and there remained, after the smoke cleared away, nothing but the bare hull, decks blown off, and covered with a mass of tangled debris from stem to stern consisting of stacks, ventilators, cage masts, and bridges. In my opinion, the ship would have been completely wiped out by such a hit, especially had there been powder in any of the magazines." Mitchell: "In about thirty minutes from the time the first bomb was dropped the battleship was under water." The *Virginia* rolled over onto her port side and disappeared from view.

With the second target demonstrably gone, Mitchell instructed the refueled planes at the Hatteras airdrome to press home another attack against the *New Jersey*, again with 2,000-pound bombs. Mitchell: "All of the bomb traps stuck a little. Every bomb overshot the target." A fifth flight was called to arms. "The two ships loaded with eleven hundred pound bombs launched their attack. The first bomb, dropped at 3:22 fell about ninety feet from the ship. The next shot, dropped by the same crew, struck close along side, but was a dud and did not detonate. Lieutenant Myers with Sergeant Nero . . . made three runs over the target to get the wind direction and velocity exactly right. On their fourth run over they dropped one bomb which struck the ship squarely. It tore open the hull and blew one cage mast from its foundation. The ship immediately began to sink and before the plane was able to make the turn and come back to drop the second bomb it had turned over."

As Grow described it, "The direct hit scored on the *New Jersey* by one 1100-lb. bomb, while not so spectacular in its result, was nevertheless quite as effective. The detonation took place below decks, and there immediately appeared along the port side a great geyser of bubbling water, indicating that the force of the concussion had blown out through the bottom, and the damage to the interior of the ship must have been terrific. In this case, also, a ship receiving such a hit and having its magazines full of powder would have been completely demolished." The *New Jersey* capsized and sank.

For a Naval officer, Grow made a sweeping commendation when he wrote, "There is no way of predicting what a direct hit with a 2,000-lb. bomb would have done, but it is apparent from the effect of the 1100-lb. bomb that a 2,000-lb. bomb would put any existing ship out of the battle."

Virginia.

New Jersey.

He concluded that "the battleship to-day is in grave danger."

Mitchell went one further: "Air Forces, with the types of aircraft now in existence or in development, acting from shore bases, can find and destroy all classes of seacraft under war conditions, with a negligible loss to the aircraft. ... The problem of the destruction of seacraft by Air Forces has been solved, and is finished."

During the summer of 1992, subsequent to diving the *Ostfriesland* and the *Frankfurt* (the German battleship and cruiser sunk by Billy Mitchell's bombers in 1921, off the Virginia Capes) Ken Clayton and I formulated plans to visit the sites of the *New Jersey* and the *Virginia*. As with many ocean diving operations, subject to the vagaries of the weather, we met with severe difficulties that curtailed our originally scheduled dive plans. By the end of the year we managed to make only one dive on the *New Jersey*, and even that might be considered by some a near miss.

The date was September 20, the place was Hatteras, the surface support vessel was the *Margie II*, captained by Art Kirchner. Also making the dive was Barb Lander, a new addition to our team. We dived as a threesome.

Due to the extreme depth we elected not to make the dive on ordinary compressed air. At 330 feet the body is adversely affected by the intense ambient pressure: oxygen becomes toxic to the body, and nitrogen induces a narcotic effect on the mind. Instead, we breathed a mixture of oxygen and helium called heliox. The mix we chose contained 12% oxygen (which is not enough to cause toxicity during the anticipated length of the dive, but enough to maintain the metabolic processes) and 88% helium (which is non-narcotic at this depth). This kind of "mixed gas" is perfectly safe to breath, but necessitates a complicated set of procedures for decompression (the amount of time required for the body to eliminate inert gas absorbed by the tissues; if this inert gas is released too fast, it bubbles in the bloodstream and causes decompression sickness, or the "bends.")

In this type of diving the anchor line literally becomes a life line. After grapneling the wreck and dropping a weighted line off the stern of the boat, a support diver established a transfer line at a depth of 70 feet, connecting the two lines. Ken, Barb, and the author jumped off the boat each wearing double tanks on our backs and two single tanks at our sides. Three tanks contained heliox-12, one single tank was filled with a gas called nitrox (36% oxygen, the balance nitrogen) for decompression purposes. One of the problems with heliox is the extremely long time required for decompression. Due to the elevated percentage of oxygen in nitrox, the decompression phase of the dive could be accelerated by breathing nitrox and oxygen.

We pulled down the anchor line against a mild current, dropping into darker and colder water as we passed through successive thermoclines. When we reached the bottom we found that the grapnel had slipped off the *New Jersey's* hull, dragged across the white sand, and snagged into a disarticulated hull plate. By looking "up current" we could make out the vague outline of what seemed to be the inverted battleship. The visibility was 75 to 100 feet, and the wreck appeared to be just at the limit of visibility. It was a huge, dark shape that rose fifty feet off the bottom, and that curved down sharply at one end with the sweep of a ship's stern.

The three of us rested on the sand and exchanged hand signals about what course of action to take: to leave the grapnel and swim closer to the wreck, or to go back up without further exploration. Our decision was one based upon safety. The grapnel was hooked by a single tine in a hull plate only a few feet across, and therefore of uncertain purchase. We elected to call the dive, and to come back another day under better circumstances.

It was a fortunate decision. We reached our first decompression stop, at 150 feet, then gradually ascended in ten-foot increments. We were only a few minutes into the decompression when the anchor line parted and the boat went adrift. If we had gone on to explore the wreck we would have been below the break, and the boat would not have been there to supply us with the rest of our decompression gases. (Support divers had yet to bring us another tank of nitrox; plus, the last hour of decompression was done on oxygen fed down to us through long hoses from storage bottles on the boat.) So, we hung onto the weighted line for a total decompression time of nearly two and a half hours. All's well that ends well.

Our determination that the wreck we dived was the *New Jersey* and not the *Virginia* was based upon the relative positions of the two battleships at the time of their sinking, i.e., the *New Jersey* was closer to the *Diamond Shoals* lightship than the *Virginia*, and in shallower water.

A new era of deep water explorers has arrived: divers armed with extraordinary training and state-of-the-art equipment that permit them to reach wrecks previously considered unreachable. We will return to the *New Jersey* and explore its massive remains. And then, the *Virginia* is only a mile away.

The *Norlavore* as the *Quantico*. (Courtesy of the Steamship Historical Society of America.)

NORLAVORE

Built: 1919

Previous names: *Quantico, Lake Fitch*

Gross tonnage: 2,713

Type of vessel: Freighter

Builder: Globe Ship Building Company, Superior, Wisconsin

Owner: Norlasco Steam Ship Company.

Port of registry: Baltimore, Maryland

Cause of sinking: Torpedoed by *U-432* (Kapitanleutnant Schultze)

Location: 35-05 North

Sunk: February 24, 1942

Depth: Unknown

Dimensions: 253' × 43' × 26'

Power: Oil-fired steam

75-20 West

Whatever horrors were suffered by the innocent men on the *Norlavore* will forever go untold. On February 22, 1942 she left her home port for Puerto la Cruz, Venezuela and never arrived.

After the war ended, German historians alleged that the *U-432* must have torpedoed the *Norlavore* late at night on February 24. The basis for such a claim is tenuous, as German records admit that " there is no attack report, but *U-432* was in the area."

Therefore, the *Norlavore* may not even have been sunk off the North Carolina coast. If she was, there is a possibility that if she landed upright on the bottom her hull could be the one reported by the USCG cutter *Gentian* as being that of the USS *Virginia* or USS *New Jersey* (q.v.) at 35-01.7 N/75-17.7 W. Or she could be the wreck known locally as the 43 Fathom Wreck, at 26864.9 and 40217.5. Only an examination of the sites can tell.

For more on the *U-432* see *Buarque* and *Marore*.

NORTHEASTERN

Built: 1901
Previous names: None
Gross tonnage: 2,157
Type of vessel: Tanker
Builder: Chicago Ship Building Company, Chicago, Illinois
Owner: Northwestern Steam Ship Company
Port of registry: Fairport, Ohio
Cause of sinking: Ran aground
Location: 26908.9

Sunk: December 27, 1904
Depth: 35 feet
Dimensions: 242′ × 42′ × 23′
Power: Coal-fired steam

40234.7

The *Northeastern* was on her way from Port Arthur, Texas to Philadelphia, Pennsylvania with a cargo of crude oil when she encountered a southerly gale that blew her off course. The first Captain W.J. Lynch knew his vessel was in trouble when she ground to a halt on the outer point of the Diamond Shoals. The time was 11 p.m. on December 27, 1904.

The ship's condition was perilous. In addition to darkness a thick fog clung to the sea, so that visibility was nil. Gale force winds whipped up tremendous waves that battered the tanker's hull with unrelenting destructive force. Distress flares were fired continuously until 4 a.m., when a signal rocket launched from shore communicated to those on board that life-savers were aware of the ship's plight.

Courtesy of C. Patrick Labadie.

There were twenty-two men on the tanker, but "owing to the dangerous surf it was impossible to launch a boat to go to the rescue." The fog lifted enough the next morning to enable the life-savers to sight the ship. "Keeper Etheridge, of Cape Hatteras station, then called away the surfboat, and the crew endeavored to launch, but at each attempt the boat was hurled back upon the beach by the resistless breakers."

The crew of the *Northeastern* were not sitting idle. They tried to save themselves in the ship's lifeboats, but each one was stove in upon launching. With their boats reduced to splinters there was nothing they could do but wait. December 28 must have seemed like a long day.

Not until 4:30 on the morning of the twenty-ninth did the wind moderate and shift to the northwest. Surfboats from both the Cape Hatteras and Creeds Hill stations were taken to Hatteras Cove, "where the crews launched them and put out to the wreck. ... The life-savers reached the scene of the wreck at 9 a.m." after four and a half hours of pulling at the oars.

"They found the vessel lying in the midst of dangerous breakers and submerged, with the exception of a portion of the stern, upon which the crew had gathered. It was decided that one surfboat should approach the wreck at a time, the other standing by in case of accident, and the Cape Hatteras boat first entered the breakers, and by means of lines rescued 10 men; after which the Creeds Hill boat pulled in and saved the remainder, 12 men. The trip to shore was successfully accomplished, and the rescued men were succored at the stations three days, being provided with clothing from the Women's National Relief Association stores."

A letter of praise was sent to the United States Life-Saving Service from the men of the *Northeastern*. It stated in part that "the ship was broken in two and in a sinking condition. We were landed safely by Captain E.H. Peel and Captain P.H. Etheridge, and we, the crew of the steamship *Northeastern*, think they ran a great risk in doing so. The kindness they showed us at the life-saving station after landing we shall never forget, as all our clothing was lost. We, the undersigned, can not speak too highly of the danger they put themselves to in saving us, for in twelve hours more we should all have been lost."

The quarter million dollar ship was pounded to pieces, and her cargo of oil was released to the sea. The beaches must have suffered from thick clots of crude coming ashore, but in those days of pre-environmental concern no mention was made of ecological disaster.

The story of the *Northeastern* has slipped into obscurity, and few today have explored her remains. The wreck's identity first came to light when Uwe Lovas and Steve Lang recovered the capstan cover, which had the ship's name cut in brass. Steve Lang later recovered the brass letters from the stern.

The wreck lies in 35 feet of water with washouts going as deep as 40 feet. The hull is upright and contiguous. The most intact portion is about

156

twenty feet of the bow; a winch sits close to the stem. Abaft the bow the hull plates have fallen outward, giving the wreck a broad width. About amidship only some of the hull plates have fallen outward, the others having fallen inward; off the port side lies the wreckage of the wheelhouse.

Between the wheelhouse area and the boilers is a pile of miscellaneous machinery. Two big, single-ended boilers are still connected by pipe work. The engine is largely buried by sand that has piled up in the stern of the wreck. The propeller shaft is not exposed, nor is the propeller. The rudder is broken off. Just inside the port stern hull is a porcelain bathtub into which two bitts have fallen. The starboard bitts are in place.

Because the wreck lies on the shoals the currents can be severe.

Below: brass letters from the stern of the *Northeastern*, recovered and photographed by Steve Lang. Left: the capstan cover, recovered by Uwe Lovas and Steve Lang.

The *Norvana* as the *York*. (Courtesy of the Institute for Great Lakes Research.)

NORVANA

Built: 1920
Previous names: *York, Lake Gatun*
Gross tonnage: 2,677
Type of vessel: Freighter
Builder: Saginaw Ship Building Company, Saginaw, Michigan
Owner: North Atlantic Gulf and West Indies Steamship Company
Port of registry: New York, NY
Cause of sinking: Torpedoed by *U-66* (Korvettenkapitan Zapp)
Location: 26913.6

Sunk: January 20, 1942
Depth: 110 feet
Dimensions: 253' × 43' × 26'
Power: Oil-fired steam

40817.0

The *Norvana* was known as the *York* when she was owned by the Merchants and Miners Transportation Company, and under that name was involved in a serious collision with *Commercial Pioneer* of the Mooremack Gulf Lines. The date was April 27, 1938. The two freighters met in a heavy fog during the dark morning hours, half a mile from the *Overfalls* lightship marking the entrance of the Delaware Bay. Except for a smashed anchor the *Commercial Pioneer* was undamaged, and proceeded on her way. But the *York* suffered a gaping wound at the water line, and had to be beached on a shoal a quarter mile from shore in order to prevent her sinking. The *York* was repaired and refloated, to steam again another day.

In October 1941 the *York* was turned over to the government. She was renamed *Norvana*, and ran under the management of the North Atlantic Gulf and West Indies Steamship Company. On January 14, 1942, the *Norvana*, Captain Ernest Thompson, and a crew of twenty-nine, left Havana, Cuba for Philadelphia.

The agony of the *Norvana's* last moments must forever go untold. She never arrived at her destination, and was reported overdue and presumed lost. What travails were suffered by the thirty men aboard her will never be known; there were no survivors.

On February 4, 1942 a Loss Committee Bulletin of the American Cargo War Risk Reinsurance Exchange noted, "We are endeavoring to ascertain whether the vessel has actually been lost and, if so, whether as a result of war or marine perils. Meanwhile, Subscribers should advise promptly lines on cargo insured against war risk."

By March 7 the owners were able to report that "a battered and empty lifeboat is the only trace of her that has been found."

Meanwhile, the Navy was investigating a derelict first spotted by a Coast Guard plane on January 20, and subsequently reported on January 21, January 28, and February 2. On February 15 "the CGC *Orchid* established qk. fl. green buoy "B" to mark the wreck as a menace to navigation. The only vessel known to have been sunk in the area at that time was the Brazilian *Buarque* which was torpedoed about 20 miles northeastward on the date the buoy was established. This coincidence of dates led to a quick and erroneous identification of the wreck as that of the *Buarque*. After discovery of this error, no guess could be made as to the wreck's identity since the only reported sinkings prior to the date of its location were more than 100 miles distant."

There matters rested for more than two years. As a confidential report later stated, "In the spring of 1944 divers of the Navy Salvage Service who were employed to remove the wreck as a menace to navigation solved the riddle. The ship's bell was brought up and found to be marked *Lake Gatun*. This was ascertained to be the former name of the American collier *York* which left Charleston, S.C. in January 1942 enroute Norfolk, Va., and had not been heard from since. What happened to her crew can only be surmised. The divers reported the wreck riddled with shell holes."

Actually, *York* was the former name of the *Norvana*, but the Office of Naval Intelligence (ONI) missed that point probably because the ship was sunk so soon after retitling that she was not listed in the next annual Lloyd's Register under her latest name. There is no explanation for why ONI gave ports of call that differed from those reported by the insurance syndicate whose job it was to know such information.

November 5, 1947: "The Loss Committee has now ruled that this vessel was lost as a result of enemy action. It has not been possible to ascertain the date of accident."

Indeed, there is still confusion as to the exact date of sinking. German records credit Zapp and the *U-66* with the kill; at the time of the *Norvana's* loss he he had already sunk the *Allan Jackson* and the *Lady Hawkins*; afterward he sank the *Empire Gem* and the *Venore*: five ships in less than a week, totaling 33,456 tons. The *Norvana* was the smallest in the bag. But German records also claim the *Norvana* was torpedoed on January 22, two days *after* the derelict later proven to be the *Norvana* was discovered.

Who to believe?

German records also claim the *Norvana* was on route from Curacao to Baltimore, again despite insurance records to the contrary. Into this morass' of claim and counterclaim only hypothesis dares tread. I opt for January 20 as the date of the *Norvana's* sinking not because of the chaos encountered in the heat of battle, during dark nights when torpedoes were flying port and starboard at dimly lit targets, but because a sunken ship cannot be spotted prior to its sinking.

Nomenclature dies hard. Still today the *Norvana* is called the *York* by local divers and fishermen. This name was reinforced in the public mind in 1991, when Mike Hillier recovered from the wreck's midship section two sets of brass letters each spelling YORK.

The wreck is large and impressive. The bow is broken off and is totally intact, with the anchors tight in their hawse pipes. It is the highest portion of the wreck, rising some forty feet above the sand. Three distinct deck levels are readily accessible from the break.

Abaft the bow is an area of sand, then the low rise of the midship section standing only fifteen feet high. There is no sign of the wheelhouse, just the supports on which it once stood. Machinery clogs the hull underneath.

The stern section is broken off and twisted to port. The boilers and engine lie under wreckage that stands twenty-five feet above the sand. The propeller is partly visible.

See *Venore* and *Empire Gem* for Zapp's depredations off the Diamond Shoals. The *U-66* returned to the Eastern Sea Frontier in the summer of 1943, under the command of Kapitanleutnant Markworth, and sank the *Esso Gettysburg* and *Bloody Marsh*. On May 6, 1944, under the command of Kapitanleutnant Seehausen, the *U-66* was sunk off the Cape Verde Islands.

Barracuda.

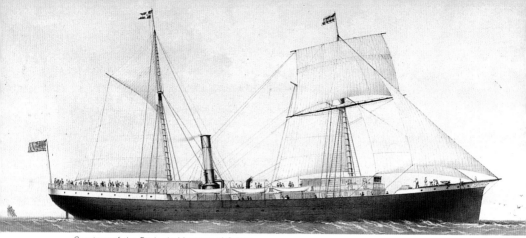

ORIENTAL

Built: 1861
Previous names: None
Gross tonnage: 1,202
Type of vessel: Iron-hulled transport
Builder: Reaney, Neafie, and Company, Philadelphia, Pennsylvania
Owner: Mora Brothers, Navarro & Company, New York
Port of registry: New York
Cause of sinking: Stranded
Location: 26949.3

Sunk: May 16, 1862
Depth: 20 feet
Dimensions: 210' × 32' × 20'
Power: Coal-fired steam

40559.1

The short career of the steamer *Oriental* lasted only nine months. Her hull was launched on June 29, 1861; her tubular box boiler contained 192 tubes, and was fired up on August 29; her trial run was conducted on September 7. Her single cylinder engine turned a four-bladed Loper patent propeller 14.5 feet across. She and her sister ship, the *Nuevitas*, were build for the Cuba trade. Auxiliary sails helped her 800 horsepower engine to drive the ship.

Due to the War of the Rebellion the *Oriental* was pressed into the service of the Federal government, at the rate of $1,000 a day, as a troop transport. One Captain Woodruff wrote home that when the *Oriental* left Annapolis for Key West on January 27, 1862 she carried some 1,200 men of the 47th Pennsylvania Volunteer Regiment. The officers had staterooms, but the steamer did not have enough bunks nor provide hammock space for such a mass of humanity.

During the voyage some of the men were forced to bed down in the dank confinement of the cargo holds, sleeping on baggage or on stretchers laid across barrels. Others had to remain on deck in the wind and spray; the first day out they encountered snow and rain. Conditions must have been horrible, especially considering the lack of toilet facilities available at the time; in those days ships had no plumbing—the men either used chamber pots or went over the side. Washing must have been impossible. Seasickness ran rampant.

The *Oriental* ran into a full gale off Cape Hatteras. Said Lieutenant Geety, "It is piteous to see 1000 sick men with one of the most wretched sicknesses imaginable." At least it staved the rush on the galley, and stretched the meager stores.

The transport returned to New York with two companies of U.S. infantry regulars, who had been relieved by the Pennsylvania Volunteers, and civilian passengers including twenty women. Another round trip voyage for Key West left New York on February 22. April 8 found the *Oriental* bound for Port Royal, Jamaica, from which she returned to New York on the twenty-second.

On May 15, 1862 the *Oriental* left New York with troops and government stores for Port Royal. Brigadier General Saxton and his staff were aboard. The steamer got off course in a heavy fog and slipped aground at midnight on the sixteenth. No one was hurt, and every one of the passengers and crew were saved. It was reported that "W.J.A. Fuller, Esq., of New-York, went sixty-five miles in a storm in a canoe across the Sound to Fort Hatteras for assistance, which by his energy was obtained."

Members of the 48th Pennsylvania Volunteer Regiment, stationed at Fort Hatteras, were involved in the rescue. "Lieutenant Ellis, assistant-adjutant quartermaster, came with the steamer *George Peabody*. Colonel Hawkins, commander of Roanoke Island, came next day and took possession of the government property, and placed a guard over it. Lieutenant Ellis and Colonel Hawkins displayed the most commendable zeal and judgment in preserving the government property, and generally promoting the comfort of the shipwrecked passengers. Both deserve the highest praise."

The *Oriental* was left where she grounded. A Custom House report dated September 28, 1878 found "the hull and machinery sanded over."

From *Frank Leslie's Illustrated Newspaper.*

The town of Oriental, on the Neuse River at the mouth of Smith Creek, was first settled in 1870 and was named after the troop transport because Rebecca Midgett, wife of the town's first settler, found the ship's nameboard. Apparently, she liked the name Oriental better than Smith's Creek, the name given by her husband, "Uncle Lou" Midgett.

The *Oriental* is known locally as the Boiler Wreck because the engine's inverted steam cylinder, protruding some eight feet out of the water, resembles a ship's boiler. The wreck lies perpendicular to the beach, bow pointing toward shore. The embedded hull is contiguous; the hull plates have fallen outward and are largely buried. The forepeak is intact, but aft of that stretches a hundred feet of debris and collapsed deck beams. The remains of the boiler are barely recognizable under coral encrustation.

Divers with tanks can easily get out of the water, sit on the top of the engine, and lean against the steam cylinder for a rest. The flywheel is quite obvious immediately aft of the engine; the propeller shaft passes through it, heads over a field of sand and scattered debris, and connects to the hub of an impressive-looking iron propeller.

The *Oriental* lies about a hundred yards offshore and is accessible from the beach. Divers can park in the lot on the west side of the road about four miles south of the Herbert C. Bonner Bridge. This is a National Seashore interpretive center, where nature trails meander through wildlife refuges. Across the road between two tall dunes is a path from which the steam cylinder is visibly obvious.

In 1973, historian Robert Burgess reported that while beachcombing about a mile north of the wreck site he found a Mexican silver eight reale dated 1843. According to Burgess, such coins were known to be in circulation in the United States as late as the Civil War. Furthermore, Navy ships carried such currency in order to purchase supplies in the Caribbean and South America. Was that single reale part of the *Oriental's* paymaster's petty cash fund, a lone soldier's pocket change, or a coin that slipped through the frayed lining in the pants of a nineteenth century beachcomber?

If you find coins in the beach or in the surf, pick them up. But the wreck is designated Site 0008PEB by the North Carolina Department of Cultural Resources, and is protected by state law. Divers may visit the remains but not remove cultural deposits from it; although, how far from the perimeter of the flattened hull one may collect souvenirs is not specified. Spearing fish is allowed.

PALESTRO

Built: 1889   Sunk: August 9, 1900
Previous names: *Palentino*   Depth: Unknown
Gross tonnage: 2,354   Dimensions: 294' × 39' × 19'
Type of vessel: Freighter   Power: Coal-fired steam
Builder: R. Thompson & Sons, Sunderland, England
Owner: Atlantic & Eastern Steam Ship Company, Ltd.
Port of registry: Liverpool, England
Cause of sinking: Stranded
Location: Outer Diamond Shoal

The *Palestro* was bound from Pensacola, Florida to Liverpool, England with a cargo of lumber. Before making the long Atlantic crossing she intended to coal in Norfolk. Due to a long period of dense fog she lost her way, and grounded easily on the Outer Diamond Shoal nearly ten miles from land. No one ashore knew of her plight. The time was seven a.m.

Captain Armstrong, master, ordered three lifeboats launched. Mild weather saw twenty-five men off safely while the captain, third officer, and three men stayed with the ship. Through the misty sea they rowed.

By two that afternoon the fog lifted enough for the lookout from the Cape Hatteras Life-Saving Station to see the wreck. According to the official report, the "Keeper sent word to Creeds Hill and Big Kinnakeet to assist, and then started for the wreck. On the way out the crew ran across two of the ship's boats with twenty men on their way ashore."

The Creeds Hill boat took them in tow to a safe landing place, while the Cape Hatteras boat continued on to the wreck site. "The vessel was a hopeless wreck and the keeper brought ashore those who had remained by." The Kinnakeet boat assisted in recovering baggage.

Meanwhile, the boat in charge of the second officer, and carrying four other men, landed unassisted about a mile from the Cape Hatteras station. "The shipwrecked crew of thirty men were sheltered at this station until the 11th, when they were transported to Norfolk by a schooner."

A less dramatic rescue can not be envisioned. If a ship had to wreck, this was the way it should be.

Ships are meant to dock, not park, and even in calm seas rivets pop and hull plates work loose. When the lifeboats first left the stranded vessel there was twelve feet of water in her holds; by that evening it had risen to twenty-seven feet. The next day the ship's decks were underwater and the hull began to break apart. Vessel and cargo became a complete loss of $300,000.

The wreck of the *Palestro* has not been identified.

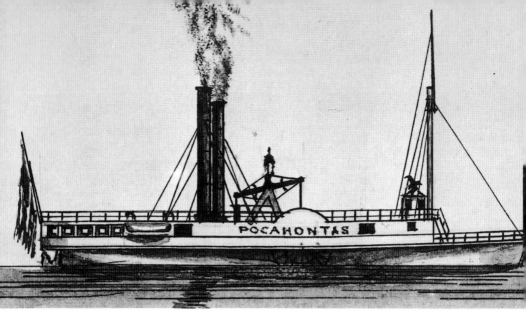

Drawing by Erik Heyl.

POCAHONTAS

Built: 1829   Sunk: January 18, 1862
Previous names: None   Depth: 10 feet
Gross tonnage: 428 (1829), 612 (1848)   Dimensions: 138′ × 30′ × 11′
Type of vessel: Wooden-hulled side-wheel steamer
Power: Crosshead engine (also called a steeple engine)
Builder: Beacham & Gardiner, Baltimore, Maryland
Owner: Powhatan Steam Boat Company
Port of registry: Baltimore, Maryland
Cause of sinking: Foundered, then drifted ashore
Location: In the surf zone off Sand Street, Salvo

    The heyday of steamboat travel was still on the horizon when the *Pocahontas* was built. Most of the great American west was unsettled; indeed, much was unexplored. The vast plains west of the Mississippi were inhabited largely by peaceful Indians and wild animals. The steam locomotive did not yet have rails to follow across the country to the thriving California coast. Conestogas and wagon trains were still in the future. And an accurate map of the North American continent had yet to be drawn.

    In the populated east coast, where the nation was becoming overwhelmed by accelerating advances in science and industry, people were held in awe by the application of machinery to waterborne commerce and by the engineered forethought of design. Consider this description from Norfolk: "The new and elegant steam boat *Pocahontas*, under the command of

Capt. John Ferguson, Senr. arrived here yesterday morning, in 17 hours from Baltimore. She was built for the Maryland and Virginia Steam Boat Company, is intended to run between Baltimore, Norfolk, and Richmond, and to take the place of the steam boat *Norfolk*. ...

"She is in all respects a boat of the first class, and being intended exclusively for the transportation of passengers, combines the most improved arrangements, as well on the score of elegance as comfort. ... In her construction particular attention has been paid to strength of frame, as well as excellence and durability of materials. The principal cabin or dining room is below deck, it is a spacious, light and airy apartment, handsomely finished and furnished, and contains thirty-two commodious births. One hundred persons may here be accommodated at table. The centre of the boat below is occupied by boilers and machinery, the former (of copper) having been placed below in order to ensure perfect safety in navigating the Chesapeake in rough weather. The front cabin contains 20 sleeping births, a bar-room, dressing room, &c. The cabin appropriated for the use of ladies exclusively, is an elegant apartment on the main deck. It is richly furnished and decorated, and contains 20 sleeping births and two state rooms. An upper deck, the loftiness of which affords abundance of light and a free circulation of air to the main and lower cabins, extends the extreme length and width of the boat, and presents a safe and delightful promenade of the most ample dimensions. The engine is of one hundred horses' power, and is remarkable for the ease of its operation. When propelling the boat at the rate of twelve miles an hour, the motion is scarcely perceptible. The machinery is from the establishment of Mr. Charles Reeder, at the south side of the basin, and is made in the workmanlike manner which has already established his reputation as a machinist."

Despite minor inaccuracies ("birth" instead of "berth," and "boilers" when in fact the *Pocahontas* had only one) the writer was obviously impressed by the classic designs of the steamboat. Note, too, the attention paid to the construction and safety of the machinery. This was a time when ship's boilers sometimes exploded because their metalworks could not handle excessive steam pressure, and the pressure relief valve had yet to be invented. Many people were killed by exploding boilers, scalded by escaping steam, or drowned as they were forced to leap overboard in mid-ocean because their ship went up in flames.

In the shipping business a voyage generally did not begin until all staterooms and cargo holds were full. One often had to pace the decks for several days waiting for embarkation. Furthermore, due to the vagaries of the wind in the days of sail, no one could predict how long a passage might take. With the introduction of the steam engine came reliability independent of becalming weather. The *Pocahontas* ran alternately with her companion ship, the *Columbus*, one leaving Baltimore as the other left Richmond, and vice versa. This regular schedule was advertised, and was the condition that defined these ships as steam packets.

Thus began a long and glorious career for the *Pocahontas*. One could travel comfortably by water (instead of overland by stage along rutted, dust covered roads) between Baltimore and Norfolk for $7.00, meals included, and between Richmond and Norfolk for $3.00. Today, that amount in cab fare would get you only a few city blocks with no meals or commodious accomodations, honking horns free.

The *Pocahontas* had her share of experiences. Several times winter gales forced her to run for shelter, thus upsetting her schedule; once there was great consternation because one of her passengers was Secretary of State Martin Van Buren. On another occasion she carried the Royal Siamese Princess, her entourage, and her pet elephant.

The *Pocahontas* also had her share of owners. As rail service became more prevalent, the steam packet companies suffered from the competition; they either went out of business or merged with other shipping lines. In 1840, the *Pocahontas* was transferred to the Baltimore Steam Packet Company. According to Erik Heyl, she "very likely . . . underwent a radical overhaul, receiving at this time a vertical beam engine and having two boilers mounted on the guards," instead of below decks. Few contemporary records are extant to substantiate such changes. Heyl's drawing is based upon "a pencil sketch in the MacPherson collection at the National Maritime Museum, Greenwich, England, made by an eye-witness and dated and inscribed 'American Steamer, Elk River, Chesapeake Bay 1840.'" It may be another steamboat altogether.

Heyl also notes that in 1841 the *Pocahontas* was "transferred to a subsidiary, the Powhatan Steam Boat Co., limited to running steamers on the James River between Richmond and Norfolk. . . . Judging by enrollment No. 21, February 21, 1848, *Pocahontas* underwent a very complete rebuilding during the Winter of 1847/48. The tonnage was increased from 428 Tons to 612 81/95 Tons; unfortunately revised dimensions of the hull were not given in the record."

Skip to 1861 and the onset of the Civil War. On July 25 the U.S. Quarter Master Department took a permanent charter on the *Pocahontas* at various rates beginning at $225 per day of use and increasing to $450 per day. On January 7, 1862 she was assigned to the Burnside Expedition at the rate of $550 per day.

Ambrose Burnside was a colonel in the United States Army when he developed a bold plan of attack against Confederate held territory. He was perhaps one of the few men in history promoted to general just because his ideas found favor with his superior officers. So exciting was his proposal that he was given an audience with President Lincoln. At this meeting, under the stern eyes of Secretary of State William Seward, General George McClellan, and Admiral Louis Goldsborough, Burnside elaborated on his plan of campaign to organize "a division of from 12,000 to 15,000 men, mainly from States bordering on the Northern sea-coast, many of whom would be familiar with the coasting trade . . . and to fit out a fleet of light-draught steamers, sailing vessels, and barges . . . with a view to establishing lodgments on the Southern coast."

The *Pocahontas* was attached to the fleet being formed under Army auspices, and known officially as the Burnside Expedition. Burnside, now a general, described how he put his "motley fleet" together: "North River barges and propellers had been strengthened from deck to keelson by heavy oak planks, and water-tight compartments had been built in them; they were so arranged that parapets of sand-bags or bales of hay could be built upon their decks, and each one carried from four to six guns. Sailing vessels, formerly belonging to the coasting trade, had been fitted up in the same manner. Several large passenger steamers, which were guaranteed to draw less than eight feet of water, together with tug and ferry boats, served to make up the fleet."

On January 9, 1862 Burnside left Annapolis with more than eighty jury-rigged gunboats and federal transports. The main cargo of the *Pocahontas* consisted of horses and their forage. The number of horses she had on board varies according to accounts, and even within the same account (103, 106, 107, and 113), the most likely number being 103. Most of them belonged to the Fourth Rhode Island Infantry, some to the 25th Massachusetts. As passengers she had sixty "men-grooms, wagon-drivers and mechanics."

The ships pooled at the mouth of the Chesapeake Bay. Since Norfolk was in Confederate hands it was widely surmised that that city was the object of the maneuver. No one, not even the ship's captains, knew for sure whither they were bound. Spies were everywhere. However, on the night of January 11 the fleet was ordered to sea. Sealed orders were not permitted to be opened until after passing Cape Henry. Then it was learned that Burnside's objective was Roanoke Island. To get there meant rounding the Diamond Shoals and entering Pamlico Sound through Hatteras Inlet.

Several ships backed out of the expedition because their captain's considered their vessels unseaworthy. Others, such as the floating batteries that were nothing more than converted canal boats, struggled along under tow and shipped quite a bit of water because of their low freeboard. As the weather thickened and the seas grew fierce, some had to be let go. When the *Grapeshot* parted her tow line in mounting seas, the men leaped overboard and were rescued by ropes thrown from the towing vessel *New Brunswick*. The *Grapeshot* was "thrown ashore to the northward of Hatteras." There was no loss of life, only the hay and oats with which the canal boat was heaped.

The *Pocahontas* did not accompany the main fleet. Instead, she left Fortress Monroe on January 16. By this time the gale was in full fury, and in addition to the calamity of the *Grapeshot*, several vessels had been blown ashore and the *Zouave* and the *City of New York* were lost. (See *City of New York* in *Shipwrecks of North Carolina: from Hatteras Inlet South*.) Into this stupendous storm the *Pocahontas* plunged.

The once elegant steam packet was now described as a "wretched old boat" and a "worthless old hulk," and "utterly unsafe," although, to be fair, these admonitions were not made until after her demise. Although

accounts differ as to the chronology of events, the circumstances are the same. On the night of the seventeenth, "when 25 miles from Cape Henry, one of her rudder-chains parted, and the boat lay-to in the trough of the sea, to repair damages. The Captain is said to have been drunk from the time of leaving the Fortress, and created great confusion on board by his orders and countermands. When within 15 miles of Cape Hatteras, an old patch blew off the boiler, the steam, rushed out and filled the boat, and the engines were stopped. A pine plug was finally driven into the hole, and the boat was got under way again. The other rudder-chain parted after they had gone 3 miles, and at about the same time the grating in the engine-room fell with a crash, and the boiler also settled down. The Captain all this while lay drunk on the cabin floor, and as destruction seemed imminent, the pilot ordered the sail set and headed the boat for the beach."

Another account has the boiler blowing out first, then the steering mechanism giving way, "when the smoke-pipe blew down, and as the vessel, from laboring in the sea, had sprung a leak, she was run ashore." In both accounts the captain was pronounced drunk.

Complete disorder reigned. "Valuable horses were thrown overboard ten miles at sea, and when the vessel struck, or was near the beach, the teamsters who had charge of the horses were so careful of their own worthless carcasses, that they refused to go down on the lower deck and cut the halters of the animals, thus leaving the poor brutes to perish on the wreck, when they might nearly all have been saved." One horse reputedly gained the beach "floating on a piece of the deck which came away when she broke up." Another account does not contradict these facts, but neither does it give the distance from shore when the horses "nearest the gangway were shoved overboard."

I suspect there was less culpability than was reported by the press. Colonel Isaac Rodman, commanding officer of the Fourth Rhode Island Infantry, was more forgiving in the official report he posted from Fort

Bartow, Roanoke Island, after the forces of the Burnside Expedition had routed the Confederate defenders: "The *Pocahontas*, on which our horses were embarked, was lost on the cape, and all the horses, except 19, perished. I am happy to say that none of the teamsters that were with them were lost, but all succeeded in getting on shore and joining the regiment." Perhaps the circumstances were insurmountable.

No mention is made of how the men reached shore: whether they rowed or swam. Those horses that did survive the savage sea "found oats and hay on the beach, thrown ashore from the wreck of the *Grapeshot*." The men "made their way along the banks ... receiving food and kind attentions from the inhabitants they fell in with; and meeting a cordial welcome from the Hawkins Zouave through whose camp they had to pass."

The "mere rotten tub, hardly holding together" was soon pounded to pieces in the surf.

Skip again, this time to 1984, when the National Park Service conducted "A Preliminary Assessment of Environmentally Exposed Shipwreck Remains, Cape Hatteras National Seashore." A site designated as 0008 NhB "is visibly comprised of the iron machinery of a steamship. The remains appear to be those of a crosshead steam engine of early to mid-19th century vintage." In-water surveys were conducted by James Delgado and his team. They inspected the machinery and made measurements of the paddlewheel shaft and hubs. The dimensions closely approximate those given for the *Pocahontas*. Furthermore, the position coincides rather well with that given for the *Pocahontas*: "twenty miles north of Cape Hatteras" is fairly close to Salvo, considering that no mile markers existed in 1862.

Local citizens call the wreck the *Richmond*, and believe it was one of the vessels lost during the Burnside Expedition. No vessel by that name is known to have been lost then or at any other time on Hatteras Island.

Is the exposed wreckage off Sand Street that of the *Pocahontas*? Follow-up surveys conducted by Richard Lawrence of the Department of Archives and History at Fort Fisher have not found conclusive evidence. Yet, by deduction, it seems likely. I can do no better than cite Delgado's admonition: "At this time a tentative identification of the wreck as *Pocahontas* is posited pending additional historical research and underwater reconnaissance."

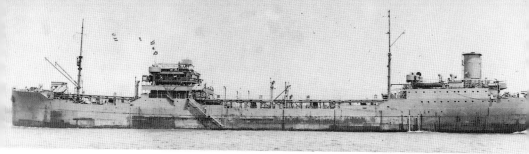

San Cirilo, sister ship of the *San Delfino*. (Courtesy of the Steamship Historical Society of America.)

SAN DELFINO

Built: 1938
Previous names: None
Gross tonnage: 8,072
Type of vessel: Tanker
Builder: Furness Ship Building Company, Haverton Hill-on-Tees, England
Owner: Eagle Oil and Shipping Company, Ltd.
Port of registry: London, England
Cause of sinking: Torpedoed by *U-203* (Kapitanleutnant Mutzelberg)
Location: 26810.2

Sunk: April 9, 1942
Depth: 200 feet
Dimensions: 463' × 61' × 33'
Power: Twin diesel engines

40622.6

By April 1942 the United States had been at war only four months. But England had been embroiled in battle for three years—and had been fighting the onslaught of German U-boats all that time. Little wonder then that the British tanker *San Delfino* was well armed. She carried "one 4-inch gun, one 12-lb. HA gun, four Marlin .30 caliber machine guns, two Hotchkiss .303 caliber machine guns, and a Lewis machine gun." A merchant ship perhaps, but she was also a small floating battery.

The tanker was on route from Houston, Texas to England, via New York and Halifax—the transatlantic crossing was to be made in convoy. In addition to 11,000 tons of much-needed aviation gas, she carried "a certain amount of ammunition for the Allied cause."

Despite her armament, four lookouts, good visibility, blacked out ports, and a zigzag course, the *U-203* found the *San Delfino* alone some ten miles east of Wimble Shoal Buoy, and stabbed her with one well-aimed torpedo.

It was ten o'clock at night when a violent explosion tore out the *San Delfino's* starboard side "near the No. 2 or No. 3 tank, between the pump room and the poop deck." Instantly "the tanker was sheathed in flames. A second explosion followed the first explosion of the torpedo and it is believed that ammunition on board the tanker was also detonated."

Captain Elbert Gumbleton, master, made an instantaneous decision to abandon ship. Within five minutes the *San Delfino* was a fiery derelict as two lifeboats struggled to get away from the flames. One boat got caught in the current and was dragged into the pool of high-octane gasoline. All twenty-eight occupants were burned to a crisp.

The other boat struggled away from the floating time bomb. Once clear of danger the crew remained near the blazing vessel in the hope that, since the radio had been damaged by the blast, the fire might attract someone to their rescue. Again Captain Gumbleton's decision was the correct one.

Only six miles away was the fishing trawler *Two Sisters*. Captain Cornelius Sanders heard the explosion of the torpedo against the *San Delfino's* hull, and "saw a sheet of flame rise over a hundred feet into the air." On his ship-to-shore radio Sanders alerted the Coast Guard of the attack as he raced at high speed for the unmistakable scene of disaster. He picked up the twenty-one survivors in the second lifeboat, many of whom were suffering from burns and injuries. He found another lifeboat, but it was empty.

The *San Delfino* was "last seen afire from stem to stern, but afloat."

On August 7, 1944 the USCG *Gentian* located a large wreck standing "about 80' high in 187' of water. . . . Fathometer soundings of 185–189 feet were obtained in the immediate vicinity of the wreck." A search of the records revealed that "no previously reported positions of wrecks lie within many miles of this position, nor had any instrument contacts been obtained by ASW vessels operating in the area." Also, "only one vessel whose wreck cannot be located with reasonable certainty was sunk near this position. This is the . . . British tanker *San Delfino*. . . . Underwater photography shows the wreck to have a wooden deck and to be sitting bolt upright. . . . The unburned lines and wooden planking would seem to make it unlikely that this is the wreck of the *San Delfino*, although the current in the area has an easterly set which may have carried the derelict to this position."

For clarification on the wreck's unusual height, "The least recorded depth over the wreck was 107 feet at M.L.W. This recording is believed to have been obtained on masts as the wreck is known to lie on an almost even keel."

Uwe Lovas was the first person to dive the *San Delfino*, but since then it has escaped the attention it deserves. The wreck is upright, intact, and visually impressive, looking from a distance very much like a ship steaming along the bottom. However, upon closer inspection one can see big holes in the sides, as if the wreck were pockmarked like Swiss cheese. Catwalks lead to where the superstructure used to be. The highest point of relief is about 160 feet.

The machinery spaces are open from above. An auxiliary boiler is visible between the bridge and the stern. A gun tub lies in the sand off the starboard side with a machine gun still inside. Artifacts abound.

Although clear blue Gulf Stream water is usually encountered on the surface, the Labrador current washes over the wreck on the bottom. The sharp thermocline can plunge a diver into unexpectedly cold conditions.

The water is clean and green, however, with visibility averaging fifty to seventy-five feet. Typical cold water marine organisms encrust the steel plates.

The wreck lies on an approximate north-south heading.

Rolf Mutzelberg and the *U-203* also sank the *Empire Thrush* (q.v.). Mutzelberg was killed accidentally on September 11, 1942. In a lull during an Atlantic patrol he and the crew were taking turns swimming and washing off weeks of sweat and grime. Mutzelberg dived off the conning tower, hit his head on the ballast tank, and broke his neck. Under the command of Kapitanleutnant Herman Kottmann the *U-203* was "lost in action against a convoy in the North Atlantic, Apr. 25, 1943, with 11 killed and 38 captured." Credit for the kill went to the HMS *Biter's* Squadron 811 A/C and the HMS *Pathfinder*.

STRATHAIRLY

Built: 1876
Previous names: None
Gross tonnage: 1,919
Type of vessel: Freighter
Builder: R. Dixon & Company, Middlesbro'
Owner: McIntyre Brothers & Company
Port of registry: Newcastle, England
Cause of sinking: Stranded
Location: 1.25 miles south of the Chicamicomico Life-Saving Station

Sunk: March 24, 1891
Depth: 20–30 feet
Dimensions: 282' × 34' × 23'
Power: Coal-fired steam

As was so poignantly described in the Wilmington *Morning Star*, "It is difficult to imagine a more desolate coast than that upon which the unfortunate steamship *Strathairly* was wrecked. For a hundred miles south from Cape Henry there extends a strip of sand cast up from the sea and separated from the main land by many miles of broad salt sounds. Sometimes this strip broadens to the width of a few miles and then shrinks to a mere thread of gray sand. Inhabitants are few in number, scattered in solitary dwellings, and without means of communicating with the world save an occasional oyster sloop or fishing boat that at irregular intervals cruise along the sounds. Their living is derived from the sea, and the strip is nearly barren of vegetation. On the sea side long sand bars run out and reefs abound, so that a vessel wrecked upon this coast is sure to strike at a distance from the shore and be speedily torn to pieces by the tremendous Hatteras surges that have made the vicinity the dread of navigators for a century and has strewn the white beaches with the timbers of numberless vessels and bodies of countless sailors."

The *Strathairly* was on route from Santiago, Cuba to Baltimore when she went aground in a dense fog. She struck at high tide more than a quarter mile from shore. With her holds full of iron ore there was no chance of lightening her load and slipping her off the shoal.

Lieutenant Failing, the district Life-Saving Service inspector, was a witness to the ensuing events. He made the following graphic report:

"As soon as the steamer struck she blew her whistle and it was quickly answered by the patrol, who then lost no time in reporting the wreck to Keeper Wescott, of the Chicamicomico Station. The latter at once telephoned Keeper Pugh, of the Gull Shoal Station, and then set out with his beach apparatus to the locality of the wreck and began operations. From the testimony of the survivors they heard a gun fired abreast of the wreck in less than half an hour afterwards. It also appears from this testimony that as soon as the vessel struck, orders were given to clear away the port or leeward lifeboat, and the crew had just got it ready to lower when the vessel gave a heavy lurch and the boat was smashed. At this time all the windward boats were also swept away, and all hope had to be given up of reaching the shore by the ship's boats. The crew then took to the rigging, as the sea was breaking completely over the vessel, the captain, the first officer, and the chief engineer going aloft aft, and the rest forward. Very shortly after this the steamer commenced breaking in two. At about daybreak the mainmast fell over the side and took with it the captain, first officer, and chief engineer, who were lost. When Keeper Wescott arrived at the wreck, which was at about 20 minutes to 6 o'clock, he sent one of his crew to notify me, as I was lying off the station in the sound, in the Government sloop." (He was aboard the *Alert*, in Pamlico Sound.)

"I arrived near the wreck at about 7 a.m. and found Keepers Wescott and Pugh with their crews, but could see nothing of the steamer through the fog, although the cries of the unfortunate men could be heard distinctly. Wescott informed me that he had made an attempt to throw a No. 7 line on board as soon as he reached the ground, although he had not seen the vessel and had nothing but the sounds of voices to guide him. The fog hung low and nothing could be seen of the steamer until 10 o'clock. Long before this, however, Keeper L.B. Midgett and the crew of the New Inlet Station had arrived. In the mean time, in addition to the beach apparatus, the surfboat, several spare shot lines, projectiles, and an extra supply of powder had been brought to the scene. When at last the vessel could be made out through the slowly vanishing fog it became apparent that she had broken in two, and that all the people alive were on the bow. The first shot after this was with a six-ounce charge. This shot fell short, the line attached being a No. 7.

"The next shot also fell short. A No. 4, or the smallest-sized line, was then brought into use, and this was landed at the forecastle. As soon as it was seen that the sailors had it, a No. 9 or a large line was bent to the smaller one, and it was drawn off in good shape until within a few yards of the vessel when the small line, unable to bear the strain exerted upon it by the longshore current, parted and the attempt had to be made over again. Being prepared for such a contingency no time was lost by the station men, the next shot carrying a No. 7 or medium-sized line. The powder charge was eight ounces. The shot struck the forward rail and the men on board got this line also. A No. 9 line was then bent to it by the surfmen, but the sailors hauled it off very slowly, the current carrying the bight so far to the leeward that gathering the line in was slow and laborious work. To this line the ship was attached, and there seemed a good prospect of success at last crowning the joint efforts of the surfmen and the sailors, but before the whip block got more than half way to the ship the stout No. 7 line broke and the situation was as bad as before. In this way effort after effort was made to send the gear off until after 3 o'clock in the afternoon, the gun being fired as fast as the lines could be faked down.

"By this time it was plain to the men on the beach that something must be wrong on board the ship as no less than five shots had been successful in landing the lines and only two or three men could be seen at work supplementing the labors of the surfmen. This is explained by the statement of the second mate, the only surviving officer, that but three were in condition to do anything, the rest having scarcely any clothing on and being too benumbed and helpless from exposure. Had the sailors succeeded in reaching the No. 9 line it was the final resolve of those on the beach to send off the whip by its single part and, if this in turn reached the ship, then send the block off and rig the gear any way that was possible. At about noon one of the seamen, Albert Smith, jumped overboard with a lifebelt on, and after a desperate struggle in the surf was pulled out by the surfmen, unconscious and nearly dead. He was promptly removed to the dwelling of ex-keeper John Allen Midgett near by, where a detail of men put into practice the method for the resuscitation of the apparently drowned, and he was finally brought to.

"Shortly after 3 in the afternoon a No. 4 line was landed on the vessel, and to this was attached the next size larger, a No. 7. Three or four men were seen hauling it off, but the smaller line snapped in two when the bend of the No. 7 line was within a few feet of the steamer, and communication was thus again broken. By this time the flood tide was again sweeping in; every shot line had been used and was wet and heavy. The surf also was so high that no boat could live in it. Under these circumstances the surfmen were becoming disheartened. They had labored hard since early morning to effect communication with the ship and rig the gear for the purpose of saving the crew, and every effort had failed. The ship was an unusually great distance from the shore; it was impossible to use the boat, and the life-saving crews seemed to have reached the limit of their resources. The day also was fast waning, and the situation of the sailors was desperate. At twenty minutes before 5 o'clock, just twelve hours after the stranding of their vessel, the sailors were heard shouting to those on shore, and then one by one they jumped into the sea for a final effort to save themselves by swimming, each man being provided with a life-belt. It appears in the testimony that at this time, in addition to the loss of the three officers previously mentioned, the second engineer and the cook were also dead. As fast as the poor fellows jumped overboard and began their struggle towards the shore they were swept by the current to the southward. The surfmen and the inhabitants of the neighboring settlements, many of whom had been present on the beach all day, at once followed them, and at great risk to themselves, in wading out into the surf, succeeded in dragging sixteen men out of the water. Ten of this number were, however, dead by the time they were reached. Immediately efforts were made to resuscitate them, but without avail. The survivors testify that before they jumped from the ill-fated vessel they were fully satisfied that such a course was their only hope, that no boat could have reached them, and that even if a large line could have reached them then they had not strength enough and were in no condition to rig the gear. Nor from the moment they reached this conclusion would there have been opportunity to do anything, for in about twenty minutes from the time they abandoned the wreck by jumping into the surf, the foremast went by the board, and very soon thereafter all vestige of the steamer disappeared. . . .

"John Northcote, ordinary seaman, was so far gone when taken from the surf that he also had to be carried to Capt. John Allen Midgett's house, where restoratives were applied, and by working on him until after midnight his life was saved. Both Smith and Northcote were moved to the station the following day. The other five men, also greatly prostrated by exposure and their struggles in the surf, were immediately taken to comfortable quarters in the station, where they were provided with dry clothing from the supply donated by the Women's National Relief Association.

"The ten bodies taken out of the surf were carried to the station, placed in boxes made by the life-saving men, a minister was sent for, and they were buried on the morning of the 26th near the station. The men saved are being well cared for by the Chicamicomico crew, and will be sent to Elizabeth City, North Carolina, by the first vessel, and thence transportation will be given them to Norfolk, Virginia."

The *Strathairly* is a beach wreck that Donny Lang has dived extensively. He says it can be found straight off the southern edge of the Hatteras Island Motel (a three story building) about twice the distance from shore as the length of the nearby Rodanthe fishing pier. He recommends using an inflatable boat because of a predominantly strong current that runs from north to south. Be careful when approaching it by rigid-hull boat because the boiler rises close to the surface and could be rammed.

The wreck lies nearly parallel to the beach with the bow facing north and closer to shore than the stern. The hull is contiguous, largely broken down, and is twisted to port about midships. The section from the boilers forward lies at a depth of 20 feet; the area is full of iron ore.

The boilers are distinguishable, but abaft of them the engine is an indescribable mass of encrustation. The remains of the shaft alley can be followed to the propeller, where it is possible to reach a depth of 30 feet.

Donny says that while the water can be clear on the bow of the wreck, the visibility from the engine back drops to about one foot due to the muddy bottom; on a good day the water clarity in the stern may reach five feet. The wreck continually sands in and out, changing from year to year. British made knickknacks are occasionally recovered by sharp-eyed divers.

U-85

Built: 1941   Sunk: April 14, 1942
Type of vessel: Type VII-B U-boat (submarine)   Depth: 90 feet
Displacement tonnage: 753 surfaced, 1,040 submerged
Dimensions: 218′ × 20′ × 15′
Power: Two diesel engines and two electric motors
Speed: 17 knots surfaced (on diesels), 8 knots submerged (on motors)
Armament: Five torpedo tubes (four bow, one stern), one 88-mm gun
Builder: Flender Werft, Lubeck, Germany
Owner: German Navy
Cause of sinking: Shelled and depth-charged by USS *Roper* (DD-147)
Location: 26917.0   40713.6

Until April 1942 the east coast U-boat war was a howling success (viewed through German eyes) and a deadly and frustrating exercise (to the men of the merchant marine and the U.S. Navy.) With near impunity torpedoes ripped through the coastal fleet with devastating effect; ships were being sunk on an almost daily basis, while the brave sailors who manned them suffered horribly and died anonymously. Those who lived

Left: the conning tower of the *U-86*. Below: the National Archives captioned this picture as the *U-85*.

through the deadly ordeals returned to the sea with the courage of their kind.

Besides engaging the enemy on two fronts (the Germans in Europe, the Japanese in the Pacific), the Navy had to fight a defensive war at home. Its resources were severely strained; men, machines, and material needed to protect shipping were in short supply. But as the war entered its fifth month the fortification of the east coast eased into high gear. Blimps, airplanes, and a mosquito fleet of small boats aided warships in pursuit of the enemy. Training and tactical exercises sharpened skills learned vicariously. Aggression became the watchword.

Meanwhile, the underwater snipers shot and submerged, torpedoed and ran, skulked by night and cowered by day.

Into this beehive of activity charged the *U-85*. Oberleutnant zur See Eberhard Greger was the U-boat's first and only captain. Greger and the *U-85* made three war patrols in the North Atlantic with very little success. On September 9, 1941 he fired a spread of torpedoes into Convoy SC-42 but made no hits. Still dogging the convoy, the following day "the U-85 made two attacks. In the first one hit was observed, and one detonation heard beyond. In the second attack two detonations were heard, but these must have been depth charges dropped by HMCS *Skeena*." Greger reported three ships sunk and one probably damaged, but only the 4,748-ton *Thistleglen* went to the bottom.

After another attack, on January 21, 1942, "the *U-85* heard two detonations and after 10 minutes observed the damaged ship in sinking condition with a heavy list." Greger tried to take credit for sinking a 9,000

Courtesy of the National Archives.

GERMAN U-BOAT
750 TON CLASS

The light flare is on the original negative of this photograph of the *Roper*. (Courtesy of the National Archives.)

ton vessel, but no Allied ships were reported lost. On February 9 Greger made his second confirmed kill: the 5,408-ton *Empire Fuselier*.

March 21, 1942 found the *U-85* on its way to the American shooting gallery. The crossing took nearly three weeks. Then the U-boat cruised offshore between New York and North Carolina, reaching as far south as Wimble Shoals. During this time it was credited with sinking the 4,904-ton *Chr. Knudsen*, which left New York on April 8, bound for Capetown, South Africa, and which disappeared without a trace. Then came the night of April 13–14, the *U-85's* time of reckoning.

Patrolling the arena was the USS *Roper* (DD-147). She was similar to the USS *Jacob Jones* (DD-130), the destroyer that was torpedoed and sunk by the *U-578* only six weeks earlier; only eleven men survived out of a crew of one hundred forty-five. (For details see *Shipwrecks of Delaware and Maryland*, by this author.) The *Roper* was a flush-deck, four-stack destroyer built a generation earlier, in 1919.

The *Roper* was no stranger to war. On April 1 she came upon the survivors of the passenger-freighter *City of New York*; the people had been adrift in rafts and lifeboats for three days. One woman gave birth in a lifeboat, and after their rescue named her son Jesse Roper in honor of the ship that saved their lives.

The night of April 13 was exceptionally clear; the stars shone bright on a calm, placid sea. The destroyer's twin propellers churned surface plankton into a bioluminescent wake. The light on Bodie Island offered a bearing point for the *Roper's* navigator. In addition to her normal complement the *Roper* had on board the Commander of Destroyer Division Fifty-four, Commander Stanley Cook Norton. The evident U-boat activity concentrated off the Diamond Shoals kept the crew on their toes, and the lookouts alert. Understandably, Lieutenant Commander Hamilton Wilcox Howe conned his ship with extreme caution.

The *Roper* plowed the sea at a steady eighteen knots, on a heading of 162°. At six minutes past midnight she made a radar contact bearing 190° at a range of 2,700 yards. "Immediately afterwards the sound man, echo ranging from bow to bow, heard rapidly turning propellers at a range and bearing that coincided with those obtained by the Radar operator. Then, almost dead ahead, the lookout picked up what appeared to be the wake of a small vessel running away at high speed. Range decreased very slowly, so the *Roper* raised her speed to twenty knots."

His suspicions aroused, Lieutenant Commander Howe rang general quarters. All duty personnel raced to their combat stations. "Orders were given to prepare the machine guns, the three inch battery, the torpedoes and the depth charges for action. As the chase began the Executive Officer went to the flying bridge to keep the Conning Officer informed of the movements of the leading ship."

No recognition signals were sent by the unknown vessel. Instead, it began a series of course changes that were obviously evasive. Although no one aboard the *Roper* knew it yet, they had a U-boat on the run; it was trapped on the surface in shallow water where it could not escape by submerging. The U-boat turned to port in increments, testing the *Roper* to determine if she had indeed spotted it. The distance between them closed.

The *Roper* was not fooled, nor was Lieutenant Commander Howe taking chances. With the fate of the *Jacob Jones* so vividly on his mind, he kept his ship slightly off the fleeing U-boat's starboard quarter. The *Roper* gradually overtook the U-boat. As the range was decreased to 700 yards and contact was imminent, Greger reacted predictably, like a cornered rabbit. He fired a torpedo from his stern tube and tried to hit the destroyer "down the throat." Howe's prescience saved his ship. Sailors held their breaths as they watched the deadly fish slide close past the port side and across the *Roper's* wake.

The U-boat made a radical turn to starboard. Its turning radius was tighter than the destroyer's, permitting it to turn inside the other's circle. Ensign Kenneth MacLean Tebo held a steady helm throughout the battle, keeping a sharp eye on the dark ghostly image.

Lieutenant William Winfield Vanous, Executive Officer, directed the training of the 24-inch searchlight and brightly illuminated the enemy's conning tower; already, German sailors were pouring out of the hatch and preparing the deck gun for action.

Chief Boatswain's Mate Jack Edwin Wright spotted his target, pulled the trigger of his 50-caliber machine gun, and with deadly accuracy poured a steady stream of tracers into the men on the deck of the U-boat. Several German gunners were picked up physically by the force of the bullets and hurled into the water. As more men scrambled to take their place they were scythed down like stalks of wheat. The conning tower became a charnel house of the dead and dying. Moreover, at such close range the projectiles penetrated the ballast tanks; the U-boat's outer skin was soon riddled with holes.

While the Germans were kept from loading and firing their deck gun, the *Roper's* 3-inch gun came on line. Coxswain Harry Hayman, "a gun captain who had never before been in charge of a gun during firing," spotted his shots with such precision that he soon landed an explosive shell at the water line below the conning tower, breaching the hull and making it impossible for the U-boat to dive.

Like rats deserting a sinking ship, German sailors poured out of the conning tower hatch and cowered behind the shearwater. The U-boat began to lose headway. The *Roper* turned at her maximum rate and prepared to fire a torpedo. Singly and in small groups the Germans jumped from the U-boat's bulbous tank on the side away from the incoming shells. The U-boat slowly came to a stop and settled by the stern, as if scuttling ports had been opened aft. By the time the *Roper's* turn brought her up behind the U-boat, it had slipped beneath the sea.

Not sure whether this was a trick maneuver, the *Roper* drove in on the spot where the U-boat had disappeared. The screams of thirty-five or forty German sailors were clearly audible to the men aboard the *Roper* as the destroyer passed through the area where they had abandoned ship, "but the *Roper* was more immediately concerned with the certain destruction of the enemy than with the rescue of the personnel." The torpedo was secured, and a barrage of eleven depth charges was laid down "at a position determined upon by an eye estimate and an excellent sound contact." Each depth charge weighed three hundred pounds, and was set to go off at fifty feet below the surface. Racks, Y-guns, and K-guns delivered the attack.

The *Roper* held a straight, steady course away from the position of the submerged or sunken U-boat. Because U-boats were known to work in consort, there was the ever-present possibility that another pack wolf lurked nearby. This "made the conduct of any rescue work before daylight far too dangerous to risk." With her antenna sweeping and sound gear pinging continuously, the *Roper* searched throughout the night for other signs of the enemy. No one got any sleep.

At dawn a Navy PBY plane flown by Lieutenant C.V. Horrigan swooped over the area to conduct a visual search. In the light of day oil slicks and a large field of debris could be seen. Horrigan dropped a depth charge on a particularly suspicious area. Two more planes appeared on the scene; they dropped smoke floats to draw attention to bodies on the surface. The *Roper* drove into the area just after 7 a.m., launched two lifeboats, "and commenced recovering bodies and floating articles." At all times at least one plane circled the destroyer for protection against other U-boats. At one time as many as seven planes of various types flew cover for recovery operations. An observation blimp arrived at 7:30. The potential situation was too serious to leave anything to fate.

"At 0750 the first boat returned with five bodies, and at 0834 hoisting of fifteen more bodies by means of a small davit was commenced. At 0850 the sound operator detected a sharp echo at a range of 2700 yards."

Was this another U-boat? Leaving the two lifeboats to continue their grisly task, the *Roper* took off at high speed toward the target. Seven minutes later she dropped four depth-charges in a straight line at seven second intervals, producing "one very large air bubble and one smaller one . . . together with fresh oil. The airship and one plane dropped flares on the spot, and the airship reported the continuation of the air bubbles." The anti-submarine action report stated, "This is believed to be same submarine depth-charged after 0006 contact."

Altogether, "twenty-nine bodies were recovered. Among other things six escape lungs were found. Two bodies had mouth-piece tubing in their mouths, indicating escape after the submarine sank. While picking up the bodies, a number of empty life jackets were noted. Two additional bodies were permitted to sink after their clothing was searched by an officer in the boat." No explanation was given for why two bodies were let go; it is likely they were so damaged by explosives that they were falling apart or that very little was left of them.

At ten o'clock two more depth charges were dropped "to further blast submarine depth-charged on previous attacks. Charges were let go over largest air bubble." The U-boat did not move, and air bubbles persisted. The *Roper* placed an orange colored buoy some two hundred fifty yards away from the largest air bubble.

That afternoon the *Roper* docked at Lynnhaven Roads. The German bodies were transferred to the Naval tug USS *Sciota* (AT-30), which later delivered them to the Naval Operating Base at Norfolk, Virginia. There they were photographed, examined, and placed in shrouds. All clothing and personal effects were saved. The next afternoon the bodies, each in a plain pine box, were trucked under escort to nearby Hampton National Cemetery. Twenty-nine graves were dug by prisoners from Fort Monroe.

As dusk approached, a select group of military personnel gathered at the grave site. Not until after dark, and in relative secrecy, were services commenced. The coffins were lowered into the ground. Two Navy chaplains officiated: Lieutenant Wilbur Wheeler read Catholic services, Lieutenant (j.g.) Rainus Lundquist read the Protestant version. In strict military fashion the vanquished enemy was saluted by three volleys while a bugler sounded taps.

The German sailors received a finer peace than they had offered to their victims.

Oddly, no mention of this decisive victory was released to the press until three weeks after the event. Even then the published account was meager and garbled, not by newspaper reporters but in the original Navy communique. By that time so many false claims had been issued for the morale of the public that the authentic account paled by comparison. The

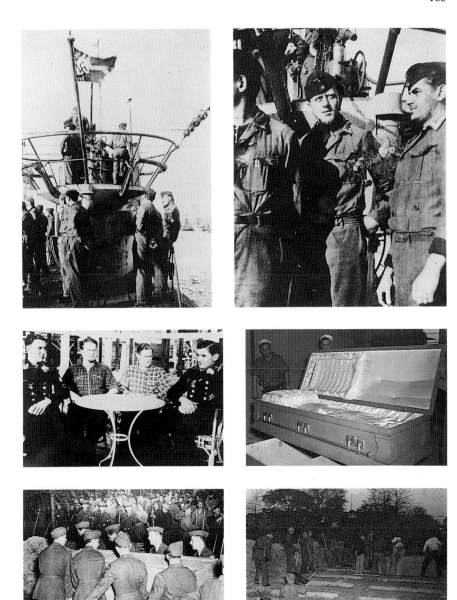

According to the War Diary of the Eastern Sea Frontier, the three photographs of German sailors were found on one of the bodies recovered from the *U-85*. (All courtesy of the Naval Historical Center.) The three burial photographs are courtesy of the National Archives.

story was spiced by the following falsity, "With the action over as suddenly as it had begun, the destroyer circled around and the crew, who minutes before had been manning the guns, went to the rails to help lift the surviving members of the submarine crew out of the water."

By coincidence, two days later part of a U-boat crew *was* captured off the North Carolina coast. (See *U-352* in *Shipwrecks of North Carolina: from Hatteras Inlet South.*) No mention of that incident was *ever* released to the public because German spies had access to American newspapers.

Not until July 23, 1942, after the U-boats had been firmly trounced and forcibly beaten out of the Eastern Sea Frontier, did the Navy announce the truth of the secret burial. Still, no mention was made of the U-boat's number; no names of deceased were made known. Outside the highest Naval circles the fate of the *U-85* was couched in anonymity.

Citations were in the offing for the alert and aggressive crew of the *Roper*. Admiral A.S. Carpender, Commander Destroyers, U.S. Atlantic Fleet, wrote, "The attack on an enemy submarine by the USS *Roper* was conducted with courage, skill, intelligence and determination, in the best traditions of the Naval Service. Its successful prosecution, which resulted in the destruction of the submarine, reflects great credit on the commanding officer, officers, and men of the *Roper*, and on the commander of Destroyer Division 54, who by his advice and guidance assisted in the conduct of the engagement."

In addition to the key figures already named, six members of the gun crew received commendations; gun captain Harry Heyman was put in for the Navy Cross. The *Roper's* forward stack was emblazoned with a large star on both port and starboard sides, to "indicate the first attack made by the vessel which resulted in positive evidence of destruction of an enemy submarine." Furthermore, every crewman was authorized to wear a distinctive sleeve device in the form of a silver star.

Diving operations on the *U-85* began almost immediately. The U.S. Navy's Experimental Diving Unit was brought in to conduct a survey and learn what it could about German submarines. Several days were spent dragging for and grapneling the sunken U-boat, and establishing mooring buoys. A diver actually alighted upon the wooden deck on April 26; he reported that the "submarine appeared to be lying on its starboard side. Inspected submarine forward to bow and returned to the descending line. No apparent damage except to clearing lines noted."

The next day the USS *Kewaydin* (AT-25) fouled the marker buoys and descending line in an increasing wind and sea. The buoy was replaced by the end of the day, but the seas were too rough to continue operations.

April 28 dawned with bettering conditions. The USCGC *Cuyahoga* relieved the British armed trawler as guardship while the *Kewaydin* repeated the laborious task of dragging, grapneling, and setting mooring lines. This time the first diver put down "made descending line fast to cleat on port side of submarine just forward of gun."

Six dives were made throughout the day, with the following conditions noted: "(a) Submarine listed to starboard practically on its side—angle of deck with bottom about 80°. (b) Forward on port side several stanchions torn away. Hull appeared intact. (c) No other damage noted except clearing lines torn loose. (d) Forward gun swung forward and to port slightly elevated with tompion in place. (e) 20 mm. AA gun aft of conning tower in place, lines and wires fouled with it. (f) Conning tower apparently undamaged. (g) Upper conning tower hatch open with lubricating oil coming up through hatch below." The *Roper's* shell damage could not be seen because the U-boat lay on the ruptured ballast tank.

Furthermore, the wood deck was intact, the conning tower showed no signs of damage by shell fire, vents to all tanks were open, salvage air lines were collapsed ("probably due to the effects of depth charges"), numerous openings in the hull were open or partially open, the lower conning tower hatch was closed but not dogged, and all compartments were flooded. The bow and stern planes and propellers were undamaged.

On April 29 the salvage tug USS *Falcon* arrived and took over diving operations. The *Cuyahoga* remained as guardship and quarters for observers. After the *Roper* fought so assiduously to send the *U-85* to the bottom, divers spent the next week trying to bring it back up. They closed the conning tower hatch, traced salvage air lines, manufactured fittings, then connected surface-supplied hoses and pumped air into the hull. Most of the external piping was collapsed; air that did pass spurted out of the compartments "like sprinkling system."

The 20-mm anti-aircraft gun was removed and recovered for study. Also brought up were the gun sights for the 88-mm deck gun, and instruments from the bridge: the night firing device, the gyro pelorus repeater, and the gyro steering repeater. One diver noted that the forward torpedo tube doors were open and ready for action. On the other hand, the ready ammunition stowage locker near the deck gun was found empty. Disassembly of the deck gun was begun but not completed.

Of historic interest was a painted picture on the forward high part of the conning tower; it depicted a "wild boar with rose in mouth."

Diving was secured on May 4 with the following recommendation: "Combining the information contained in the USS *Roper* report of action with that gained by divers, it is my opinion that this vessel was thoroughly and efficiently scuttled by her crew, and that successful salvage can be accomplished only by extensive pontooning operations."

The Navy had better things to do. The machine of destruction was abandoned to the greatest of all destructive forces: the elements of nature.

Although there are no other reports about activity on the sunken U-boat, the wreck as it exists todays seems to have undergone further damage than that observed by Navy divers in 1942. The bow truncates sharply at the end of the pressure hull; the forward portion of the outer hull, or skin, is missing. The torpedo tubes protrude from the end and are separated so that the parts with the outer doors and massive hinges lie loose in the sand, partially or completely buried. A field of debris lies in front of the main wreckage and is scattered back along the starboard side. Rumor has it that the bow was blown off by private salvors.

Oddly, the angle of tilt is no more than 45°. Sand has built up high on the port side of the wreck, while the starboard side is exposed to a much deeper depth. Ocean currents scour the stern somewhat, but most of the time the propellers are covered with sand. However, this condition can change from year to year, and the amount of exposure can vary considerably. Due to the prevailing current, the sand has drifted against the port side of the hull nearly level with the tilted deck, while the starboard side drops down a good ten feet.

Most of the thin, outer skin has rusted through to reveal the pressure hull underneath. When I first dived the wreck in the 1970's a spare torpedo was exposed forward of the conning tower; it was stored outside the pressure hull but inside the outer skin. Sometime during the past several years this torpedo disappeared. Since a G7a T1 compressed-air torpedo weighs 3,369 pounds, this was no simple salvage task. Yet no one has come forward to take credit for the job.

The forward torpedo room is accessible through the torpedo loading hatch, but after penetrating six or eight feet forward the room is filled with sand to within a foot of the overhead.

The control room can be accessed through the large damaged area below the starboard side of the conning tower. The interior at this point is a complicated maze of pipes and beams strung together with a cat's cradle of electrical wires. Explorers beware. The conning tower hatch is open, but very small; because the lower hatch is also open it is possible to crawl through the conning tower and into the control room. The conning tower is in the process of separating from the hull; already it is possible to get an arm in the gap.

From inside the control room one can head aft around the periscope housing and go through the after control room hatch all the way to the galley hatch; however, it is a bit of a squeeze due to interior dunes.

Complete silt-out must be expected behind a diver crawling through such close confines.

One can either exit through the galley hatch, or duck under it and go further aft, at least until one is pressed up against the overhead by sand that seems to build up higher with each passing year. The silt inside is thick. Divers have recovered china and other odds and ends by digging in the sand both forward and aft of the galley hatch. Due to this build-up of sediment, much more undoubtedly awaits the persistent diver with an airlift.

The after torpedo loading hatch is open, but an iron bar bolted across it from the inside prevents a diver wearing tanks from entering. Only by removing all paraphernalia and using a long breathing hose can one squeeze past the barrier. Think twice before you try it.

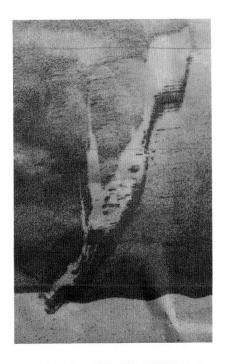

Left: side-scan sonar image of the *U-85*. Below: notice the cold water marine growth around the torpedo loading hatch. Bottom: this spare torpedo was stowed outside the pressure hull; notice the stainless steel inspection cover with cutouts for the adjustment settings.

U-701

Built: 1941
Type of vesse: Type VII-C U-boat (submarine)
Displacement tonnage: 769 (submerged), 1,070 (surfaced)
Dimensions: 218′ × 20′ × 15′
Power: Two diesel engines and two electric motors
Speed: 17 knots surfaced (on diesels), 7.6 knots submerged (on motors)
Armament: Five torpedo tubes (four bow, one stern), one 88-mm gun
Builder: Stulcken Sohn, Hamburg, Germany
Owner: German Navy
Cause of sinking: Aerial depth-charge
Location: North of the Diamond Shoals

Sunk: July 7, 1942
Depth: 115 feet

The *U-701* had a special mission when it came to America: to lay mines in the shipping lanes off the Chesapeake Bay approaches. That area was so well protected by Allied mines that enemy incursion was considered not only impractical, but insane. The protective minefield extended more than thirty miles to sea. A zigzag channel resembling a lightning bolt twisted and turned through the moored explosive devices. Only an experienced pilot could read the lighted buoys, and lead convoys and independent merchant ships through the swept channel.

The danger of drifting outside the prescribed safe zone was loudly emphasized when the American tanker *E.H. Blum*, waiting for escort one fog-shrouded morning, blundered into a mine and was blown in two. There was no loss of life, and the ship was salvaged and reunited, but the lesson was obvious to all. The shipping lanes were well defined, and had to be adhered to rigorously.

While it seems suicidal that the enemy would send a valuable warship and its crew on such a daring and deadly exploit, consider this exposé. Neutral ships whose papers were inspected after docking in Baltimore were found to have routing instructions different from those issued by the Allies. They were quite specific as to which routes to follow and which to avoid upon entering the Chesapeake Bay. That area to be avoided was exactly where German mines had been swept up. The implication is obvious: German intelligence was trading information with neutral nations to the benefit of both.

So, when Kapitanleutnant Horst Degen conned the *U-701* through the

American minefield to lay his own nest of explosives, he very likely already knew the safe way through.

Choosing Degen for such a venture was no accident. As a graduate of the German naval academy with eight years at sea, he was already experienced when he left the destroyer division to join the U-boat arm. Before getting his own boat he served with the redoubtable Erich Topp on the *U-552*. (Topp sank seven ships in the Eastern Sea Frontier; see *Byron D. Benson*.) The Office of Naval Intelligence (ONI) described Degen as daring and reckless, "which are the peculiar attributes of the more successful U-boat commanders, ... a philosophy of combat which insists on retention of the offensive, admitting little evasive action."

The brand new *U-701* experienced teething troubles right from the start. It failed sea trials in the Baltic and was returned to the shipyard to have its faulty construction overhauled. Among other things the air and oil lines were not properly fitted, and the electrical circuits were wired wrong. This resulted in a three-month delay in acceptance. After a month's target practice and torpedo practice the *U-701* underwent another stint at the ship builder's before being cleared for duty. Thus five months were wasted before its first war cruise.

Degen's sole success on his first patrol (the 3,657-ton *Baron Erskine*) was offset by the loss of one of his officers washed overboard in a heavy sea. On his second patrol to the North Atlantic he torpedoed and sank two anti-submarine trawlers: the 541-ton *Notts Country* and the 440-ton *Stella Capella*. Although his record was not admirable, it showed promise because of the aggressive nature of his attacks—in broad daylight and in the presence of armed escorts.

The *U-701's* fuel tanks were topped off at Lorient on May 20, 1942; it left immediately for the American coast and for its encounter with destiny. The Atlantic crossing took three weeks. During that time the U-boat "passed and exchanged signals with a three-masted Portugese sailing ship, the *Gazella Primera*, bound for the Newfoundland Banks to fish." Due to Portugal's neutrality the *Gazella Primera* went unmolested. Today that ship is a treasured tourist attraction owned by the Philadelphia Maritime Museum, and displayed on the Delaware River at Penn's Landing, in Philadelphia.

Two large liners were chased. One turned out to be the Swedish *Drottningholm* traveling under diplomatic immunity, the other went unidentified because she outran the U-boat.

According to Degen's initial interrogation after capture, he received a vicious and prophetic reception upon his arrival off the east coast. He was caught on the surface by a patrol plane. The U-boat crash-dived but reached a depth of only forty feet when five depth charges straddled its hull. "Lights failed and instrument glasses were smashed in the control room, but the damage was slight and quickly repaired." The men were thoroughly shaken up.

The date of this attack was given as June 12. After the war, Degen conceded that on that very same day he was skulking submerged toward Cape Henry, and during that night unloaded his cargo of mines. Several similar variances between admission and actuality will be noted in the ensuing text; the reason for Degen's subterfuge was to deceive ONI about his real activities lest it affect future mining operations.

All Degen's statements are suspect unless verified from other sources. If such an aerial attack did occur, it could not have happened when he said it did. In fact, Degen later contradicted himself by bragging that prior to laying his mines he ran openly on the surface and experienced no alerts from either aircraft or anti-submarine vessels.

Nevertheless, Degen's undertaking was audacious in the extreme. He had to circumvent the defensive minefield, avoid prowling patrol boats, and deposit his mines in the shipping lane exactly where he was most likely to be spotted by inbound or outbound traffic. His navigation had to be precise or he would either be sunk, or fail in his objective.

Degen pulled it off supremely. Triangulating the lights on Cape Charles and Cape Henry, he reached a position only a few miles off the coast of Virginia Beach where (in his words), "we could see the dark shadows of dunes, with lights here and there . . . even cars and persons and lighted houses." In fact, coastal blackout had been in effect for months. The night was dark with a new moon.

When the beacon of the Cape Henry lighthouse was directly off the U-boat's port side the first mine was ejected from its tube. Unlike World War One minelaying U-boats that were specially designed with rails and minelaying tubes, the *U-701* utilized its existing tubes to carry out the task. Each tube held three magnetic mines constructed to fit production-line torpedo tubes. As each mine was pushed out an internal timer was activated. The mine armed itself after sixty hours of sleep.

In the midnight tranquility the U-boat's diesels must have sounded dreadfully loud to the crew. Degen played tag with a sentinel ship as he dropped his mines at one minute intervals until all fifteen were sowed. Then he hurried out of the area, running surfaced until dawn. The tubes were reloaded with torpedoes and in short order the *U-701* was ready for the next phase of its destructive mission. Two and a half days later, when the mines woke up, the *U-701* was operating far out to sea off Cape Hatteras.

At 5 p.m. on June 15 an inbound convoy of thirteen ships running in single column ran afoul of the *U-701's* mines. First struck was the tanker *Robert C. Tuttle*. The massive steel hull activated the magnetic detonator causing an explosion directly under her belly; seams were opened and her plating was strained. As her bow settled to the bottom, the rest of the convoy was ordered to zigzag and avoid suspected enemy torpedoes. The tanker *Esso Augusta* ran over another mine that blew off her rudder and stern post and shifted her engine mounts; she stopped dead in the water. (Both tankers were salvaged.)

The escorting destroyer USS *Bainbridge* (DD-246) laid down a defensive pattern of depth charges. The concussion detonated one of the German mines nearby and knocked the destroyer out of action; she limped into port for repairs.

Three hours later the British armed trawler *Kingston Ceylonite* ran over another mine and was literally blown apart. Minesweepers were called in to clear the area. They found all the mines but one. That one was discovered by the *Santore* on June 17. (For complete details of these events see *Shipwrecks of Virginia*, by this author.)

Meanwhile, the *U-701* sought other prey by night, submerged from sight by day. With all the men and machinery generating heat, and with the tepid water preventing its loss, the temperature inside the steel hull was sweltering. When resting on the bottom in the Gulf Stream the powerful current pushed the U-boat so that the rumbling and grating kept the men awake. For a week Degen had no opportunity to use his torpedoes. The crew was getting restless from inactivity, and the close confinement led to short tempers.

So eager was he to make a kill that he nearly torpedoed a sunken ship. Not until the second pass of his set-up approach did he realize that the unlighted vessel had not moved; then he realized his mistake. Afterward, he noticed several ships whose masts and superstructures dotted the Diamond Shoals like grisly steel corpses. They were a galling reminder that preceeding U-boat commanders had reached American shores when the country was unprepared for war. Now it was different.

The spell of idleness was broken the night of June 19–20, when the *U-701* chanced upon the guardship *YP-389* (q.v.) off the Diamond Shoals. The patrol boat was too small to be worthy of a torpedo, so Degen surfaced and gave his crew some target practice. "Apparently the gun crew, groping over-anxiously in the dark, seized every available shell in the ready-use lockers without descrimination." The *YP-389* was pummeled with an unorthodox mixture of shrapnel, high explosive, and incendiary shells, "a wasteful and untidy piece of work" but successful nonetheless. The *YP-389* was set afire and duly sunk.

Then came another week of languor. U-boat warfare alternated between short periods of intense excitement and long days of utter boredom; there was no in between. On June 27, Degen and his crew got more than they bargained for.

The sound man clapped his earphones tighter to his ears. Faintly he heard the sound of approaching screws—lots of them. Degen brought the *U-701* up to periscope depth. The bright sun shone down on a juicy southbound convoy. KS-514 comprised thirty-one ships arranged in nine columns. The convoy was supposed to be moving at eight knots, but because of stragglers was making only a little more than six: a covey of sitting ducks to any U-boat commander worth his salt.

Degen chose his target, got its bearing, and launched two electric torpedoes. One hit the tanker *British Freedom* just forward of the bridge. The explosion "ripped a hole at least 15 ft. long in starboard side, sprung main deck over area of 30 ft. square and demolished bulkhead in No. 3 and 4 tanks, also main pipe line." Captain Francis Main, master, ordered abandon ship. Ten minutes later the *British Freedom* hove to while the crew evacuated the ship in lifeboats. After another ten minutes the captain and chief officer reboarded, found the ship in seaworthy condition, and signalled the crew to come back. She got up steam and headed back for Norfolk.

The *U-701* did not fare as well. The converted yacht *St. Augustine* (PG-54) picked up the U-boat on her sounding gear and drove in with a well-executed depth charge attack. She dropped five cans so close to the descending U-boat that the "electric motors were put out of commission temporarily and the glass of gauges in the conning tower was broken." After effecting repairs the *U-701* dived deep and ran silent.

After several hours of careful searching the *St. Augustine* re-established contact. She dropped a pattern of four depth charges with unerring accuracy. Air bubbles rose to the surface along with four-inch discs of white wadding. This time the U-boat's air-circulators were knocked out; down below the crew started to stifle from the build up of heat.

Once again the persistent patrol boat found her target. This time she rolled four depth charges off her stern racks, each set to detonate at a different depth: one hundred feet, one hundred fifty, two hundred, and three hundred. This vertical "stradling" further damaged the cowering U-boat but did not sink it. However, damage sustained in this uneven battle caused considerable alarm and discomfort.

The next day, June 28, Degen brought the U-boat to the surface. With the air-circulators still out of action he needed to ventilate the hull. The men were nauseated by the heat and humidity; they suffered headaches and vomiting. It was important to run the diesels for several minutes with the main induction vent closed and the hatches open in order to force a draft through the damp, sticky compartments.

Warily, the *U-701* patrolled at periscope depth. At noon a large tanker came into view. Failing to notice the Coast Guard cutters and aircraft that provided escort, Degen launched a torpedo that ran true and found its mark. The cargo of bunker oil was ignited by the explosion; great tongues of flame licked the sky. That was all Degen saw before a concerted depth-charge attack forced him to crash dive.

A type J2F-5 Coast Guard plane dropped two explosive cannisters on the U-boat, then circled and dropped two more. By that time the *U-701* was too deep to feel any harmful effects. Coast Guard cutter *470* laid a seven depth-charge pattern that Degen heard explode far off.

The tanker was the 14,054-ton *William Rockefeller* (q.v.). The crew abandoned ship in the lifeboats and were soon picked up by the *CGC 470*.

The *William Rockefeller* remained afloat throughout the day, burning furiously. When Degen surfaced that night he spotted flames on the horizon and drove in to deliver the coup de grace.

For the next nine days the *U-701* was stuck in the doldrums. The crew suffered boredom and sickness. The only routine out of the ordinary was the periodic surfacing to ventilate the boat; the air-circulators could not be repaired at sea. For that reason the U-boat was cruising on the surface in the midafternoon on July 7.

The sky was clear and the sea smooth. Four lookouts clustered in the conning tower, each scanning a ninety degree quadrant through binoculars. In addition to Lieutenant Degen were Lieutenant (j.g.) Junker, Ensign Bazies, and Warrant Quartermaster Kunert.

Suddenly Junker shouted, "Airplane, there!"

Without a word Bazies and Kunert dived down the hatch.

Degen said, "You saw it too late."

"Yes," Junker replied.

The awful whine of screaming airplane engines chased them down the hatch. The ballast tanks were flooded and all vents closed. The *U-701* went into a crash dive. All too soon came the terrible explosions of two aerial depth charges.

The plane was an Army A-29 bomber with the impersonal designation #9-92-392. It was attached to the 396th Bombardment Squadron. When it left Cherry Point Field, North Carolina for a routine anti-submarine patrol off Cape Hatteras it carried a crew of five: Second Lieutenant Harry Kane (pilot), Second Lieutenant Murray (Navigator), Corporal C.E. Bellamy (bombardier), Corporal L.P. Flowers (radio operator), and Corporal P.L. Broussard (engineer). The plane was armed with one 50-caliber and five 30-caliber machine guns, and held three 325-pound depth charges in its bomb carriage.

For four hours the plane's engines droned noisily fifteen hundred feet above a calm and placid sea. Murray dead-reckoned their course as he spotted landmarks. A lively chatter kept the crew alert to their task. It was like every other patrol they had flown.

Kane: "I was flying in lower broken clouds with visibility about ten miles when off to my left at a distance of about seven miles, I first sighted this boat through an opening in the clouds. Its heading was between 300 and 330 degrees. I immediately made a sharp turn to the left in order to get a closer look and investigate."

It took only moments to realize that the vessel was a U-boat running with decks awash. Instantly the men prepared for action. Kane began his descent for a bombing run.

"At a distance of approximately two miles, the submarine commenced to dive, taking about fifteen seconds to get under the water. When we got over it, we were at an altitude of 50 feet and our speed was about 220 mph. The submarine was then about 10 to 15 feet under water and his swirl from diving was quite pronounced. The navigator and bombardier could easily discern all its outlines and superstructure. We dropped three depth charges, in train; the first fell 25 feet short, the second 100 feet further on, and the third 50 feet beyond the second. Both second and the third depth charges either fell on the submarine or slid off the left side. The second was aft of the conning tower and the third between the bow and the conning tower.''

The effect on the U-boat was devastating. A summary of Degen's interrogation states that ''the submarine was approximately five meters under surface when the first bomb made a direct hit on the topside of the stern of the submarine, tearing a large hole which put out of commission the first engine and caused water to rush in. The second bomb made a direct hit on the topside just aft of the conning tower which tore a large hole and put out of commission all of the engines and mechanisms.''

Other detail comes from the Translation of Statement Prepared by Kapitanleutnant Horst Degen While Held as Prisoner of War at Camp Devens, Mass. ''2 bull's eyes—air bombs. All instruments out of order. Tanks blown. Within 1 to 2 minutes control room and conning tower filled with water. Ship had list to starboard of approximately 20 degrees. C/T hatch opened easily. Ship is at a depth of about 15–20 meters and no longer able to surface. Depth of water about 80–100 meters.''

Elsewhere, Degen noted that the U-701 settled on an even keel listing to starboard at 30 degrees, and that the depth was 60 meters.

Accounts of escape from the sinking U-boat are incoherent and contradictory, in one sense understandable considering the circumstances of stress, in another purposely obfuscatory. As water cascaded into the compartments through massive holes in the pressure hull, and spurted out of disjointed seats and sprung valves, the U-701 headed down on its last dive. So fast did it plummet, and so intent on escape were the survivors, that there was no time to pull the lever that released the rubber life raft. They were literally burped out of the conning tower hatch in the last remaining bubble of air, most without life preservers or escape lungs.

Kane: ''About fifteen seconds after the depth charges were released, a light blue substance appeared about 25 feet to the left of the slick caused by the third depth charge. This started a slight bubbling on the surface. As it increased in intensity, a man popped up in the middle of it.''

The bomber crew was ecstatic. They shouted and cheered madly at what was absolute proof that they had sunk their sub. One man after another popped up through the glistening air bubble, until eighteen of them floated together on the blue Atlantic swells.

An ONI summary of interrogations stated that ''one torpedo man stated he was asleep in the bow compartment at the time of the attack. He said the main lighting failed, but the emergency lights were still on. He made his way to the control room to ask whether they were to abandon ship. He then struggled back to the bow compartment—perhaps to get lifesaving apparatus or some treasured personal possession—and when he again reached the control room water was waist deep.''

Kane: "As we continued to circle, at an altitude of about 300 feet, we noticed another group of men about 100 yards from the first group. There were also about fifteen men in this group. Quite a few of the men were wearing what appeared to be black swimming trunks. I would venture to say that they were Germans. Their complexion was rather light and one of them was exceedingly bald. While circling around the survivors, we dropped four life vests. All this time, Corporal Flowers, the radio operator, was transmitting in detail just what had happened."

The passage of time between the appearance of the first group of men and that of the second is unclear, but may have been as long as thirty minutes—implying that the U-boat lay unmoving on the bottom.

Because a sea was kicking up, the two groups were prevented from seeing one other; each assumed they were the only survivors. The group that escaped through the conning tower hatch consisted of eighteen men; the group that escaped from the bow numbered approximately fifteen. The remainder of the complement of forty-three men must have drowned in the stern and gone down with the boat.

The men were ill-prepared for survival at sea. Most wore only trunks because of the U-boat's opressive heat. Degen: "We had three escape lungs and one life preserver, and in addition two small life preservers which had been thrown to us by the airplane (landplane). Force of sea, 4. The plane circled about several times, threw smoke floats into the sea and then departed." Ironically, Degen recognized the plane as the same type that attacked the *U-701* when it first entered the Eastern Sea Frontier.

According to one official document Kane, "upon sighting a Panamanian freighter left scene of attack and signalled the freighter to follow and pick up the survivors of the destroyed submarine. The freighter acknowledged receipt of the message but failed to comply with instructions." Was this a deliberate act of disobedience? The merchant marine surely had no love for the curs who sank their ships and left their crews to die. "The plane then returned to the attack area but was unable to locate survivors. Large quantities of oil, however, were visible for four or five miles."

Another official document states that Kane spotted a Coast Guard vessel five miles away. After dropping the smoke bomb he "proceeded to the vicinity of this craft. He quickly informed the Coast Guard by aldis lamp and radio, of the sinking of the submarine and the plight of the survivors and then returned as nearly as possible to the site of the sinking and the survivors. The crew of the bomber did not see the men again but they circled the area until the Coast Guard patrol vessel was right below, that is, in the area of the sinking. Kane then informed the vessel that he would have to leave the area because of shortage of fuel, which he reluctantly did at 1630, two and one half hours after the attack."

Degen; "We sighted the plane again, apparently in search of us, but it was unable to find us again because of the rough sea, even though we had remained close together."

With his crew looking on, Kane points to a position on the chart where he believes the *U-701* went down. (Courtesy of the National Archives.)

A cruel combination of circumstances left the German sailors stranded in the broad reaches of the sea; the Gulf Stream current propelled them northward at nearly two knots; the slight chop made indescernible low-lying heads from whitecaps; either Murray's navigation was off, or he did not take the drift into account.

The *CGC 472* searched diligently without success. The *PC-480*, which was escorting a convoy twenty-five miles away, was called off duty to help locate the U-boat's survivors.

As evening settled in, Boatswain's Mate Hansel and Midshipman Lange decided to swim to shore, estimated by Degen as thirty miles away. (Perhaps they intended to reach one of the half-sunken derelicts. Or perhaps Degen's measure of distance was intentionally overestimated.) Neither Hansel nor Lange were ever seen again. Then came the darkness, and the uncertainty. With as many as five men clinging to one life preserver their physical resources were severely strained. Around nine o'clock Coxswain Etzweiler was unable to support himself any longer, and drowned. In group one, eighteen was whittled down to fifteen.

The long, dark night dragged on. The men kicked, coughed, gagged, and fought to keep their heads out of the water. The loneliness was interminable. Degen: "We consoled ourselves with hope in the morrow. A few of us were ready to give up, but these we cheered up, so that we were all still together when it became light again."

But with light came heat. The men were smeared with oil: an irritant that got into their eyes and the pores of their skin, but which mitigated the effects of sunburn. They had no food and, worse, no water. Salt stung their lips and sickening sea water found their tongues and throats. Their suffering was horrible.

Degen: "Around 1200 a Coast Guard ship passed within 2,000 meters of us at slow speed. Despite our cries and waving we remained unnoticed. The ship passed out of sight. Although we all hoped that it would return, some of the men now gave up. Damrow and Schmidtmeyer were delirious as though in fever. Around 1400 the following drowned, one after another: Damrow, Schmidtmeyer, Grundler, Bahr, Weiland, Schuller." Half the group was dead. "We saw many airplanes—apparently we were still being sought."

A massive air-sea rescue operation was taking place. Army, Navy, and Coast Guard planes were alerted about the situation; they flew in a steady treadmill past the reported sinking position, which already was in doubt. Both the *CGC 472* and the *PC 480* were combing the ocean off the Diamond Shoals, or following an oil slick some fifteen miles long.

For the beleaguered German sailors the entire day passed without relief of their fears, their waning strength, their growling stomachs, their parched throats. They lay on their backs clinging to the few bits of jetsam they possessed, and clenched shut their eyes against the hot, blinding sun. Time and again waves washed over faces burnt raw. The salt got into eyes, nose, and mouth: a constant anguish. Two firemen died: Bosse and Fischer. And then there were seven.

Sometime late in the day the men from group one received a revelation when a man from group two appeared in their midst. Degen: "We came across apprentice seaman Laskowski, who wore two escape lungs and who was still very fresh. He reported that several more of the crew had escaped, among others the first and second watch officers."

Despair set in. "With the oncoming darkness we huddled close together in order to survive in this way also the second night. Fortunately the sea subsided. We found a lemon and a cocoanut. Each man received a swallow of cocoanut milk, a piece of the meat and everyone had the opportunity to suck the lemon. A tremendous refreshment! Our thirst was awful, and the large quantities of salt water burned mouth, nose, and stomach. (The cocoanut was opened by Vaupel after the greatest exertion with the help of the oxygen flask from the escape lung.)"

A believer would claim divine intervention, but the food was more likely flotsam from a torpedoed merchant ship and was therefore the offering of innocent men killed for the sake of Germany's territorial expansion. Besides, the meager repast was not the savior of all the enemy aggressors. Despite Laskowski's freshness and double buoyancy, he died, as did Leu and Michalek. "All three were delerious and yelled terribly." They were down to five.

"At dawn my strength began to leave me too. I seem to recollect that I talked nonsense and that Kunert kept on quieting me. As the sea was still like a pond, I kept up the practice of discarding my life preserver, saying that I would swim to shore. I assumed that with a few strokes I would feel bottom under my feet and would be able to stand up, but every time I tried this I went under. That would bring me up again and I would swim back to my life preserver. This occurrence must have happened many times. Then I lost consciousness."

About the time that Degen passed out, another patrol left the Naval Air Station at Elizabeth City, North Carolina to go look for him. Belonging to Squadron ZP-14, the *K-8* was a lighter-than-air craft better known as a blimp. It's pilot was Ensign G.S. Middleton. The *K-8* proceeded southeast to the Wimble Shoals Light Buoy, then picked up an oil slick which it followed northward.

At 11:55 a.m., the *K-8* became the Germans' salvation when it "located the first survivor, who appeared to be strong and uninjured. The search was continued in the same area and two more survivors were located within a short time. Information, giving position, and the state of the survivors, was sent to the Coast Guard Station, Elizabeth City, including the fact that weather conditions were such that a Coast Guard plane could

Courtesy of the National Archives.

land at sea. The search continued and survivor number four was located approximately one-quarter of a mile from the group of three. A life raft was then lowered to the strongest survivor hoping that he would be able to help other survivors, and shortly thereafter food, blankets, first aid kit, knife and water were lowered to the survivors in the raft. The first survivor to board the raft was directed to the other survivors and picked all of them up. The search was then continued east about 15 miles following the slick and debris to its source.

"Along this route, three dead men in life jackets were found. They were being attended by several sharks. There were many life jackets noted to be floating among the seaweed, slick, and debris. While returning to the life raft, three other survivors were located by the *K-8* approximately five miles from the raft, also separated by one-quarter to one-half miles." The survivors were found ninety miles from where the *U-701* went down.

Degen: "I awakened as though I had been asleep when I suddenly heard myself called. About 30 meters away sat Kunert, Vaupel and Grootheer making for me in a white rubber boat. I was taken into the boat as Kunert was about to open a can of pineapple with a knife. Out of a can already opened Grootheer gave me tomatoes to eat, and all the while a Zeppelin airship circled about us."

Meanwhile, Elizabeth City was a beehive of activity as word circulated about the German survivors and plane No. 167 prepared for take-off. The pilot of the J2-F5 was Lieutenant Commander Richard Burke, the same man who had flown to the rescue of the only two survivors from the torpedoed freighter *Chenango* (q.v.).

"He located the *K-8* at 1423 and after scouting the vicinity for a few minutes, he also saw the seven survivors scattered over an area of eight miles. Landing on the water where the *K-8* had dropped flares to indicate wind direction and to spot the first survivors, he first proceeded to pick up the three individual scattered survivors and then taxied about five miles west to the life raft and took on board the remaining survivors. Rescue operations were completed at 1535, and during the actual operation, another Coast Guard plane, Type J-4F, Flying Fortress, circled the area taking pictures."

Degen was completely naked, and so far gone that his memory of the rescue was faulty. "As the coastal waters are thoroughly oily, we were completely covered with a thick black layer of oil. Now, while in the boat, the sun shone down upon us, and this resulted in a terrible sunburn. ... A large flying boat arrived and took us on board. We were given water and hot coffee. All four of us were completely finished. ... We were delivered to the Navy Hospital at Norfolk where we were treated with the greatest care and attention and made into human beings once more. There we found three other survivors: Seaman Seldte, Apprentice Seaman Faust, Seaman Schwendel." All three were from group two. While Degen was in delirium Kundt passed away.

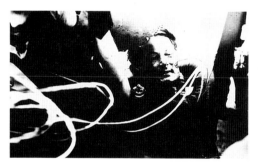

All courtesy of the National Archives.

After surviving the forty-nine-hour ordeal afloat, at the end of which he slipped into and out of consciousness, it is understandable that he never noticed the other three men already on the plane, or that he believed he had not gotten sunburned until the final hour, or that he did not realize that he was covered with oil from his own U-boat, and that the major oil spills came from the tanker he had sunk and from other ships torpedoed by his fellow pack wolves.

Perhaps upon reflection Degen accepted the deaths of his shipmates as just retribution for the suffering they and their kind had inflicted upon so many innocent men, women, and children whose greatest crime in life was the occupation of land which Germany desired to annex.

Degen's memory also failed to record the medical attention offered by the Coast Guard Pharmacist's Mate aboard the plane. "All were given mild stimulants, water, coffee, whiskey, and sandwiches. A hypodermic was administered to Captain Degen. ... One of them badly weakened and exhausted stated 'you come joost in time, odderwise, I die.' All except the Captain asked for cigarettes."

Other than their skins the German sailors saved surprisingly little. The records are unclear. "Four of the survivors were naked and three had no bathing trunks." Elsewhere, "Four pairs of swimming trunks and two escape lungs and one rubber life jacket constituted the sole effects." Did one man have swimming trunks swathing his forehead?

Within three hours of rescue the U-boat crew underwent interrogation at the Norfolk Navy Yard. ONI reported that the men "with one exception, were fairly security-minded, but not to the degree generally encountered. Degen had probably admonished his crew not to divulge matters of military importance, but a number of factors—his own garrulousness, his independent interpretation of security, the swiftness of the sinking, and the prompt preliminary interrogation—contributed to weaken the resistance of the survivors to incisive questioning."

From the U-boat crew was learned the entire history of the *U-701's* construction, trials, and first two missions—although selectively left out was the loss of the officer washed overboard in the North Sea. Degen related the highpoints of his background in the German navy, including names, dates, and places of negligible intelligence value. Degen was proud to be Erich Topp's protege: he "taught me all I know."

ONI noted that "the condition of the survivors unquestionably weakened their resistance to questioning. As the prisoners recovered, their defenses against interrogation stiffened."

Little did ONI know how devious was Degen's apparent candor. He readily admitted to attacking ships on dates that coincided with the attacks against the *YP-389, British Freedom,* and *William Rockefeller,* but left out all mention of his mine-laying operations in the Chesapeake Bay approaches. He did not brag about the four ships that ran afoul of his

202

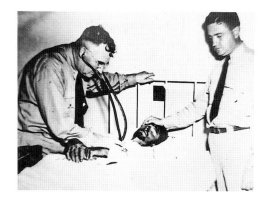

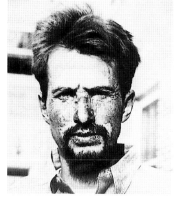

All courtesy of the National Archives.

"infernal devices" even though a radio transmission from headquarters praised him for the success of that phase of his mission.

On the contrary, "Degen held the opinion that shallow waters presented opportunities to mine-laying U-boats, both in the paths of convoys and at harbor entrances. He admitted the possibility of large U-boats carrying mines, but said such matters are held secret."

By such deceptive sincerity did Degen keep the biggest secret of all. Not until after the war did he receive credit for his "kills" off Virginia Beach, and for the unholy ruckus caused by enemy incursion into a supposedly protected area. In that he was a true patriot to his country.

On July 11, after two days in the hospital, Degen received an unexpected honor. Kane and the entire crew of the bomber that sank his boat visited him at his bedside "and inquired after our well being." Little was recorded of this historic event unique in the annals of war.

The next day the crew of the U-701 boarded a train bound for Fort Devens, Massachussetts, "where we shall now pass the days of our detention as prisoners of war. We are being correctly handled and receive good treatment. There is plenty of good food to eat."

Certainly, German prisoners received better treatment than American POW's received at the hand of the Nazis.

Although the U-701 did not reach its first birthday (July 16), its crew celebrated four birthdays in American POW camps. During that time Degen wrote to Admiral Carl Doenitz requesting decorations for the surviving crew members. (The Red Cross reported the men's names through Axis contacts.) For Quartermaster Gunter Kunert, who held Degen's head out of the water for so many hours and saved his captain from drowning, he requested the Iron Cross, First Class. For the others he requested the Iron Cross, Second Class. His gratitude and love for his men were unfailing.

In June 1946, all seven men were repatriated in good health.

An interesting postscript to the U-701 saga occurred forty years later. On the anniversary of the sinking, Harry Kane flew to West Germany and met once again his former adversary Horst Degen. They spent a week reminiscing about that time long ago when, with their nations at war, they had met as enemies. This time, in peace, they emerged from their engagement as friends. A luxury, of course, that only survivors can afford.

What of the sunken U-boat? An analysis of the various positions given by Kane and Degen make it clear that neither one knew precisely where he was at the time of the attack. Kane thought he was off Avon, Degen claimed contradictorily that his boat went down in either 80 to 100 meters (265 to 330 feet) or 60 meters (200 feet); at either depth the boat was beyond easy salvage. ONI evaluations based upon direction and time of drift placed the U-701 somewhere off the Diamond Shoals. A plot of these locations on a navigation chart yields a triangular area tens of square miles in area. Somewhere within that three-sided boundary the U-701 lay rusting away.

Over the years there has been much speculation among wreck divers concerning the evidence contained in the testimony of the participants. Which of it was mistaken, which of it was intentionally misleading, and which of it, if any, was accurate? Conclusions were hotly debated. About the only item agreed upon was the approximate depth: between 100 and 150 feet. (This despite Degen's admonitions to the contrary. One would expect him to deceive ONI in order to dissuade the Navy from locating and salvaging the U-boat and recovering its secret coding equipment.)

But there is another reason for assuming the depth to be shallower than stated: the number of survivors. All submariners undergo rigorous underwater escape training; those who fail are weeded out of the program. Germans were well trained in the use of the Drager lung: a breathing device built into an inflatable vest that recirculates oxygen supplied from a small pressurized flask. With it there have been some miraculous escapes.

Consider the case of the *U-550*. It torpedoed the *Pan Pennsylvania* on April 16, 1944, south of Nantucket. Blown to the surface by depth charges from the U.S. destroyer escort *Joyce* (DE-317), it was then rammed by the destroyer escort *Gandy* and the *Peterson* (DE-172). Some of the U-boat crew were cut down by machine gun bullets; thirteen were rescued; the rest went down with the boat in some 270 feet of water. Nearly three weeks later three bodies were found floating on the surface; all wore escape lungs, one was sitting in a raft. Autopsies revealed that they had died only recently, leading to the conclusion that they had escaped from the U-boat subsequent to its sinking.

But they had escape lungs. Most of the men of the *U-701* made it to the surface unaided by either flotation or breathing apparatus: a practical impossibility from the depth ascribed by Degen. One man might make it, possibly two or more, but not thirty-three out of forty-three men. The high rate of successful escape implied shallow depth.

Many people have talked about looking for the *U-701*, some have even gone out on the ocean to search for it (including the author). There was considerable competition to be the discoverer. However, if there is one characteristic necessary for finding previously unlocated shipwrecks, that characteristic is dedication. Then, when all the common search methods fail to yield positive results, devise creative alternatives.

This was the tack taken by Uwe Lovas, along with his brother Ron and friend Alan Russell. When Lovas took up diving it was with the specific intention of discovering long lost shipwrecks; and, the highest priority among those wrecks he wanted to find were U-boats. In both quests he has succeeded admirably.

Lovas did not go the way of the average wreck diver, by joining clubs and signing up on charters. He bought his own boat, equipped it with all the best electronics, and set out to explore "hang" numbers: loran coordinates that come from trawler and dragger captains; these are the obstructions on which boats have "hung" their nets. During the revelation stage on the path to discovery, not only did Lovas and his companions have to learn to operate a small boat, they had to become proficient at interpreting the readouts of their electronics.

The quest began in earnest in 1986, and almost immediately Lovas found his first U-boat, in the Potomac River: the *U-1105*. It was brought to the U.S. after World War Two because the Navy wanted to study the German innovation that made U-boats invisible to sonar: a rubber skin laminated onto the outside of the hull. After a thorough examination the U-boat was scuttled in 80 feet of water, and forgotten—until Lovas began compiling a list of U-boats lost in diveable depths. A photograph taken while the *U-1105* was sinking revealed trees in the background; examination of the records revealed a typographical error in which two digits of the lat-lon position were transposed. After such intense archival research, Lovas found the actual field work deceptively easy, and discovered the wreck almost immediately.

The search for the *U-701*, however, was a long one that required great patience—years of patience. Nevertheless, Lovas maintained his focus and never lost sight of his goal. It was *U-701* or bust. First came bust. His boat was destroyed in a highway crash as he was trailering it home after a fruitless day running grid patterns with a depth recorder. Repairs took the rest of the dive season and part of the winter. That was when he decided that the grid pattern method was not going to work; it was too time consuming and left too much cause for doubt. Besides, there was an awful lot of territory to cover.

Deep contemplation decided him upon a different means to his goal. He had to cut a broader swath across the ocean floor during electronic sweeping operations than a depth recorder would allow. The obvious tool for this kind of work on a bottom that is relatively flat and without rock piles or high relief is side-scan sonar. But due to the shifting nature of the sand and the height of the underwater dunes, Lovas decided that his needs would be better served by a magnetometer: a device that detects anomalies in the Earth's magnetic field such as those produced by large masses of iron or steel of which ships' hulls are constructed.

Lovas did not just go out and buy a unit off the shelf, however. He built his own. After long conversations with Richard Lawrence, director of the North Carolina Division of Archives and History, at Fort Fisher, he decided to design a unit similar to the one Lawrence had used with such success in locating archaeological shipwreck sites in rivers. Instead of utilizing a towfish that is dragged through the water by a cable, this model incorporates a sensor head mounted on the bow of the boat.

Lovas also wrote the computer program to drive the magnetometer. This was no easy task: it took forty versions in the software before he developed a program without bugs. By interfacing the magnetometer's computer program with the boat's loran he could recreate his daily plot at home, see exactly what ground was covered, review the ''hits'' that signified anomalies, and return to each "hit" with precision and reliability. Instead of hauling nets and "hanging" on a wreck, he dragged an electronic web whose return signal pinpointed magnetic masses. The strength of the anomaly determined the size of the target. What's more, a magnetometer can detect anomalies that are buried in the sand and, therefore, hidden from the beams of scanners and depth recorders.

Even with all this electronic gadgetry, however, you still can't find wrecks unless you're looking in the right place. By carefully reading all the available reports and weighing each piece of evidence in light of its probable accuracy, Lovas made some deductions that he hoped would steer him in the right direction. Crucial to finding the *U-701* was locating the *Empire Thrush* (q.v.). Just prior to being sunk, Degen claimed to have seen the funnel and masts of a sunken ship toward shore. A review of the Eastern Sea Frontier records revealed that of the four wrecks still visible at that time on the Diamond Shoals, only the *Empire Thrush* showed its funnel and both masts. If he could find the British freighter he could then concentrate his search efforts eastward of the wreck, gradually working out to deeper depths.

To make a long story short, his detective work eventually paid off. Not only did he find the *Empire Thrush*, he found several other wrecks in the process. The end of a search that rivaled in enterprise the quest of the golden fleece came on June 25, 1989. Unfortunately, neither Lovas nor his companions realized at the time that they had driven over the *U-701*. It was only one of several targets they had "magged" that day, and not the highest on their list of priorities for checking out. It was at the extreme edge of the grid square drawn around the U-boat's most likely position.

It was not until weeks later, while reviewing the data in his computer files, that Lovas decided that the "hit" recorded that day should be checked out. A wreck is not officially identified until it is seen with the eye and touched by the hand. Then came bad weather and other distractions, not the least of which was Alan Russell leaving the country because of his job.

So it was that on August 27, only Uwe and and brother Ron were on the boat when they returned to the site first located two months previous. Conditions were fine, there was no current, the depth recorder showed a spike, but time after time the grapnel would not catch. Finally, Ron went down the buoy line—and into the history books. He set the hook, popped up, swam back to the boat, and breathlessly told his brother that the wreck was a U-boat, or, at least, what appeared to be a U-boat. He thought there was a conning tower.

Uwe could not understand his brother's lack of certainty, but he was so excited by the prospect of closing the book on the *U-701* that he started hyperventilating even as he donned his dive gear. He had to force himself to calm down. As he neared the wreck he knew that the quest was over: he saw the outline of the saddle tank. Then, he saw the grapnel in the conning tower, the radio direction finder (RDF) antenna, and forward of that, the

Above: the conning tower is practically all that is exposed. Below: behind the RDF loop (ratio direction finder) is the open conning tower hatch. (Both photos by Dave Sommers, via Uwe Lovas.)

Above: the forward deck gun, with the conning tower in the background. Below: Steve Lang examines the 88-mm deck gun. (Both photos by Dave Sommers, via Uwe Lovas.)

88-mm deck gun. There was no doubt that it was the *U-701*, but what had caused his brother's disorientation was the boat's state of interment: the wreck was nearly completely buried, with only those parts just described being visible above the surface of the sand.

The following month Hurricane Hugo disturbed the bottom so heavily that most of the pressure hull aft of the conning tower became exposed. Now the damage holes were obvious. Then slowly over the course of the next several months the sand filled back in and covered most of the wreck except for the gun and conning tower and part of the ballast tank. Since the conning tower hatch and the forward torpedo loading hatch are both open, it can readily be seen that the interior of the boat is choked with sand right up to the level of the hatches.

The wreck lies in an area of migrating dunes which move in the same fashion as ocean waves but at a much slower pace. During the deposition phase the bottom can rise as much as ten feet in comparison to nearby scours. That explains why the hull comes and goes: more is exposed when the wreck is in the trough of a dune than when it is in the crest.

Why is the wreck only 105 feet deep despite Degen's continued claim (even after the war, when the reason for deceipt no longer had meaning) that the depth was 200 feet or more? Lovas asked him about that. Degen's comment was that his belief was based upon the reading on the U-boat's depth gauge, which possibly had been knocked out of calibration by concussion from the severe depth charging: a plausible line of reasoning considering the circumstances.

Uwe Lovas denies that he was "obsessed" with finding the *U-701*, unless you define obsession as driving to North Carolina every weekend (he lives in Fredericksburg, Virginia) for three years, towing a boat, and then exploring the offshore waters for hours on end in the hot sun and churning waves, fighting off seasickness. Perhaps. If nothing else, he is persistent. And that persistence has paid off.

Photo by Uwe Lovas.

The *Venore's* sister ship. (Courtesy of the National Archives.)

VENORE

Built: 1921   Sunk: January 23, 1942
Previous names: *Charles G. Black, G. Harrison Smith* Depth: Unknown
Gross tonnage: 8,017   Dimensions: 550′ × 72′ × 43′
Type of vessel: Bulk ore carrier   Power: Oil-fired steam
Builder: Bethlehem Ship Building Corporation, Sparrows Point, Maryland
Owner: Ore Steam Ship Company
Port of registry: New York
Cause of sinking: Torpedoed by *U-66*
Location: In the vicinity of the Diamond Shoals

The *Venore* was designed as a hermaphrodite vessel whose cargo compartments were built as ore holds that could be converted to oil tanks. For the first nineteen years of her life she served the Standard Oil Company of New Jersey as a tanker, with a carrying capacity of 140,050 barrels that she could pump at the rate of 5,000 barrels per hour. She mostly plied the coastal route between the Texas oil fields and the New Jersey refineries.

While war raged in Europe, the Esso tanker and her crew received official praise from no less a person than Admiral Chester W. Nimitz. "The Commanding Officer, USS *Satterlee*, has stated that in his opinion the intelligence, initiative, cooperation, and the faculty of acting instinctively in a logical manner, in unforseen circumstances, shown by Lt. Comdr. Frank Irving Shaw, Merchant Marine Reserve, upon this occasion, are deserving of special commendation. The Bureau of Navigation takes pleasure in commending you for your prompt and efficient performance of duty in an unusual situation."

The incident deserving of such homage was described by Captain Shaw, master of the *Venore* when she was the *Charles G. Black*. "While this vessel was en route from Corpus Christi, Texas, to New York, April 17, 1940, the destroyer USS *Satterlee* (DD 190), Lieutenant Commander Harold R. Demarest, USN, commanding signaled this vessel in Latitude

28°57′ North, Longitude 79°39′ West. We were informed that they were in need of bunker fuel and were requested, if we could, to supply approximately 500 barrels of bunkers, which would be sufficient to carry them to Norfolk, Va., their port of destination.

"The *Black* was stopped, the destroyer *Satterlee* came along our port side; 528.8 barrels from our bunkers were discharged into her fuel tanks without incident. Our detention was 2 hours, 23 minutes. As all communication was accomplished by wig-wag and international code, Second Mate Aksel Selvik and Third Mate Frederick Austin are to be commended for the efficient manner in which signals between the vessels were sent and received."

On September 26, 1940 the Ore Steam Ship Company bought the combination bulk cargo carrier and converted her for use in the ore trade. In that capacity, "on December 16, 1941, the steamship *Venore*, light, stout, staunch and strong and in every respect seaworthy, under the command of Captain Fritz Duurloo sailed from Baltimore bound for Cruz Grande, Chile. She arrived at Cruz Grande on January 4, 1942, and on the same day, with a full cargo of 22,250 tons of iron ore, she sailed for Sparrows Point, Maryland, via the Panama Canal. She was through the canal on January 16 and the voyage continued uneventful or without mishap until the evening of January 23."

All forty-two men aboard the *Venore* undoubtedly hoped that the remainder of the voyage would be as boring. At nine knots the ship proceeded "on a zigzag course with only dimmed side lights in good weather." The tanker *Empire Gem* (q.v.) overtook the *Venore* just before reaching the Diamond Shoals, and, because of her faster speed, became the first of the pair to run the U-boat gauntlet.

A protest signed by three surviving officers and a seaman stated, "Those on the *Venore* heard a report which sounded like an explosion, immediately after which the *Empire Gem* which was forward of the *Venore's* starboard beam burst into flames. Captain Duurloo who was on the bridge ordered a hard left rudder, and the *Venore's* side lights were turned off. And as the *Venore* was swinging to port with the *Gem* astern, he as well as others who were on the vessel observed a submarine round the *Gem's* stern proceeding fast toward the *Venore*. The *Venore* continued on at full speed toward the shore in a westerly direction, those on her bridge last observing the submarine off her port quarter as the *Venore* ran out of the illumination from the burning tanker, and after entering the darkness, the *Venore's* course was changed to starboard."

Radio Operator Vernon Minzey began a continuous transmission of distress calls.

Some fancy maneuvering must have been occurring at this time. The *Venore* initially turned to the west, but was forced by the shoals to head north. The *Empire Gem* was out of control and slowly veering to westward across the *Venore's* track. At attack speed the U-boat curved past one victim and chased after another. Instead of being trapped between the proverbial rock and a hard spot, the *Venore* was caught between a shoal and a submarine.

The survivors' protest claims that "not very long after the *Venore's* course was changed to starboard, those on her bridge observed an amber flashing light off her port bow. After counting the flashes and checking the bearing of the light, they concluded it might be the light at Cape Hatteras, but in a little while it was gone." They suspected afterward that the U-boat was imitating the Cape Hatteras light buoy in order to lure the ship to destruction.

Whether or not that was true, the *U-66* caught up with the *Venore* and launched a torpedo into her port side forward. The impact was slight and damage insignificant. With half the crew at their duty stations Captain Duurloo once again swung the *Venore's* bow toward shore, where the U-boat might not follow. However, "the strain of the impending attack was too much for some members of the crew and panic broke out among them. In direct violation of the Captain's orders, some of the crew, mostly negroes, began to lower the lifeboats. Due to the headway, two boats were lost at once, one of them containing a large number of men. Another seaman jumped overboard and was lost. In fact, only one of the three lifeboats remained afloat and in this boat there were only two colored seamen."

The U-boat dogged them all the way. Zapp raced ahead and reached a good firing angle before launching another torpedo. Thirty-five minutes after the first attack "there was a terrific explosion on the *Venore's* port side at No. 9 ballast tank. Smoke, flame and water shot high into the air. The vessel lurched and listed to port, her hatches being brought under the water." (No. 9 ballast tank was aft of the bridge and forward of the poop.)

The ship's lights were knocked out by the blast. With his vessel listing at forty-five degrees, Captain Duurloo had no choice but to order abandon ship.

Vernon Minzey stayed at his key. Instead of broadcasting warnings about the attack on the *Empire Gem*, he kept the authorities up to date on the condition of his own ship: "Torpedoed twice 15 miles south of Diamond Shoals. . . . 15 miles south of Diamond Shoals torpedoed twice no news yet still listing badly. . . . Cannot stay afloat much longer want help immediately. . . . Still here got Norfolk message listing more now. . . . " Then came a long, neverending silence.

"In a well-disciplined manner" the fourth lifeboat was lowered to the surface of the sea. According to the official Navy report, "it was not until the lifeboat had cast off that it was first realized that the Captain and Radio Operator were not accounted for. By that time, however, it was physically impossible to return to the stricken ship. The third mate, Andrew Johnson, related after his rescue that he and the radio operator were in the pilot house with Captain Duurloo, when the Captain ordered him to get into the boat.

'I went aft with the wireless operator to get into the boat,' he said. Jackson further told how he slid down the forward falls and became entangled in the falls as he plunged head first into the boat. 'When they had gotten me untangled from the falls, I found they had cast off and the wireless operator was not in the boat. I don't know what became of him.' The third mate did not know what had become of the Captain either.''

The men in the lifeboat had their own troubles: playing tag with the killer U-boat. As the giant hulk of the *Venore* rolled over by degrees, the *U-66* drove up to within a few hundred yards of her port quarter and blinked "a light which appeared to have the strength of a good-sized flashlight. It shone from about ten feet above the water and it seemed to be trying to locate victims of the attacks. This lasted only a few minutes and then the submarine was swallowed by the darkness.''

After falling prey to one ruse, the *Venore's* men suspected another that might prove more deadly. Said Allen Horten, able bodied seaman, "Those Boches are plenty smart. . . . Those dirty Germans have a habit now, you know, of coming up alongside a lifeboat and machine-gunning the men. We weren't going to take any chances, so we stayed in the bottom.'' Such strong beliefs lead to extreme caution.

All night long the lifeboat bobbed on the gentle Atlantic swells, hovering near the stricken ship. The men expected rescue at any moment. However, the surfboat dispatched from Ocracoke in response to the *Venore's* calls for help was diverted by the flames of the *Empire Gem*, which was on the way to the site of the *Venore*. According to Navy Staff Duty Notes, "C.G. *Frederick Lee* and *PC453* ordered to scene of action. *Frederick Lee* on patrol about 30 miles north of Diamond Shoals at time of torpedoing.''

The Navy summary of the incident is contradictory about the condition of the foundering vessel. "The next morning, the *Venore* was seen lying on her side, like a crippled giant. She had capsized after the attack by the second torpedo.'' Capsize means to flip over in an inverted position, upside down; to turn turtle. "On her side'' means lying on her beam ends—ninety degrees over, not one hundred eighty. No clarification comes from the American Marine Insurance Syndicates notice of loss: "She was either lying on her side or had completely turned over with her bottom up.''

After standing by their ship for more than twelve hours, the twenty-one crewmen decided to shift for themselves. They "pulled away from the scene in their lifeboat, and about noon the same day sighted the lifeboat containing the two negroes. Efforts to rescue these men failed; their boat had been swamped by heavy seas; both were believed to have been lost. The survivors also sighted a patrol plane, which apparently did not see the survivors.'' Of the two patrol boats sent after them there was no sign.

Thus the men were forced to spend a second night enduring the cold in their open boat. The Gulf Stream current carried the lifeboat northward. Staff Duty Notes record that at 3 a.m. "about 70 miles south of Cape

Henry survivors of *Venore* heard what was believed to be surf roaring. Saw two lights on water 3 miles away and identified the sound as sub recharging batteries."

Finally, "the next morning, January 25, at 1035, the SS *Tennessee*, a Texas Oil Company tanker approached from the south and the 21 men in the remaining lifeboat were rescued." They had spent thirty-eight hours adrift. Despite the cold air, the temperate Gulf Stream water undoubtedly saved the men from suffering more than they did.

The loss of the *Venore* cost her reinsurers $2,250,000 for the hull alone, exclusive of cargo. No policy could replace the twenty-one lives.

The *Venore* sank unobserved with her position in doubt. After so many twists and turns her second engineer thought she finally sank six or seven miles east of the Diamond Shoals. In 1944, a Coast Guard survey team did an extensive analysis of the various reported positions of both the *Empire Gem* and the *Venore*, and of their tracks and speeds, and concluded that the wreck they found on June 29 was that of the *Venore*.

"Wreck is lying on its side and provides a fathometer target 63' deep in 95' feet of water." The position was given as 35-04.8 N/75-23.6 W. "No other wreck can be located in a position which would make its identification as the *Venore* logical. Underwater photographs indicate that the vessel is a war casualty. . . . One frame shows plates which have been ripped by a violent explosion."

It was deemed no hazard to navigation and was not wire-dragged or otherwise demolished. Oddly, the identity of the *Venore* has not been established by modern day divers.

The *U-66* returned to the Eastern Sea Frontier in the summer of 1943, under the command of Kapitanleutnant Markworth, and sank the *Esso Gettysburg* and *Bloody Marsh*. On May 6, 1944, under the command of Kapitanleutnant Seehausen, the *U-66* was sunk off the Cape Verde Islands.

Venore. (Courtesy of the National Archives

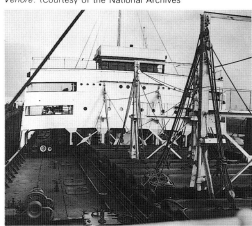

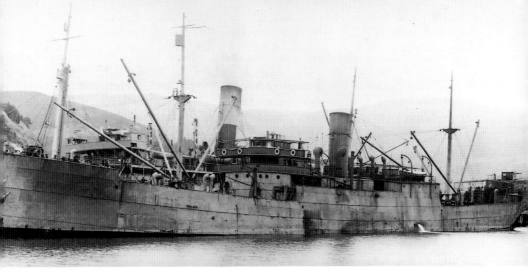

Verdun, sister ship of the *Veturia*. (Courtesy of the Steamship Historical Society of America.)

VETURIA

Built: 1912
Previous names: None
Gross tonnage: 5,554
Type of vessel: Freighter
Builder: Russell & Company, Pt. Glasgow, Scotland
Owner: Veturia Steam Ship Company, Ltd. (Gow, Harrison & Company)
Port of registry: Glasgow, Scotland
Cause of sinking: Ran aground
Location: 26895.6

Sunk: February 20, 1918
Depth: 30 feet
Dimensions: 424′ × 56′ × 28′
Power: Coal-fired steam

40246.4

The British schooner *Veturia* got lost in a thick fog on the morning of February 20, 1918 and suddenly found herself stranded in shoal water. Her situation was precarious: she was slowly being pounded to pieces by the crashing waves.

Cruising off the Diamond Shoals was the Coast Guard cutter *Onondaga*. At 9:00 a.m. she picked up the *Veturia's* SOS and immediately changed course to assist. The *Onondaga* also relayed the message to the radio station at Beaufort, which then telephoned the Coast Guard stations in the vicinity of the wreck. The life-savers pooled their resources. A surfboat was launched and "worked in surf for some time, but the Sea being rough and tide strong was unable to cross the outer bar." However, the staunch efforts of the four crews did not come to naught. By firing rockets from shore they elicited a response from the stranded steamer, and were able to pinpoint her location on the outer shoals.

For thirteen hours the *Onondaga* searched for the grounded vessel which, because of the unusually oppressive fog, could not be located. It was not until ten o'clock that night that the cutter succeeded in hailing the *Veturia*. Heavy seas prevented the *Onondaga* from approaching any closer than two hundred yards. Captain Frank Mills, master of the *Veturia*, signalled that it was his desire to abandon ship. The *Onondaga* then lowered boats which fought through the surf to the *Veturia's* side. Seven trips were required to take off the crew, and it was not until two o'clock in the morning that the last of the forty-seven men (and three cats) safely boarded the cutter. The daring rescue operation was a complete success.

Captain Mills saved his papers and the ship's log, but "none of the effects of the officers and crew was saved except a few articles carried in the hands." It was not until 10 a.m. that the shifting wind blew out the fog and laid down the seas enough for a surfboat to reach the scene of the wreck. By that time, of course, the *Veturia* was abandoned.

The *Onondaga* took the *Veturia's* crew to Wilmington, North Carolina, and there a curious situation arose. Captain Mills and his officers were put up at the Orton hotel, the British seamen at the Imperial, and the twenty-two Chinese crew members at the Stonewall. Follow-up events were described thus:

"According to the English seamen's law, the pay of a sailor on board a British merchantmen ceases in the event the ship on which he is serving is wrecked, and he is paid off and given his liberty, if he so desires. Otherwise, if he wishes to remain in the service, he must so inform his officer. Then provision will be made for his return to the home port of the vessel upon which he was serving, and the owner of the ship becomes responsible for his keep. All of the British members of the crew declared their intention to remain in the service of the company and will be maintained here, although their pay ceases.

"The Celestial contingent of the crew presented a rather different aspect. According to the immigration laws of America, Chinese are not allowed to enter this country. Those doing so by indirection, as is the case with the Chinese members ... are to be held under close surveillance until arrangements can be made for their return to the country of their nativity.

"Those landed yesterday were placed under a guard from the United States naval reserve force here. They were quartered at a hotel, and a restaurant keeper given instructions to provide dishes dear to the Celestial heart for their nourishment. The guard had orders to allow their charges all liberties consistent with the regulations, and to permit them to walk about the streets. Only one of their number is able to speak intelligible English."

The *Veturia* eventually broke apart and became a total loss. The cargo of nitrates taken on in Colon, Panama never reached its destination at Hampton Roads, Virginia. The vessel sank into obscurity. Furthermore, the ship's name was erroneously reported in Coast Guard documents as the *Ventura*, the *Vintura*, and in the newspapers as the *Eturia*; was listed alternately as a tramp steamer and as a schooner; and was given the wrong tonnage.

As great as these difficulties present for the researcher, the remains of the steel wreck located by Uwe Lovas yielded its secrets with uncommon ease. Although only a four-foot high chunk of encrusted metal the size of a van protruded out of the sand, that chunk was the extreme tip of the bow and possessed the ship's bell. Steve Lang spotted it right away, and together he and Lovas recovered the bronze prize. It was engraved with the ship's name.

The depth of water over the wreck varies due to alternating cycles of scouring and dune development. The water may sometimes be five feet shallower, in which case no part is exposed at all.

For now, at least, the bulk of the *Veturia* is interred in the pure white sand of the outer Diamond Shoals, marked by a small steel tombstone from which the epitaph has been removed for safekeeping. Perhaps someday the wreck will reappear in its entirety. It bears watching.

Photo by Steve Lang.

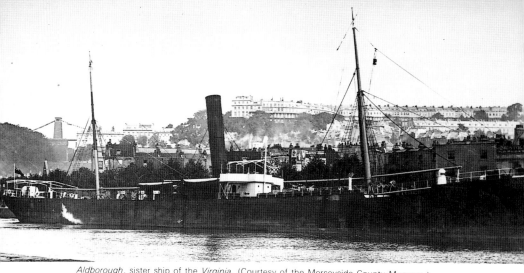

Aldborough, sister ship of the *Virginia*. (Courtesy of the Merseyside County Museum.)

VIRGINIA

Built: 1888
Previous names: None
Gross tonnage: 2,314
Type of vessel: Freighter
Builder: Russell & Company, Pt. Glasgow, Scotland
Owner: S.S. Virginia Co., Ltd. (F. Woods)
Port of registry: London, England
Cause of sinking: Stranded
Location: Outer Diamond Shoals

Sunk: May 3, 1900
Depth: Unknown
Dimensions: 289' × 38' × 19'
Power: Coal-fired steam

Knowing that his ship was approaching the vicinity of Cape Hatteras, Captain Charles Samuels ordered the sounding lead thrown. He found no bottom at fifty fathoms. Since no land was visible through the haze, and because the open sea was rough, he changed course to the northwest: into the wind. Farther up the coast he expected to turn into the Chesapeake Bay so he could deliver his cargo of iron ore from Daiquiri, Cuba to the loading docks at Baltimore.

Three hours later came the awful cry from the bow lookout, "Breakers ahead."

The wheel was turned hard aport and the engine thrown into reverse. The ship responded to the turn, but before she could slow down she bottomed out. Captain Samuels was eating supper at the time. He raced to the bridge and took over command. Since the *Virginia* still had way on, he decided that she must have passed over a lump. He ordered full speed ahead. Before the steam valves were opened the ship crashed hard aground, and stuck. No amount of reversing and forwarding of the engine could move her.

According to a Life-Saving Service report, "Her location at this time . . . was on the southeast point of the dreaded Outer Diamond Shoal, 9 nautical miles southeast by south from Cape Hatteras Life-Saving Station and about the same distance east-southeast of the station at Creeds Hill. She immediately began to pound with great violence and to fill with water.

"The master knew pretty well where he was and, being aware of the slues and gullies between the shoals, feared that the steamer might slip into deep water and sink at once. Therefore he quickly ordered both anchors to be let go, and himself ran forward to superintend the operation, but before he could get back to the bridge the vessel broke in three pieces and sank to the rail, giving him barely time to leap for his life to the midship section. Without further ado he ordered the boats out and all hands to abandon ship.''

The captain, twenty-four crewmen, and one stowaway scrambled for their lives. "The crew hastily attempted to launch the two starboard boats, but both were smashed to pieces—the large lifeboat in the water alongside, and the longboat at the davits. Then the men rushed to the port lifeboat, which was safely lowered away and manned by fifteen persons, Second Mate Moore in charge. Mr. Moore states that it was his purpose to return to the ship and stand by the master, but that it was impossible to do so, and therefore he ordered the oarsmen to pull away straight out for the open sea. The port longboat was now put into the water with seven men in it, but before it could be cleared from the ship's side it was rolled over, and six of its occupants were quickly drowned. Mate Wyness, who was in charge, was hauled back on board the steamer by means of a bowline thrown to him by one of the four men who still remained on the wreck, but had intended to go in the boat.

"There were now five on board, and, as then seemed to them, in far worse plight than the boat's crew who had pushed out aimlessly and unprovisioned into the ocean—hardly more fortunate than their shipmates who had already perished. The steamer's hull was awash, and there was no better place of refuge than the main rigging, to which the survivors speedily betook themselves. All about them was the impenetrable haze or fog, while their eyes rested upon a most disheartening scene below. From the forecastle all the way to the stern the hull was submerged, except that the forecastle head stood 8 or 10 feet out of water. The vessel was broken athwartships into three pieces, and through the rents in its jagged sides the water hissed and foamed, and at intervals spouted upward in great volumes 15 or 20 feet high. Save the bit of the forecastle head, nothing showed above the sea but the two masts, the bridge and funnel, and a few feet of a flagstaff far aft. All this dreadful havoc had been wrought in little more than thirty minutes.

"The survivors now turned their thoughts to some means of making a signal of distress. Night was close at hand, and they knew that they could not be discovered from the shore before morning, even if the weather should clear up, unless they could burn some sort of a night signal. They were aware that there were inflammable materials away forward in the forecastle head, but the sea was so high that nobody could go to the place even if when there the materials should be accessible. All they could do was to hold their perilous places and almost despairingly hope that in some way relief might come, and thus they passed the tedious hours of the night. When morning broke they cast their eyes forward to the bridge, which was still above water, and believing that if they could reach it their safety would not be less, while they would have space to stretch their cramped limbs and move about, they determined to make the attempt. The plan devised was to rig a sort of boatswain's chair on the mainstay by which they could slide down and lower themselves to the bridge, a contrivance similar to the breeches-buoy apparatus. This they succeeded in accomplishing with less difficulty than might be imagined, and all passed down without trouble except the captain, who was the last to make the venture, and was for some minutes suspended in mid-air by the fouling of the gear. Finally there proved to be no recourse but to cut the halyards, which was done, letting the "chair" slide down with great velocity some 35 or 40 feet. The captain was considerably bruised in making the passage, but all hands being at last where they could exercise themselves a bit, their spirits were somewhat revived.

"Although it was now broad daylight, they could perceive no signs of land, and therefore knew that unless the hazy condition of the atmosphere should pass away they could not be seen, and would be obliged to endure another night on board the wreck. The master still had it in his mind to make the first possibly feasible effort to reach the oil and turpentine stored in the forecastle head, and as the forenoon wore on and the tide fell he concluded that as favorable an opportunity as they should ever have had arrived. Therefore, at very great personal danger, he jumped from the bridge and swam forward with all his power, beset by a strong current and with the sea continually breaking across the forewaist. However, he reached the goal, and encouraged by his success the chief mate followed. By the aid of a line thrown by the master he succeeded also, and together the two men explored the dark repository of the treasure upon which their lives seemed wholly to depend.

"Throughout the entire day the haze continued, but when night came on the two officers eagerly set fire to their signal. In the meantime, however, the tide had risen, as well as the wind and the sea, so that only with the greatest difficulty could the blaze be kept up, being often entirely extinguished by the waves that broke over the wreck. Frequent heavy showers also conspired with the sea to thwart the purpose of the careworn men, but nevertheless they kept their pitiful signal burning at every possible favorable interval during the night. Altogether they had used up by the time day dawned 30 gallons of oil and turpentine, although much of it, priceless as it was to them, was wasted by the action of the ruthless sea.

"Two nights and one day had now passed without food, and under such a tension of excitement and apprehension as to seriously impair the resources of the strongest and bravest of men, and it was doubtful whether they could hold out much longer. But fortunately, although they did not know it, their forlorn signal had been seen by some of the crews of both life-saving stations, and also the Hatteras Station had responded with a red rocket, which, however, proved not to have been visible on the wreck. Indeed the light shown on the wreck was so dim at the stations that the keepers were by no means sure of its import. Lights are often seen in the vicinity of the shoals, borne sometimes upon vessels which, during the summer, often pass through the slues between the Inner and Outer Diamonds, and also upon fishing vessels which frequently anchor under the lee of shoals.

"Nevertheless Keeper Etheridge was suspicious of trouble, and at daylight turned his telescope toward the point where the signal had been seen. The weather was still a little thick, but at 7 a.m. it lighted up, and the telescope then revealed the funnel and masts of the wreck. Etheridge then knew all. His many years' experience told him well enough what his eyes could not see. He quickly ordered out the Monomoy surfboat, called up Keeper Styron, of Creeds Hill Station, and requested him to start at once for the Outer Diamond, as the Hatteras crew were about to do. The boats of both stations got away at about the same time, and as soon as they cleared the beach made sail. The wind was now blowing a gale from the northward, and the sea was running high, but there was no faint heart among the life-savers, although all knew full well the peril of their undertaking. By 9 o'clock the five wretched men on the wreck made out the gleaming sails of the two surfboats, but they could scarcely believe their own eyes, for they had little confidence that any men would venture out to the Diamond Shoals in such weather as then prevailed. But there were the lifeboats—help was coming at last. For forty-two hours the poor fellows had endured hunger and thirst, and contemplated without sign of weakness almost certain death, but now that deliverance was at hand they gave way to tears—the brave man's last tribute to joy as well as to sorrow.

"The Creeds Hill boat arrived first at a point within about a quarter of a mile of the wreck, but seeing the tremendous sea running over the treacherous shoals, and realizing the perils that an attempt to rescue would surely involve, Keeper Styron wisely decided to wait for his mates to come up. The Hatteras boat was soon on hand, sail was taken in, and the two keepers conferred a few moments regarding the best plan of action, deciding, in order to minimize the danger of disaster to either boat, that the Hatteras crew should take the three men from the bridge, and the Creeds Hill crew the captain and the mate from the bow. The breakers were so heavy that the boats could not cross the shoals, and therefore they proceeded under oars around the southwest point of the Outer Diamond, and each approached its appointed place as near as the keepers deemed it prudent to venture. Both were masters of surfmanship, and by their skillful and judicious maneuvering soon had the grateful survivors safely in their boats according to the plan agreed upon, without the most trivial mishap. Sail was then made, and both boats started for home, where they arrived at about 5 p.m., having performed one of the most noteworthy rescues ever effected in the vicinity of stormy Cape Hatteras."

The report goes on to state that "Had the entire ship's company remained on board none would have perished. Happily the fifteen men who put to sea in the port lifeboat were sighted and picked up twenty-four hours after they went afloat by the steamer *El Paso*, bound from New York to New Orleans, where they were landed and properly cared for by the British consul. When taken on board the *El Paso* they had been without food or water for twenty-four hours, and were nearly worn out by constant bailing of the leaking boat and their arduous labor at the oars."

The wreck of the *Virginia* has not been identified.

Arrow crab.

Newcastle City, sister ship of the *Wetherby*. (Courtesy of the Steamship Historical Society of America.)

WETHERBY

Built: 1883
Previous names: None
Gross tonnage: 2,129
Type of vessel: Freighter
Builder: W. Gray & Company, West Hartlepool, England
Owner: Furness, Withy & Company, Ltd.
Port of registry: West Hartlepool, England
Cause of sinking: Stranded
Location: Southwest point of the Outer Diamond Shoal

Sunk: December 2, 1893
Depth: 30 feet
Dimensions: 285′ × 36′ × 24′
Power: Coal-fired steam

It was 9:30 on a brisk December morn when surfman D.W. Barnett spotted a steamship on the Outer Diamond Shoal. So far off was she that he could not be sure that she was stranded. Barnett raced as fast as he could back to the Cape Hatteras Life Saving Station, and alerted the keeper, Captain P.H. Etheridge.

The keeper was not a good speller and disdained of punctuation, but he *was* a man of quick action. As he later wrote in his Log, "I went up the Lookout of the station and satisfied myself that the ship was stoped Immediately ordered the boat out and the mules put to the carrage which was promptly dun   in the meanetime called Creeds Hill and Big Kinnekeet Life saving station and told them of the wreck on the shoals   the ship was seen to moove astern a little and then go ahead agane which caused sum delay leaving a a chance to suppose the ship wold get off but a few minutes later satisfide me the ship had stoped and starte was made for the seen of the wreck the boat was launched at 10 am we arived alongside the ship at 12 noon   when we arived along side the ship she was on her starbard beam ends and rapidly filing with water the ship was laying head to the sea theare was no lee to the ship at the time of our arrival along side   I lay off from the ship and talked with the capt and tride to persuad him to leave the ship as the position he was in was dangerous but he took no head to what I sed so I went abord the ship and privalled with him to leave the ship which he did after sum pursuasion'' Privalled? This is all hand-written, you understand, in great Gothic scrawl.

Captain John Wilson, master of the *Wetherby*, had little choice in the matter. The engine room and after hold were stove in, the decks were sharply canted, and he had the lives of this crew to consider. Yet, it must have been a difficult decision to make; a captain does not yield lightly his command. The awful responsibility of losing his ship must have weighed heavily upon his heart. But bad weather was on the way. Lightering $50,000 worth of phosphate rock so the freighter could be pulled off the shoal seemed an impracticality under the circumstances. His voyage from Fernandina, Florida to Norfolk, Virginia was permanently terminated. Reluctantly, he ordered abandon ship.

"At sum time when I was along side the boat something unnone to me broke in one planke and the ships Life Boats was launched and A portion of the crewes effects put in there and at about 1 PM A start was made for the shore   I took 4 men   the capt chief engeneer and stuard and mess boy put D.W. Barnett surfman no 1 in our of the ships boat with the 2dmate and J.L. Jennett no 4 in the boat with the 1st mate shortley after we left the ship we met Keepe styron   styron was in about 1/4 of a mile of the ship when we met him we took the ships boats in towe and styrou took the other Keeper where we got abrest of this station   Keeper styron took our of the boats and 13 men to the Creeds Hill Life saving station   Then capt Gray took the boat that I had been towing and towed her to the outer bare and landed the crew in his surf boat   My boat was leaking   I pumped until the boat filled to the deck then I came to the beach in that condition   My Boat was in such bad conditione I told Capt Gray to land the men out of ships boat in his surf boat which he did the   plase of E.F. stowe surfman no 2 was filled by W Barnett   stowe was home on privilege."

Both the *Wetherby* and Captain Wilson's hopes for saving her were dashed as thickening weather brewed into a heavy storm. The $100,000 steamer became an unsalvageable wreck. The twenty-four survivors spent four days at the Cape Hatteras and Creeds Hill stations, "when they were transferred from Durants Station to the schooner *Lizzie S. James*, which carried them to Norfolk."

Such rescues were commonplace among the men of the Life-Saving Service: men who were paid not for their literary eloquence but for braving the perils of the sea. When Captain Etheridge and his crew launched their boat through the pounding surf and rowed twelve miles from their station to the stranded *Wetherby*, they carried on a tradition that others less versed in the hazards of such an undertaking have come to take for granted.

What of the *Wetherby*? Consider this notice issued by the Lighthouse Board in July 1894. "The United States Lighthouse board has established, in 18 feet of water on the SE. edge of the shoals, the 'Outer Diamond Shoals Beacon,' an iron structure rising 20 feet above mean highwater, above which a mast, with cross boards, rises to a height of 52 feet above mean high water. The position of this beacon is shown on the charts 8½ miles SE. ⅞ S. from Cape Hatteras light. The wreck of the steamer *Weatherbee*, showing an iron mast above water, has been located, and is shown on the charts 6 ⅞ miles S. ⅞ E. from Cape Hatteras light."

The beacon is no longer there, but no doubt the hull of the *Wetherby* still is. By deductive reasoning it has been identified by Steve Lang's recovery of the helmstand dated 1882, and stamped "Paisley," the Scottish manufacture of the instrument. Furthermore, the wreck had a two-cylinder engine as the *Wetherby* did.

At the present time a fair amount of the wreck is exposed. A small piece of the bow with eight to ten feet of the tip broken off still holds the winch. Little more than jumbled hull plates connect the bow with the two boilers, one of which has rolled off to the starboard side. The engine is upright. The propeller shaft comes off the end of the engine, is exposed as far as a broken coupling, then the rest of the lower hull is buried. The rudder is hard over to port.

As with all the wrecks on the shoals, the amount of wreckage visible varies with time.

Amberjack.

WILLIAM ROCKEFELLER

Built: 1921

Previous names: None

Gross tonnage: 14,054

Type of vessel: Tanker

Builder: Newport News Ship Building & Dry Dock Company, Virginia

Owner: Standard Oil Company of New Jersey

Port of registry: Wilmington, Delaware

Cause of sinking: Torpedoed by *U-701* (Kapitanleutnant Degen)

Location: 35-16 N

Sunk: June 28, 1942

Depth: Unknown

Dimensions: 554′ × 75′ × 43′

Power: Oil-fired steam

74-56 W

By a strange coincidence the *William Rockefeller* was named after a ship that was torpedoed in the Great War, then suffered the same fate one world war later.

When World War Two began in Europe the *William Rockefeller* was already heavily engaged in the transport of oil. By the time of her demise she had successfully delivered 7,209,524 barrels (302,800,008 gallons) of cargo for the war effort. For the most part she picked up crude oil at

Courtesy of the National Archives.

Corpus Christi, Texas and took it to the refineries in northern New Jersey.

During one voyage in mid-March 1942 she was steaming off the Diamond Shoals while Johann Mohr in the *U-124* was wreaking havoc among merchant shipping. (Mohr sank the *Kassandra Louloudis* (q.v.) and the *E.M. Clark* (q.v.) on the night of 17–18.) The *William Rockefeller* made it through the shooting gallery unscathed.

Afterward, she took an errant cruise from Curacao to Cape Town, South Africa, traveling twenty-nine days alone. She delivered her fuel oil without a hitch, and returned by the same route. On June 19 she picked up 136,697 barrels of fuel oil in Aruba and headed for New York.

According to Captain William Stewart, master, "We proceeded according to routing instructions received from the British naval authorities at Aruba, steering various courses as prescribed. The vessel was blacked out at night.

"On June 27 we arrived off Ocracoke Lighthouse at about 3:30 p.m. and were ordered to heave to. Within a short time we were approached by a U.S. Coast Guard patrol boat which instructed us to proceed toward our ultimate destination. The commanding officer of the patrol boat escorted us to a designated haven, where we anchored overnight.

"Early in the morning of June 28 we hove anchor and proceeded for several hours under the escort of the same Coast Guard vessel that had left us the night before. We were then met by another patrol boat which took over as escort. Several planes were observed overhead.

"At 12:16 p.m., while I was in the chart room, a torpedo suddenly struck the tanker without warning on the port side amidships in way of the pumproom. I went into the wheelhouse and ordered the general alarm sounded and the engines stopped. The fuel oil valves were closed and the steam smothering lines opened. Our position was then 16 miles east northeast of Diamond Shoal Lighted Buoy, Latitude 35°11' North, Longitude 75°02' West."

The concussion felt on the bridge was insignificant, but closer to where the torpedo struck the force of the explosion blew an oiler right off his feet. Several men were as inundated with oil "as if they jumped into a tank of fuel oil." Hissing steam escaped from ruptured pipes with such violence that voice communication was impossible.

One plane peeled off to deliver two depth charge attacks; both missed the target, but forced the offending U-boat, the *U-701*, to submerge and run for it.

The *William Rockefeller* was left with a hole below the water line twenty feet in diameter. "Deck plates above were buckled and the pump room and No. 5 tank room flooded immediately. Fire broke out in the damaged area and while the ship did not list or settle, the fire burned briskly."

Captain Stewart: "I went to the lower bridge and walked to the after end of the midship boat deck, but could determine little as to the damage because of the dense smoke and fire. Practically the whole after end of the ship was shut off from view."

The excitement was evident among the *William Rockefeller's* forty-four crewmen. On his own initiative Chief Engineer Edward Snyder "stopped the port engine by means of the deck hand control and also closed the starboard engine. Later, with the assistance of First Assistant Engineer John V.F. Brown, I opened the deck steam smothering lines."

The six-man armed guard assembled on the stern platform that supported the 3-inch gun, but could find no target for their shells. Neither had any of the three lookouts seen signs of the enemy.

Captain Stewart: "At first I concluded that there was no emergency requiring the abandonment of the ship and was planning to turn the *Wm. Rockefeller* landward and beach her if necessary."

The crew had other thoughts. Cut off from their emergency stations by the fire that bisected the ship, the men rushed to the nearest lifeboats and started launching them. Captain Stewart gave no order to abandon ship, although he realized that the fire amidships prevented communication between the forward and the after parts of the vessel. With his crew leaving him, he had no alternative but to go along with their plan. The helm was thrown hard over in order to take off way.

The forward falls of two davits were handled with undue haste, dropping the boats perpendicularly into the water and causing them to fill up. While some of the men knocked the emergency life rafts off their skids, Captain Stewart supervised the launching of lifeboat No. 2.

"I instructed them to lower the boat away easily, evenly; when they started to lower away, to do so easy and equally, and the boat was launched successfully. While they were launching the boat and getting into it, I had another look around, and the fire seemed to be subsiding slightly, and when I came back on the bridge I could hear them shouting on the boat for me to come on. Then I went and took a look around to satisfy myself that none of the crew was being left behind, perhaps disabled, and after being satisfied that no one was left aboard, I left the ship."

Captain Stewart "thought it would still be possible for me to return later, when the fire had subsided, with a view to deciding whether the *Wm. Rockefeller* could be navigated and beached if necessary. However, about 20 minutes after a Coast Guard patrol boat had picked up the last man, the fire on the vessel increased considerably, extending over at least half of the ship and burning fiercely until we lost sight of her."

The *CGC 470* chased after the U-boat, laid a pattern of seven depth charges, then return to rescue the men in the lifeboats and rafts. She took them to Ocracoke.

Captain Stewart: "Some of the men who were smeared with oil, which had got into their eyes, and others with minor cuts and bruises, were treated at the Coast Guard Station."

Two escort vessels stayed by the *William Rockefeller's* side throughout the day, awaiting the arrival of salvage tugs. Red flames and black clouds of smoke continued to ravage the hull. After dark, blazing oil lit the sky like a huge funeral pyre. Not to be cheated of his prize, Kapitanleutnant Horst Degen, captain of the *U-701*, sneaked past the guardships in the bleak minutes before midnight and launched another torpedo, striking the tanker in the engine room.

Degen: "A half minute later the stern sank down and the bow rose high up into the sky like a torch out of a terrible nightmare. It stood there for a few moments and suddenly the whole ship just went down over the stern in a gentle slide, hissing all over. The giant fire went out instantly and the crew on the deck found themselves in a completely dark night. It was eerie, as if someone had switched off the light in a bright room."

A Navy memorandum stated that "the position of the *William Rockefeller* at the time of the attack . . . was 35-07 N/75-05 W, which is about 16 miles ENE of Diamond Shoals Lighthouse. The ship drifted about 15 miles NE of the position where attacked before sinking." A Navy extrapolation gave the final resting place as 35-16 N/74-56 W.

The wreck of the *William Rockefeller* has not been located. If indeed it did go vertical, as Degen stated, then the wreck lies in very deep water.

For the demise of the attacking U-boat, see *U-701*.

Eyes in the dark.

YP-389

Built: 1941
Previous names: *Cohasset, AMc-202*
Gross tonnage: 170
Type of vessel: Patrol craft
Builder: Bethlehem Steel Company Shipbuilding Division, Quincy, MA
Owner: U.S. Navy
Cause of sinking: Shelled by *U-701* (Kapitanleutnant Degen)
Location: South of the Diamond Shoals, five to eight miles northeast of
        buoy No. 4 of the Hatteras mine area

Sunk: June 19, 1942
Depth: Unknown
Dimensions: $102' \times 22' \times 10'$
Power: Diesel engine
Official designation: YP-389

   The case of the *YP-389* is a strange one in the annals of naval warfare not because of the uneven battle she fought against an overpowering enemy, but due to the bureaucratic ignorance that contributed to her loss and the political absurdity that resulted from it.

   The *YP-389* was built as the fishing trawler *Cohasset* for R. O'Brien & Company of Boston, Massachussetts. In consequence of a Congressional directive enacted on December 12, 1941 (five days after the Japanese attack

Courtesy of the Hart Nautical Museum, MIT Museum.

Courtesy of the National Archives

on Pearl Harbor), the Navy proceeded to acquire privately owned vessels that could serve in the capacity of coastal protection in the absence of warships that were pursuing the war in the far-flung seas. The *Cohasset* was acquired on February 6, 1942.

Conversion from a fishing vessel to a minesweeper began on the twelfth, at the shipyard of the Marine Basin Company in Brooklyn. The *Cohasset* emerged nine days later adorned with a 3-inch bow gun, two 30-caliber Lewis machine guns, and two depth-charge racks astern with six depth charges each. Her steel hull housed the latest in radio direction finding equipment. She was placed in service on the twenty-second as a coastal minesweeper, the *AMc-202*.

On May 1 the more pressing need for coastal patrol craft saw her reclassified as the *YP-389*. She served on escort duty, but her ten-knot speed was too slow to provide adequate coverage for her charges: not only could she barely keep up with the convoys, should a U-boat appear she did not have to speed to prosecute an effective chase. New employment found her warning merchant shipping away from the shoals and protective minefields between Morehead City and the Diamond Shoals.

On his first four-day patrol Lieutenant Roderick Philips, commanding, tested the 3-inch gun and found it inoperative. When he returned to Section Base at Morehead City a Chief Gunner's Mate "examined the gun and stated that he thought the cause of its failure to fire was due to a combination of a defective firing pin spring and bad ammunition but he believed the gun would fire with good ammunition, although they had no opportunity to test it." The part and the tools with which to replace it were unavailable, and placed on order.

In the mean time the *YP-389* was ordered out on patrol. For two days and nights she slowly swept back and forth offshore of the Hatteras minefield. The twenty-four-man crew took their jobs seriously. They kept a sharp eye for unwary merchantmen straying too close to danger.

The early hours of June 19 found the *YP-389* "proceeding on a southwest course bearing between the Diamond Shoals gas buoy and Buoy No. 4, her speed reduced to 6.2 knots." Five men were on watch: Lieutenant Philips as officer of the deck, "the quartermaster on the wheel, a signalman on the bridge, a lookout on the flying bridge, and another lookout on the stern." The ship was blacked out.

At 2:20 a.m., machine-gun tracer bullets streaked out of the dark from a position some four hundred yards inshore of the patrol boat, followed by incendiary shells that raked the starboard hull with unerring precision. Lieutenant Philips sounded the general alarm, and the crew raced to their battle stations. Seaman C.F. Hensley and Fireman J.C. Doucette were cut down as soon as they stepped out of the forward companionway to man the deck gun; Hensley died instantly. Lieutenant Philips sent a distress call to the Coast Guard, and received acknowledgment.

The patrol boat was soon aflame from stem to stern. "The enemy, who still could not be seen in the darkness of the night, now shelled the victim with the heavy gun, using a combination of common and shrapnel shot, and the two .30 caliber machine guns of the *YP-389* blazed away at the source of the tracer bullets whenever that target was opened."

With the suspicion that his deck gun might misfire, and with the deadly enfilade tearing up the patrol boat's decks, Lieutenant Philips put his stern to the enemy and veered westward, thus presenting as small a target as possible while heading in the direction from which he expected help to arrive. Ramming was out of the question because the U-boat had nearly twice his speed. In fact, the U-boat crisscrossed the patrol boat's wake and fired upon both aft quarters of the *YP-389*.

The patrol boat's machine guns nipped away ineffectively at the zigzagging U-boat. In order to deter the enemy from approaching too close astern, Fireman W.B. Cole rolled depth charges off the racks until he was shot down by enemy gunfire. The four explosives went off but did not damage the U-boat.

The *YP-389* soon became a mass of flames, a floating crematorium. She had no chance in this unequal battle against superior firepower. She was, after all, nothing more than an unarmored fishing boat with a few guns. Furthermore, her main armament was out of action. As the crew fought fires that raged out of control, the brightly lit patrol boat was an unmistakable target that fell prey to a hail of fire. She was being picked to pieces by high explosives; shrapnel scythed through the hull and superstructure with devastating effect.

Above the clamor of screeching shell fire, roaring machine guns, and crackling flames, after an hour of fighting a losing battle, with his command about to sink from under him, Lieutenant Philips gave the order to abandon ship. He maintained his station at the helm and kept the U-boat off his starboard quarter while the men assembled on the protected side by the forward winches. His instructions were explicit.

He held a steady course and maintained full speed. In groups of twos and threes the men went over the side, the wounded aided by the uninjured. Lieutenant Philips held steadfast in his exposed position as the blazing pilot house was peppered with shot. Not until he was the last man aboard did he leap over the side.

The trick worked; the U-boat chased after the burning craft and continued to pummel her with shellfire until just before she sank. It then disappeared into the darkness.

Five men did not get away from the *YP-389*. The survivors bobbed in the gentle swells: their bodies buoyed by lifejackets, their hopes buoyed by the thought that help was on the way. Thirteen men suffered from burns and shrapnel wounds, six of them seriously. Doucette died in the water.

At 7:30 that morning two Coast Guard boats came upon the ragged file of men and picked them up one by one. Most had to be hospitalized. It was a night of action that they would never forget.

For Lieutenant Philips, perhaps even more unforgetable—and at least as insensible—was the Court of Inquiry that followed. Three retired Naval officers led by a Naval reservist as Judge Advocate formed the opinion that "Lieutenant Philips failed to close the enemy and ram him or force him to submerge; and further, that he failed to do his utmost to 'take, capture, and destroy the said enemy as it was his duty to do so, by reason of which failure the said USS *YP-389* was sunk and the enemy submarine escaped.' The Court of Inquiry further rendered the opinion that Lieutenant Philips was culpably inefficient in the performance of his duty in that 'he failed to have his vessel ready for enemy action by reason of which inefficiency the USS *YP-389* was brought under heavy enemy fire and eventually sunk.' The Court recommended that Lieutenant Philips be brought to trial by General Court Martial on the charges: (1) Failure to seek encounter with the enemy; and (2) culpable inefficiency in the performance of his duty."

The war ended with "no record that the General Court Martial has taken place." Thus a man who should have received a U.S. medal for his actions got only German metal.

The wreck of the *YP-389* has not been identified. The best position the Navy could given on its location was south of the Diamond Shoals and five to eight miles northeast of buoy #4 of the Hatteras mine area. A careful reading of the after-action report seems to indicate that this was where the attack occurred. If Lieutenant Philips ran his ship westward for an hour at full speed, the *YP-389* could have gone down ten miles from the indicated position.

See *U-701* for the circumstances of its eventual loss.

SUGGESTED READING

Berman, Bruce D. (1972) *Encyclopedia of American Shipwrecks*, The Mariners Press, Boston, Massachusetts.

Bunch, Jim (1986) *Diving the U-85*, Deep Sea Press, P.O. Box 48, Kitty Hawk, North Carolina 27949

Clark, William Bell (1929) *When the U-boats Came to America*, Little, Brown, and Company, Boston, Massachusetts.

Gentile, Gary (1990) *Shipwrecks of Delaware and Maryland*, Gary Gentile Productions, P.O. Box 57137, Philadelphia, PA 19111 ($20 postage paid).

—— (1988) *Shipwrecks of New Jersey*, Sea Sports Publications, Box 647, Belden Station, Norwalk, Connecticut.

—— (1992) *Shipwrecks of North Carolina: from Hatteras Inlet South*, Gary Gentile Productions, P.O. Box 57137, Philadelphia, PA 19111 ($20 postage paid).

—— (1992) *Shipwrecks of Virginia*, Gary Gentile Productions, P.O. Box 57137, Philadelphia, PA 19111 ($20 postage paid).

—— (1989) *Track of the Gray Wolf*, Avon Books, New York, NY.

Heyl, Erik (1952–1969) *Early American Steamers* (six volumes) Eric Heyl, 136 West Oakwood Place, Buffalo, New York 14214.

Keatts, Henry, and Farr, George (1991) *Dive into History: Submarines*, Gulf Publishing Company, Houston, Texas.

—— (1986) *Dive into History: U-boats*, American Merchant Marine Museum Press, Kings Point, New York.

—— (1990) *Dive into History: Warships*, Gulf Publishing Company, Houston, Texas.

Lonsdale, Adrian L., and Kaplan, H.R. (1964) *A Guide to Sunken Ships in American Waters*, Compass Publications.

MacNeil, Ben Dixon (undated) *Torpedo Junction*, Time Printing Co., Manteo, North Carolina.

Navy Department, Office of Naval Records and Library, Historical Section, (1920) *German Submarine Activities on the Atlantic Coast of the United States and Canada*, Publication Number 1, Government Printing Office.

Newton, John; Pilke, Orrin; and Blanton, J.O. (1971) *An Oceanographic Atlas of the Carolina Continental Margin*, North Carolina Department of Conservation and Development, Raleigh, NC.

Offley, Edward (1982) *War Cruise: U-701*, privately printed screenplay by Edward Offley, 505 Redgate Ave. #10, Norfolk, VA 23507.

Standard Oil Company (1946) *Ships of the Esso Fleet in World War II*.

Stick, David (1952) *Graveyard of the Atlantic*, The University of North Carolina Press, Chapel Hill, North Carolina.

U.S. Coast Guard (undated) *War Action Casualties Involving Merchant Tank Vessels*, prepared by the Merchant Vessel Inspection Division.

LORAN NUMBERS — ALPHABETICAL

1250 Rocks	26810.0	40410.0
14 Buoy	27040.5	39572.4
1700 Rock	27043.0	39709.8
210 Rock	27069.7	39493.1
240 Rock	27079.0	39495.3
43 Fathom Wreck	26864.9	40217.5
4A Buoy (Airplane)	27087.6	41125.2
Aeolus (439' cable layer)	27081.4	39489.7
Airplane	27087.6	41125.2
Alexander Ramsey	27268.0	39106.5
Alton Lennon (150' barge)	27217.7	39082.9
Amagansett	27025.3	39724.3
Ann R. Heidritter	26965.5	40197.0
Ario	27043.2	39712.9
Ariosto	26975.1	40179.4
Artificial Reef	27128.2	39661.5
Ashkhabad	27037.1	39617.6
Asphalt Barge	26868.5	40458.8
Atlas	27023.6	39721.5
Australia (stern)	26883.3	40250.4
Australia (bow)	26883.5	40250.2
Barge (130 feet long)	26975.1	40689.1
Barge (130 feet long)	26975.0	40690.0
Barge (130')	27019.4	40133.0
Barge (60 feet long)	27127.5	39660.2
Barge (60 feet long)	27127.3	39662.5
Barge (Steel)	27103.0	41284.1
Bedfordshire	27048.6	39562.1
Bedloe/Jackson	26940.8	40687.3
Big Boiler Wreck	26919.3	40085.4
Big Rock	26990.0	39535.0
Big Rock	26985.0	39585.0
Big Ten Fathom	27079.6	39555.2
British Splendour	26976.7	39957.4
BT-6400 (104' barge)	27019.4	40132.4
Buarque	26843.5	40999.3
Buarque	26844.1	40999.8
Byron D. Benson	26923.6	40864.9
Cape Henry	27176.9	41286.2
Captain Rick	27035.7	41244.9
Caribsea	27042.5	39741.0
Cassimir	27128.6	39250.1
Chenango	26872.3	41104.8
Chenango	26872.2	41105.0
Chesapeake Tower Reef	27103.1	41286.2
Chesapeake Tower Reef	27103.9	41286.2
Ciltvaira (false)	26847.8	40450.8
City of Atlanta	26894.8	40399.7
City of Birmingham	25959.2	41130.2
Classroom	27217.7	39082.9
Coast Guard Cutter	26940.8	40687.3
Concrete (480 tons) 200' S	27267.4	39161.0
Concrete Sections	27224.5	41261.3

Consols	27042.8	41011.2
Consols	27042.8	41011.7
D Wreck	27042.5	39740.8
Danny's Wreck	26943.7	40560.2
Diamond Tower	26875.2	40278.8
Dionysys	26940.7	40575.7
Dixie Arrow	26949.7	40038.3
Dixie Arrow	26951.5	40038.6
Dolly Parton Wreck	27066.4	41275.1
Dredge Wreck	27241.2	39046.0
Dredge Wreck	27241.2	39046.8
E.M. Clark	26905.3	40062.2
Ea	27063.2	39623.1
East Tanker	26981.8	39793.0
Eastern Slough Buoy	27075.0	39670.4
Ed's Lobster Wreck	27110.7	39236.3
Empire Gem	26903.3	40172.7
Empire Gem (stern)	26903.5	40172.6
Empire Gem (bow)	26903.5	40173.0
Equipoise	26863.7	40932.9
Equipoise	26863.9	40933.2
Esso Nashville	27156.3	39163.8
F.W. Abrams	26967.3	40073.6
Far East Tanker	27981.3	39788.9
Fenwick Island	27064.0	39607.9
Fishing Vessel	26904.5	40148.6
Florida	27285.7	41255.3
Four-A Buoy (airplane)	27087.6	41125.2
Francis E. Powell (bow?)	27014.1	41270.0
Freighter	27133.2	39180.0
Frying Pan Tower	45165.2	59220.0
George Summerlin (130')	27062.2	39683.3
Grainger Wreck	27160.0	39175.0
Green Buoy Wreck	26847.8	40450.8
Gulf Hustler	27069.8	41273.0
Hanks (trawler)	27048.2	41188.8
Hesperides	26910.1	40236.5
Hyde (215' dredge)	27218.2	39081.9
Isle of Iona	26978.6	40174.2
Jackson/Bedloe	26940.8	40687.3
John D. Gill (bow)	27198.5	39085.3
John D. Gill (stern)	27199.5	39083.5
Kassandra Louloudis	26886.9	40274.7
Keshena	26959.8	40085.2
Kingston Ceylonite	27131.5	41218.1
Knuckle Buoy	27061.2	39618.7
Lancing	26897.2	40182.3
LCM (55 feet long)	27267.5	39160.8
LCU-1468, 100' S of buoy	26941.4	40685.5
Liberator	26888.7	40218.8
Liberty Ship	27268.0	39025.0
Lighthouse Wreck	27117.0	41276.9
Little Ten Fathom	27081.1	39560.6
Malchace	26941.1	39881.4

Train Cars (10) 550′ SW	27233.1	39224.5		Unknown	27101.9	41244.5
Train Cars (10) 550′ SW	27214.7	39226.0		Unknown	27145.4	41268.1
Train Cars (10) 350′ SW	26979.1	40726.0		Unknown	26857.9	41270.4
Train Cars (5) 250′ SW	27243.1	39077.2		Unknown	27066.5	41275.0
Train Cars (5) 300′ NE	27243.1	39077.2		Unknown	27103.6	41282.3
				Unknown (barge)	26897.–	41217.–
				Unknown (lost net)	26851.–	41271.–
Train Cars (8)/Concrete	26945.0	40175.0		Unknown (Norman Miller)	26928.8	39922.6
Train Cars (9)/Concrete	26951.0	40182.0		Urn Wreck	26940.1	40191.4
Trawler	27092.3	39633.3		Valley Moon	27028.7	39995.7
Tug (65 feet long)	27267.8	39161.6		Veturia	26895.6	40246.4
Tug, Tanker, Two Barges	27268.0	39107.0		Virginia (BB-13)	26863.4	40212.0
U-352	27063.5	39491.5		W.E. Hutton	27143.2	39524.3
U-85	26917.0	40713.6		W.E. Hutton	27143.6	39524.3
Unis	26940.1	40191.4		Wanderer	27236.5	41274.3
Unknown	26900.3	40403.6		West Rock	27072.1	39515.7
Unknown	26869.5	41137.6		West Rock	27077.4	39521.5
Unknown	26859.5	41168.4		Western Slough Buoy	27083.3	39654.9
Unknown	27141.4	41217.7		Winthrop	27145.0	41268.0
Unknown	27138.8	41218.6		WR-2	27128.6	39250.1
Unknown	27138.8	41220.1		WR-4	27198.3	39085.4
Unknown	26882.5	41229.7		Wreck	26906.2	40242.3
Unknown	26875.5	41244.2		Wreck	26906.8	40242.8
				Yard Oiler (174′)	27039.3	39574.6
				York	26913.6	40817.0
				Zane Grey	26940.7	40574.3
				Zerida	27436.5	41267.6
				Zerta	27436.5	41267.6

LORAN NUMBERS — DESCENDING 4 AND 3 LINES

Chesapeake Tower Reef	27103.9	41286.2		Zerta	27436.5	41267.6
Chesapeake Tower Reef	27103.1	41286.2		Zerida	27436.5	41267.6
Cape Henry	27176.9	41286.2		Concrete Sections	27224.5	41261.3
Barge (Steel)	27103.0	41284.1		ODU Wreck (good)	27224.5	41261.2
Unknown	27103.6	41282.3		River Front Junction	27024.3	41260.3
Prince of Peace	26866.1	41281.5		Florida	27285.7	41255.3
Nike's #2	27188.1	41280.1		Stormy	27116.4	41249.6
Santore	27117.0	41276.9		Ricks Trawler	27035.7	41244.9
Nancy	26864.4	41276.9		Captain Rick	27035.7	41244.9
Lighthouse Wreck	27117.0	41276.9		Unknown	27101.9	41244.5
Dolly Parton Wreck	27066.4	41275.1		Unknown	26875.5	41244.2
Unknown	27066.5	41275.0		Salty Sea II	27087.7	41241.1
North of Trestle	27205.3	41274.7		Unknown	26882.5	41229.7
Wanderer	27236.5	41274.3		Unknown	27138.8	41220.1
Gulf Hustler	27069.8	41273.0		Unknown	27138.8	41218.6
Unknown (lost net)	26851.–	41271.–		Kingston Ceylonite	27131.5	41218.1
Unknown	26857.9	41270.4		Unknown	27141.4	41217.7
Francis E. Powell (bow?)	27014.1	41270.0		Unknown (barge)	26897.–	41217.–
Stanchion Wreck	27064.2	41268.2		Pinar Del Rio	26590.9	41216.9
Unknown	27145.4	41268.1		Tiger	27101.9	41189.2
Winthrop	27145.0	41268.0		Margaret P. Hanks	27048.3	41189.0
Nike's Wreck	27145.0	41268.0		Margaret P. Hanks	27048.2	41188.8
				Hanks (trawler)	27048.2	41188.8
				Tiger	27101.6	41188.6
				Unknown	26859.5	41168.4

Nordhav	26838.1	41155.8
Unknown	26869.5	41137.6
City of Birmingham	25959.2	41130.2
Four-A Buoy		
(airplane)	27087.6	41125.2
Airplane	27087.6	41125.2
4A Buoy (Airplane)	27087.6	41125.2
Morma Kite	26456.–	41113.–
Robert Graham		
Dunn	26513.–	41109.–
Chenango	26872.2	41105.0
Chenango	26872.3	41104.8
Consols	27042.8	41011.7
Consols	27042.8	41011.2
Buarque	26844.1	40999.8
Buarque	26843.5	40999.3
Equipoise	26863.9	40933.2
Equipoise	26863.7	40932.9
Russian Trawler		
(130′)	26849.5	40886.1
Byron D. Benson	26923.6	40864.9
York	26913.6	40817.0
Norvana	26913.6	40817.0
Train Cars (10)		
350′ SW	26979.1	40726.0
U-85	26917.0	40713.6
Train Cars (10)		
350′ SW	26975.0	40690.0
Barge (130 feet long)	26975.0	40690.0
Barge (130 feet long)	26975.1	40689.1
Jackson/Bedloe	26940.8	40687.3
Coast Guard Cutter	26940.8	40687.3
Bedloe/Jackson	26940.8	40687.3
LCU-1468, 100′ S of		
buoy	26941.4	40685.5
San Delfino	26810.2	40622.6
Dionysys	26940.7	40575.7
Zane Grey	26940.7	40574.3
Danny's Wreck	26943.7	40560.2
Oriental	26949.3	40559.1
Marore	26885.6	40505.3
Marore	26885.2	40504.2
Mercel	26894.6	40502.3
Moriana 200	26868.5	40458.8
Asphalt Barge	26868.5	40458.8
Mirlo	26847.0	40450.8
Green Buoy Wreck	26847.8	40450.8
Ciltvaira (false)	26847.8	40450.8
1250 Rocks	26810.0	40410.0
Unknown	26900.3	40403.6
City of Atlanta	26894.8	40399.7
Phil's Wreck	26857.1	40340.5
Tires (16,280)	26950.0	40280.0
Diamond Tower	26875.2	40278.8
Kassandra Louloudis	26886.9	40274.7
Merak (?)	26869.7	40273.1
Australia (stern)	26883.3	40250.4
Australia (bow)	26883.5	40250.2
Point Shoals Buoy	26891.4	40250.0
Veturia	26895.6	40246.4

Wreck	26906.8	40242.8
Wreck	26906.2	40242.3
Norlavore	26878.3	40237.6
Hesperides	26910.1	40236.5
Northeastern	26908.9	40234.7
Southeast Rocks	26861.0	40234.0
Tenas	26888.8	40219.2
Liberator	26888.7	40218.8
43 Fathom Wreck	26864.9	40217.5
New Jersey (BB-16)	26864.9	40217.4
Virginia (BB-13)	26863.4	40212.0
Ann R. Heidritter	26965.5	40197.0
Urn Wreck	26940.1	40191.4
Unis	26940.1	40191.4
Nevada	26940.1	40191.4
Slick Wreck	26897.2	40182.3
Lancing	26897.2	40182.3
Train Cars		
(9)/Concrete	26951.0	40182.0
Ariosto	26975.1	40179.4
Train Cars		
(8)/Concrete	26945.0	40175.0
Monitor	26887.6	40174.7
Monitor	26887.4	40174.5
Isle of Iona	26978.6	40174.2
Smell Wreck	26903.5	40173.0
Empire Gem (bow)	26903.5	40173.0
Empire Gem	26903.3	40172.7
Empire Gem (stern)	26903.5	40172.6
Squirrel's Rock		
(220′)	26891.1	40160.9
Regulus	26942.5	40159.0
Mr. J.C. (105′ long		
tug)	26957.0	40155.0
Fishing Vessel	26904.5	40148.6
Barge (130′)	27019.4	40133.0
BT-6400 (104′ barge)	27019.4	40132.4
Big Boiler Wreck	26919.3	40085.4
Keshena	26959.8	40085.2
F.W. Abrams	26967.3	40073.6
Rock Pile	27903.0	40070.0
E.M. Clark	26905.3	40062.2
Pinnacle	26953.5	40039.9
Dixie Arrow	26951.5	40038.6
Dixie Arrow	26949.7	40038.3
Train Cars (10)		
400′ SW	26987.0	40024.0
Train Cars (10)		
300′ SE	26995.9	39998.0
Powell	26949.4	39997.4
Valley Moon	27028.7	39995.7
Proteus	26949.6	39960.6
Tarpon	26946.0	39959.2
British Splendour	26976.7	39957.4
Unknown (Norman		
Miller)	26928.8	39922.6
Manuela	26945.2	39916.8
Malchace	26941.1	39881.4
East Tanker	26981.8	39793.0
Far East Tanker	27981.3	39788.9

Name		
Tamaulipas (bow)	26981.3	39788.8
Tamaulipas (stern)	26980.7	39773.9
Caribsea	27042.5	39741.0
D Wreck	27042.5	39740.8
Amagansett	27025.3	39724.3
Shad	27025.3	39724.2
Atlas	27023.6	39721.5
Ario	27043.2	39712.9
1700 Rock	27043.0	39709.8
George Summerlin (130')	27062.2	39683.3
Eastern Slough Buoy	27075.0	39670.4
Barge (60 feet long)	27127.3	39662.5
Steel Framing	27127.7	39661.9
Artificial Reef	27128.2	39661.5
Theodore Parker	27127.8	39660.9
Barge (60 feet long)	27127.5	39660.2
Thistleroy	27078.8	39656.8
Western Slough Buoy	27083.3	39654.9
Portland	27056.1	39652.2
Novelty (140' menhaden)	27138.5	39636.9
Trawler	27092.3	39633.3
Senateur Duhamel	27092.8	39633.3
Ea	27063.2	39623.1
Knuckle Buoy	27061.2	39618.7
Russian freighter	27037.1	39617.6
Ashkhabad	27037.1	39617.6
Fenwick Island	27064.0	39607.9
Northwest Rock	27037.2	39595.4
Panam	26975.5	39585.0
Big Rock	26985.0	39585.0
Northwest Place #1	27090.4	39577.6
Northwest Place #2	27089.1	39574.8
Yard Oiler (174')	27039.3	39574.6
14 Buoy	27040.5	39572.4
Northwest Place #3	27089.1	39570.0
Train Cars (10) 350' SW	27139.7	39569.5
Bedfordshire	27048.6	39562.1
Little Ten Fathom	27081.1	39560.6
Big Ten Fathom	27079.6	39555.2
Suloide	27146.1	39550.1
Train Cars (10) 200' SW	27177.0	39549.8
Train Cars (10) 350' SW	27162.4	39545.3
Big Rock	26990.0	39535.0
Train Cars (10) 250' W	27160.2	39524.8
W.E. Hutton	27143.6	39524.3
W.E. Hutton	27143.2	39524.3
South Wreck	27143.6	39524.3
South Wreck	27143.2	39524.3
West Rock	27077.4	39521.5
West Rock	27072.1	39515.7
240 Rock	27079.0	39495.3
210 Rock	27069.7	39493.1
U-352	27063.5	39491.5
Aeolus (439' cable layer)	27081.4	39489.7
Rock South of 13	27134.3	39470.0
Schurz	27067.7	39463.8
Papoose	27074.0	39431.1
Naeco (bow)	27053.7	39422.8
New River (80' vessel)	27225.7	39403.7
Southeast Naeco	27035.0	39391.0
Semaeco	27035.0	39391.0
Naeco (stern)	27065.4	39387.8
Train Cars (10) 275' SW	27210.0	39324.4
Tires (48,700)	27256.9	39252.5
WR-2	27128.6	39250.1
Cassimir	27128.6	39250.1
Ed's Lobster Wreck	27110.7	39236.3
Train Cars (10) 550' SW	27214.7	39226.0
Train Cars (10) 550' SW	27233.1	39224.5
Train Cars (10) 500' SW	27211.7	39195.0
Normannia	27143.3	39180.5
Normannia	27142.8	39180.5
Freighter	27133.2	39180.0
Grainger Wreck	27160.0	39175.0
Esso Nashville	27156.3	39163.8
Tug (65 feet long)	27267.8	39161.6
Concrete (480 tons) 200' S	27267.4	39161.0
LCM (55 feet long)	27267.5	39160.8
Tug, Tanker, Two Barges	27268.0	39107.0
Socony 8	27268.7	39106.8
Ramsey	27268.0	39106.5
Alexander Ramsey	27268.0	39106.5
Stone Brothers (105' tug)	27269.4	39105.7
WR-4	27198.3	39085.4
John D. Gill (bow)	27198.5	39085.3
John D. Gill (stern)	27199.5	39083.5
Train Cars (10) 525' W	27127.7	39082.9
Classroom	27127.7	39082.9
Alton Lennon (150' barge)	27217.7	39082.9
Hyde (215' dredge)	27218.2	39081.9
Train Cars (5) 300' NE	27243.1	39077.2
Train Cars (5) 250' SW	27243.1	39077.2
Train Cars (10) 300' SW	27261.0	39068.7
Pocahontas (105' tug)	27240.4	39048.3
Dredge Wreck	27241.2	39046.8
Dredge Wreck	27241.2	39046.0
R.R. Stone (86' tug)	27241.4	39045.8
Liberty Ship	27268.0	39025.0

Books by the Author
Fiction

Vietnam
Lonely Conflict

Action/Adventure
Mind Set

Supernatural
The Lurking

Science Fiction
Entropy
Return to Mars
Silent Autumn
The Time Dragons Trilogy:
A Time for Dragons
Dragons Past
No Future for Dragons

Nonfiction

Advanced Wreck Diving Guide
Shipwrecks of New Jersey

Track of the Gray Wolf
Wreck Diving Adventures

Available (postage paid) from:

Nonfiction

GARY GENTILE PRODUCTIONS
P.O. Box 57137
Philadelphia, PA 19111

- $25 *Andrea Doria: Dive to an Era*
- $20 *Ultimate Wreck-Diving Guide*
- $20 *USS San Diego: the Last Armored Cruiser*
- $25 Video (VHS): *The Battle for the USS Monitor*
  The Popular Dive Guide Series:
- $20 *Shipwrecks of Delaware and Maryland*
- $20 *Shipwrecks of Virginia*
- $20 *Shipwrecks of North Carolina: from the Diamond Shoals North*
- $20 *Shipwrecks of North Carolina: from Hatteras Inlet South*

Fiction

- $20 *The Peking Papers*